Hand Book of
Spices and Packaging with Formulaes

with directories of plant and equipments and importers/exporters & Manufacturers of Spices/Masala

Hand Book of
Spices and Packaging with Formulaes

with directories of plant and equipments and importers/exporters & Manufacturers of Spices/Masala

Written By

Eiri Board Of Consultants & Engineers

Compiled By

Sudhir Gupta

ENGINEERS INDIA RESEARCH INSTITUTE

4449, Nai Sarak, Main Road, Delhi - 110006 (India)

Ph: +91-11-23918117, 23916431, 45120361, 23947058, 64727385

* E-Mail: eiritechnology@gmail.com & eiriprojects@gmail.com

*Website: www.eiriindia.org & www.industrialprojectreports.com

PRINTED & PUBLISHED BY

ENGINEERS INDIA RESEARCH INSTITUTE

4449, Nai Sarak, Main Road, Delhi - 110006 (India)

Ph: +91-11-23918117, 23916431, 45120361, 23947058, 64727385

* E-Mail: eiritechnology@gmail.com & eiriprojects@gmail.com

*Website: www.eiriindia.org & www.industrialprojectreports.com

Distributors:

EIRI Project Consultants and Publishers
Roop Nagar, Delhi-110007
and
Industrial Technologies, India
Nai Sarak, Delhi-110006

Revised and Englarged Edition

ISBN: 9788186732311

Printed in New Delhi (INDIA)

₹ 900/- or US $90

Printed & Published by Sudhir Gupta for "Engineers India Research Institute", 4449 Nai Sarak, Main Road, New Delhi -110006

Preface

Spices are widely used all over the world as food flavouring ingredients as well as treating variety of ailments. The market for spices is classified into straight spices and value added spices. Straight spices are spices in their natural form while value added spices consist of masalas, oils and oleoresins of spices. The global production of spices is about 8 million MT, out of which India's share is 35 per cent. The main spices growing countries are India, China, Pakistan, Sri Lanka, Chile, Egypt, Mexico etc. The global trade of spices is estimated to be about 0.5 million MT valued at US$ 1.500 million India's share of global trade is 47 per cent and 26 per cent by volume and value respectively. The demand of spices are gradually increasing day by day as this is a consumable product and it has also got a wide scope in overseas countries. Despite of many producer of this product, still there is a huge demand supply gap.

The book named **HAND BOOK OF SPICES AND PACKAGING WITH FORMULAES** covers new formulaes of various kinds of Spices. The major chapters of the book are Ajowan, Amchur, Aniseed, Asafoetida, Chilli, Caraway, Cardamom, Cassia, Celery Seed, Cinnamon, Clove, Coriander, Cumin Seed, Fennel, Fenugreek, Garlic, Ginger, Nutmeg, Pepper, Tamarind, Turmeric, Drying of Red Chilli, Dry Ginger, Onion Dehydration, Garlic Powder, Mustard Powder, Turmeric Powder, Formulaes of Different Kinds of Ground Spices, Packaging of Spices, Methods of Tests, Agmark, Details of Machinery, National Standards, Importers/Exporters of Spices, Plant & Equipment Suppliers & Manufacturers of Spices etc. etc.

The book has been written for the benefit and to prove an asset and a handy reference guide in the hands of new entrepreneurs & well established industrialists.

Director

ENGINEERS INDIA RESEARCH INSTITUTE

Nai Sarak, New Delhi (INDIA)

E-Mail : eirisidi@bol.net.in

Website : http://www.startindustry.com

CONTENTS AND SUBJECT INDEX

1

INTRODUCTION

Spices are widely used all over the world as food flavouring ingredients as well as treating variety of ailments. The market for spices is classified into straight spices and value added spices. Straight spices are spices in their natural form while value added spices consist of masalas, oils and oleoresins of spices.

Spices and condiments need no introduction, since India is known the world over as 'The Homes of Spices'. Spices constitute an important group of agricultural commodities which are virtually indispensable in the culinary art. They also play a significant role in our national economy and so also in the national economies of several spice producing, exporting and importing countries. Besides, huge quantities of spices are also being consumed within the country for flavoring foods and are also used in medicine, pharmaceutical, perfumery, cosmetics and several other industries.

According to the International Organization for Standardisation (ISO), there is no clear-cut division between spices and condiments and as such they have been clubbed together. The term 'spices and condiments' applies to "such natural plant or vegetable products or mixtures thereof, in whole or ground form, as are used for imparting flavour, aroma and piquancy to and for seasoning of foods".

There are over 80 spices grown in different parts of the world and 50 spices are grown in India. Spices may comprise different plant components or parts such as :

Spices Plant Components		*Examples*
Aril or **Bracket** covering seed	:	Mace or Jalvatri
Barks (of tree branches)	:	Cassia, Cinnamon
Berries	:	Allspice or Pimento, Black-Pepper, or Juniper,
Buds (unopened flower-bud)	:	Clove
Bulbs	:	Onion, Garlic, Leek, and Shallots
Floral Parts (Pistil or female parts)	:	Saffron
Fruits	:	Cardamom, Chillies/ Paprika
Kernels	:	Nutmeg or *Jaiphal*
Leaves or Leafy spices	:	Basil or *Tulsi*, Bay, Mint, Peppermint, Marjoram, *Tejpat*,
Rhizomes (underground stem)	:	Ginger, Turmeric
Exudation, latex or oleogum resin from the **Rhizome**	:	Asafoetida
Roots	:	Angelica, Horse-radish, Lovage
Seeds	:	Ajowan, Aniseed, Caraway, Celery seed,

Coriander, Dill, Fennel, Fenugreek, Mustard & Poppy Seeds, etc.

The above table shows the extent of heterogeneity in spices. Spices are well-known as appetisers and are considered essential in the culinary art all over the world. They add tang and flavour to otherwise insipid foods. Some of them also possess antioxidant properties, while others are used as preservatives in some foods like pickles and chutneys, etc. Some spices spices also possess strong antimicrobial and antibiotic activities. Many of them possess medicinal properties and have a profound effect on human health, since they affect many functional processes. For instance, spices intensify salivary flow and the secretion of amylase, neuraminic acid and hexosamines. They favour the cleansing of the oral cavity from food adhesion and bacteria; they help to check infection and caries, and protect the mucous membrane against thermic, mechanical and chemical irritation. Spices increase the secretion of saliva rich in ptyalin which facilitates starch digestion in the stomach, rendering the meals which are rich in carbohydrates, more digestible. Spices possibly activate the adreno-cortical function and fortify resistance and physical capacity. Stroke volume, blood pressure, and stroke frequency can be markedly diminished or augmented by means of spices. The significance of these possibilities is evident with regard to the ailing, on the one hand, and to the performance conscious sportsman, on the other. Spices inhibit thrombus formation and accelerate thrombolysis. All these important physiological and medicinal aspects of spices and condiments deserve our serious consideration and further thorough probe whereever necessary.

Uses of Spices

The people of those times used spices, as we do today, to enhance or vary the flavours of their foods. Spices were also flavour disguisers, masking the taste of the tainted food that was still nutritious, but would, if unspiced, have to be thrown away.

2

AJOWAN OR BISHOP'S WEED

Bot. Name : *Trachyspermum ammi* (L) Sprague
Syn. : *Carum copticum* Heirn
Family : *Umbelliferae*
Indian Names : **Hindi**: *Ajowan;* **Bengali**: *Jowan or Joan*; **Gujarati**: *Yavan*; **Kashmiri**: *Jawind*; **Kannada**: *Oma*; **Malayalam**: *Omum*; **Marathi**: *Onva*; **Oriya**: *Juani*; **Punjabi**, **Urdu**: *Ajowain*; **Sanskrit**: *Ajamoda Yavanika*; **Tamil**: *Omum*; **Telugu**: *Varnu*.

Description and Distribution

Ajowan is an annual herbaceous plant bearing the greyish-brown fruits (seeds) which constitute the spice. It belongs to the family 'umbelliferae' comprising 270 genera and 2,700 species mostly grown in the temperate regions of the world except for a few species which are cultivated in the tropics, especially India and North Africa. In addition to ajowan, caraway *(Carum carvi)*, celery *(Apium graveolens)*, coriander *(Coriandrum sativum)*, cumin *(Cuminum cyminum)*, dill *(Anethum graveolens)*, and fennel *(Foeniculum vulgare)* are the other spices which also belong to the family 'Umbelliferae' and are discussed individually later. All these umbellifers are aromatic and possess a characteristic aroma and taste.

Ajowan is grown in Iran, Egypt, Afghanistan and chiefly in India (largely in Uttar Pradesh, Bihar, Madhya Pradesh, Punjab, Rajasthan, Bengal, Tamil Nadu and Hyderabed, etc.).

It is generally grown in October-November and harvested in May June.

1

8

2

5

9

3

6

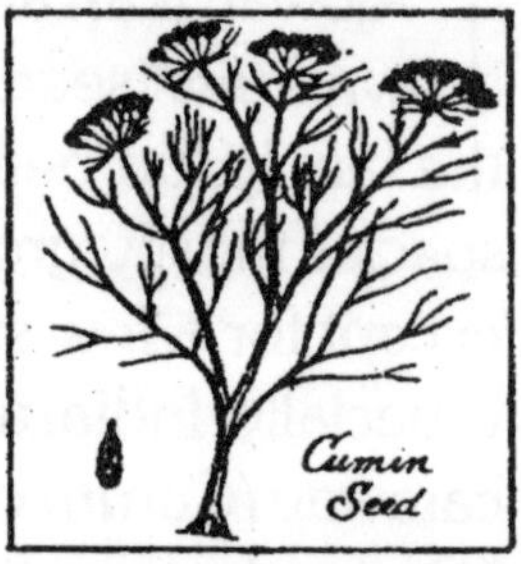

10

4

7

11

12

13

14

15

16

17

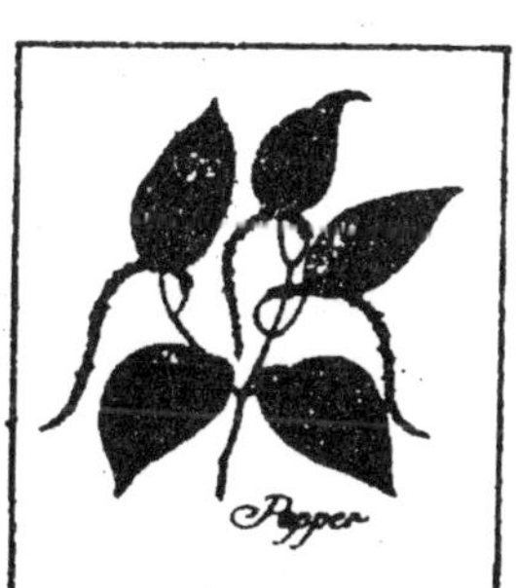

18

19

20

21

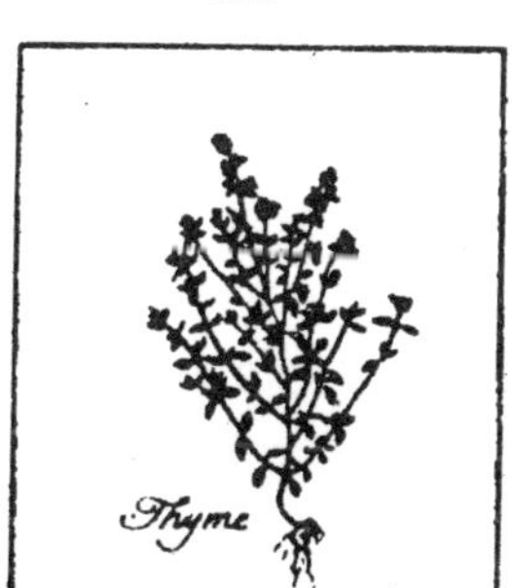

22

Recently two new high-yielding varieties of ajowan have been developed at the Agricultural Research Station, Andhra Pradesh. Selections I and II yield 1,140 & 1,170 kg/ha. as compared to only 750 kg/ha. by local variety, i.e., over 50% high yield. Such varieties should be encouraged on a commercial scale.

Composition

Ajowan seeds, like other spices, are not viewed nutritionally. They are more known as adjuncts used in small quantities for flavouring numerous foods, as antioxidants, as preservatives, or in medicine or for the manufacture of essential oils for ultimate use in perfumery, essences and medicine, etc. However, for the purpose of enforcement of quality standards with the ultimate object of detection of adulteration, information on physico-chemical composition is often sought which, in brief, is as follow-moisture: 8.9%; protein: 15.4%; fat (ether extract): 18.1%; crude fibre: 11.9%; carbohydrates; 38.6%; mineral matter (total ash): 7.1% calcium: 1.42%; phosphorous: 0.30%; iron: 14.6 mg/100 g; calorific value per 100 g: 379.4.

Uses

Essential Oil : Steam distrillation of crushed seeds yields 2.0 to 4.0% essential oil which is valued considerably in medicine on account of the presence of thymol therein. Ajowan seed is distilled in India, partly in primitive native stills and partly in more modern and large-scale distilleries located in Rao (Indore) Gwalior and Dhar. Prior to and during World War I, considerable quantities of ajowan seed were exported from India for distillation in Europe and USA. The oil was for a long time the principal source of thymol or '*ajowan ka phool*'. However, since the introduction of synthetic thymol, the distillation of ajowan oil outside India has partially ceased, and the oil lost its former importance.

In Medicine: Ajowan seeds are reported to be useful in flatulence, colic, atonic dyspepsia, diarrhoea, cholera, hysteria and spasmodic affections of the bowels. They produce feelings which accompany bowel disorders. They are most frequently used in conjuction with asafoetida, myrobalan and rock-salt. Externally, ajowan is applied in mixtures to relieve rheumatic and neuralgic pains. A teaspoonful of the seeds with a little salt is a common domestic remedy for indigestion, the seeds with a little salt is a common domestic remedy for indigestion from irregular diet. For stomachache, cough and indigestion, the seeds are masticated, swallowed and followed by a glass of hot water. They are also useful in skin diseases. A hot poultice of the seeds is used as a dry fomentation to the chest in asthma and to the hands and feet in cholera and fainting. They check chronic discharges such as profuse expectoration from bronchitis. Extracts of seeds in 70% and 40% alcohol are toxic to *Staphylococci* and *Escherichiacoli*. The leaves are used as a vermicide. Ajowan is one of the most valuable spices for use in medicine, thereby improving human health in a number of ways mentioned above. Even the roots of ajowan plant are reported to be diuretic and carminative.

3

AMCHUR

Bot. Name : *Mangifera indica* Linn.
Family : *Anacardiaceae*
Indian Names : **Bengali**: *Kachukacha Aam*; **Gujarati**: *Keri*; **Hindi**: *Kachcha Am (Keri), Amchur*; **Kannada**: *Mavina Kayi*; **Malayalam**: *Manga (Pacha)*; **Marathi**: *Amba*; **Oriya**; *Kancha Ambu*; **Punjabi**: *Kachcha Aam; Amchur*; **Tamil**: *Mangai*; **Telugu**: *Mamidi Kayi*; **Urdu**: *Kachcha Aam, Amchur*.

Description and Distribution

Amchur is the dried or dehydrated product prepared from unripe mango flesh in the form of peeled slices or powder used for acidification of curries etc. Mango is the most important fruit of India and is grown in many states of India. Invariably, under-ripe and wind-fallen seedling or country mangoes are utilised for the manufacture of amchur. No particular varieties are in demand for this purpose. Generally, the cheapest immature raw acidie fruits that are dropped by storms/winds are utilised for the preparation of amchur. Amchur is produced mostly in the northern states of India and constitutes as an '*acidulant spice*'.

The unripe fruits are peeled and the flesh cut into thin slices. The slices are then dried in the sun and packed in gunny bags for sale. Amchur is also marketed in the form of powder by crushing or powdering the dried peeled raw mango slices. Sometimes slices fresh and peeled are seasoned with powdered turmeric and then sun-dried in order to avoid insect and pest attacks during preparation and storage.

Composition

Analysis of a commercial sample of amchur showed the following composition-moisture: 14.7%; total acidity (as citric acid): 15.2%; reducing sugar: 3.0%; ash: 5.4%. The analysis of a typical sample of fresh raw mango revealed-moisture: 90%; protein: 0.7%; fat: 0.1%; carbohydrates: 8.8%; mineral matter: 0.4% calcium: 0.01%; phosphorous: 0.08%; iron:4.5 mg/100g; carotene (vit. A): 150 I.U./100g; vit. B2 (riboflavin): 30mg/100g; vit C: 8mg/ 100g; calorific value: 39/100g. Amchur is rich in citric acid. Recently, a sample of amchur was found to be adulterated with added synthetic citric acid. Quality standards have recently been fixed for amchur by any standard-laying body.

Uses

Amchur is used as an *'acidulant'* or a *'souring agent'* for curries, like similar to the use of tamarind pulp extracts in the South Indian curries *sambar* and *rasam*. It is also used in chutneys, soups and certain specific vegetable curries. The main purpose of its addition is to lower the pH of gravy whereby, the destruction of spoilage organisms in the vegetable curry, etc. is made much easier at boiling point.

It is further reported that unripe mango is useful in opthalmia and eruptions. The rind is astringents, stimulating, tonic in debility of stomach.

The kernel, too, is astringent, used in haemorrhage and diarrhoea and is anthelmintic; its juice, if snuffed, can stop nasal bleeding.

4

ANISEED

Bot Name : *Pimpinella anisum* Linn.
Syn. : *Anisum vulgare* Gaertner.
Anisum officianalis Moench
Family : *Umbelliferae*
Indian Names : **Bengali**: *Muhuri, Mitha jira*; **Gujarat**: *Anisi, Sowa;* **Hindi**: *Imported or Valaiti Saunf or Sawonf, Badian*; **Kannada**; *Sompu*; **Malayalam**: *Shombu; Marathi; Somp, Badishep*; **Oriya**: *Sop*; **Punjabi**: *Valaiti Sounf*; **Sanskrit**: *Shetapusapa*: **Tamil**: *Chombu*: **Telugu**: *Kuppi Sopu.*

Description and Distribution

Aniseed is an annual herbaceous plant belonging to the ajowan family and a native of the East Mediterranean region. It is widely cultivated in Bulgaria, Cyprus, France, Germany, Italy, Mexico, South America, Syria, Turkey and Russia. In India, it is grown to a small extent as a culinary herb or as a garden plant. It appears that the reports of its cultivation and production are not correct since aniseed has often been confused with fennel *(Foeniculum vulgare)* because of the common Indian name *Saunf* applied to both. Even the commodity commonly available in the Indian market under the name of *Lucknow Saunf* is called *'Indian aniseed'*.

Composition

The chemical composition of aniseed varies with the origin of the fruits; the reported ranges of values are-moisture :

9-13%; protein: 18%; fatty oil: 8-23%; essential oil: 2-7%; sugars: 3.5%; starch: 5%; N-free extract: 22-28%; crude fibre: 12-25% and ash: 6-10%. Choline is also present.

Distillation of Oil

Aniseed, on steam distillation, yields an essential oil, known as *'oil of anise'* which has now replaced the fruit for medicinal and flavouring purposes. Anise oil is a colourless or pale-yellow liquid having the characteristic odour and taste of the fruit.

The yield of oil generally varies from 1.9 to 3.1%. Higher values upto 6% have been reported from Syrian aniseed. Crushing of fruits prior to distillation gives better yields of oil. The material should be distilled soon after crushing to prevent any loss of oil due to evaporation. Anise oil is a highly refractive liquid which solidifies on cooling. The congealing point depends much on the anethole content and is a valuable criterion for evaluating the oil. Exposure of the oil to air causes polymerisation, and some oxidation also takes place with the formation of anisaldehyde and anisic acid.

Uses

A Flavourant: Aniseed possesses a sweet, aromatic taste and emits, when crushed, a characteristic agreeable odour and is used for flavouring food, confectionery, bakery products, beverages, 'anisette' and other liquors.

In Pledicene: The fruit is considered a mild expectorant, stimulating, carminative, diuratic and diaphoretic and is used in flatulent colic, in the preparation of asthma powders and in veterinary medicine. Alcoholic extract of aniseed possesses fungicidal activity.

In Perfumery and for Flavouring Anise Oil: Essential oil is used in perfumery, soaps and other toilet articles for flavouring culinary preparations, confectionery, beverages and liquor anisette. It is used in perfuming sachets, dental preparations and mouth washes; it is also used in the manufacture of liqueurs.

In Medicine: Oil of anise is also reported to be used as an aromatic carminative to relieve flatulence, and as an ingredient of cough-lozenges in combination with liquorice. It is a mild expectorant and is used as an antiseptic, and for the treatment of cholera. It may be used in the preparation of gripe water. The distillation 'water of anise' is sold in Indian markets as *'Araq badian'* or *'Araq saunf'* and is reported to be used in medicine.

Essential oil is also used externally as an insecticide against small insects such as head-lice, mites and vermin. It also has fungicidal properties.

5

ASAFOETIDA

Bot. Name : *Ferula asafoetida* Linn.
Family : *Umbelliferereae*
Indian Names : **Bengali, Gujarati, Hindi, Hindustani, Marathi, Punjabi** and **Urdu**: *Hing;* **Kannada**: *Ingu*; **Kashmiri**: *Yang, Sap*; **Malayalam** and **Tamil**: *Perungayam*; **Oriya**: *Hengu*; **Sanskrit**: *Badhika, Agudagandhu*; **Telugu**: *Inguva, Ingumo.*

Description and Distribution

Asafoetid or Asafoetida is the dried latex or oleogum oleoresin exuded from the living rhizome or rootstock or taproot of several species of Ferula, three of which grow in India, mainly in Kashmir. These are the perennial herbs belonging to the genus Ferula which are the sources of the oleogum resins used as condiment as well as in medicine. The species are distributed from the Mediterranean region to Central Asia. The more important ferula oleogum resins imported into India, chiefly from Iran and Afghanistan, are (a) asafoetida, (b) galbanum and (c) sumbal. Of these, asafoetida is the most important. A part of the imported resin is re-exported from India to various countries. The trade name asafoetida is based on the scientific name of a related species, *'Ferula asafoetida'*. Nearly a crore of rupees worth of asafoetida is being imported annually into India. The gross value of the sales, especially of the compounded asafoetida, mostly as consumed in South India, is probably many times more.

Types/Varieties of Asafoetida

Asafoetida of commerce is available in three forms, viz. '*tears*', '*mass*' and '*paste*'. The tears, constituting the purest form of the resin, are rounded or flattened, 5-30 mm in diameter and greyish or dull yellow in colour. The two types are recognised according to whether the tears retain the original pale colour for years or gradually become dark or reddish-brown. Mass asafoetida is the common commercial form. It consists of tears agglutinated into a more or less uniform mass usually mixed with fragments of root, earth, etc. The paste form also contains extraneous matter,

There are several varieties of asafoetida which come under different classification and are priced accordingly. There are two major varieties of asafoetida, namely '*Hing*' and '*Hingra*'. Hingra is said to be inferior to Hing which is richer in odour and is the most fancied. Hing is further classified as '*Irani Hing*' and '*Pathani Hing*', according to their country of origin, the former being from Iran, and the latter from Afghanistan. Among them, again, there are several varieties. Of these, '*Hadda*' is the most priced and the strongest. The two varieties of Irani asafoetida are '*sweet*' and '*bitter*' asafoetida. Sweet asafoetida is obtained from the horizontal cutting of the stem. Its colour is brown, transparent or turbid, and contains pieces of stem. The bitter asafoetida is obtained from the cutting of the plant root. No pieces of wood exist. It is similar to amber-coloured separated grains or a dough of white and red colour.

The two broadly recognised classes of asafoetida sold in the market with which most of the consumers may be familiar, are the white or pate variety and the dark or black variety. The former is water soluble and the latter is oil soluble. The question often asked is: What is the real difference between these two varieties? If one gets to know the chemical composition of asafoetida there is not much difference. After all, asafoetida is an oleogum-resin; where the gum portion preponderates, as in Hing, it is water soluble, and where the resin portion preponderates, as in Hingra, it is oil soluble. Thus, depending upon the extent to which one component or the other preponderates, a sample of asafoetida is water-soluble or oil-soluble. The components to which asafoetide owes its characteristic odour, reside in the oil portion and are believed to be due to two classes of compounds. One of them is ferulic ester and the other-the more important one-is a volatile oil consisting of different sulphur compounds, some of which are similar to those found in garlic and onion. Briefly, Hingra is the exudate of *Ferula foetida* Regel *(Syn F. scorodosma)*, while Hing is the exudate of F. *asafoetida* (Syn: *F. alliacea Boiss*). Irani Hing samples mostly contain woody residue but Pathani ones are camparatively free from wood. Specimens with a wet surface and agglutinated appearance occur in Pathani, but none in Irani. Hingra is heterogeneous in colour, and consistency, etc.

Composition

Asafoetida contains resin, 40-64%; gum: about 25%; volatile oil, 10-17%; and ash, 1.5-10%. The resin portion consists chiefly of asaresinotennol, free or combined with ferulic acid. Umbelliferone seems to be present in the combined state.

According to the latest amendment of Food Adulteration Act, 1954, amended up to date, the definition for Hing or Hingra and Bandhani Hing is as under:

Asafoetida *(Hing or Hingra)* means the oleogum resin obtained from the rhizome and roots of *Ferula alliaces, Ferula* rubricaulis and other species of Ferula. It should not contain any colophony resin, galbonum resin, ammoniaccum resin or any other foreign resin.

Bandhani Hing or compounded asafoetida is composed of one or more varieties of asafoetida *(Irani or Pathani* Hing or both) and gum arabic, edible starches or edible cereal flour. It should not contain colophony resin, galbonum resin, ammoniaccum resin or any other foreign resin, coal-tar dyes, and mineral pigment.

Uses

As flavourant: Asafoetida is extensively used in India for flavouring curries, sauces and pickles in conjuction with onion and garlic. In Iran (Persia), the natives rub asafoetida on warmed plates prior to placing meat on them. Besides, the large cabbage like tops of the plants are relished raw by the natives.

In Medicine: Medicinally, it stimulates the intestinal and respiratory tracts and the nervous system. It is useful in asthma, whooping cough and chronic bronchitis. It is used as an enema for intestinal flatulence. It also administered in hysterical and epileptic affections and in cholera. Asafoetida is often employed in veterinary medicine. It is a very useful remedy for relieving spasms and in indigestion and colic. It is applied externally on the stomach to stimulate the intestines.

Recent studies have shown that (1) asafoetida oil has antibiotic properties and inhibits growth of microbes, (2) asafoetida has sedative properties and its possible use in heart disease has been suggested.

In the Ayurvedic systems of medicine, the well-known recipe called *Hingashtaka* contains asafoetida as one of the important ingredients. However, the important question still remains as to whether such a reputation which asafoetida enjoys as a medicine is scientifically well-founded. If so, the precise mode of its action is yet to be understood clearly. Likewise, there is also need for rigorous implementation of purity standards as well as for the development of rapid and reliable analytical methods for the detection of adulteration. According to the Prevention of Food Adulteration Act (PFA), asafoetida (Hing or Hingra) shall not contain any colophony resin, galbonum resin, ammoniacum resin or any other resin, but it is generally felt that these standards do not fully reflect the true quality of asafoetida. The estimation of the odoriferous principles may be a truer measure of odour and hence the quality of asafoetida. There is need for intensification of reseaches in this direction. Further, knowing that there is considerable internal demand for asafoetida in India, particularly for medicinal and culinary purposes, there is need to encourage its cultivation in suitable areas in the inner Himalayas in order to be self-sufficient and thereby to avoid the heavy drain of valuable foreign exchange from India.

6

CAPSICUMS OR CHILLIES

Bot, Name : *Capsicum annum* Linn.
Bird Chilli : *Capsicum fruitescens* Linn.
Tabasco Chilli : *Capsicum fruitescens* Linn.
Family : *Solanaceae*
Indian Names : **Bengali**: *Lanka, Lanka-Morich*; **Gujarati**: *Marcha*; **Hindi**, **Punjabi, Urdu**: *Lal Mirch*; **Kannada**: *Menasina Kayi*; **Kashmiri**: *Martsu, Waungum*; **Malayalam**: *Mulaku*; **Marathi**: *Mirchi*; **Oriya**: *Lanka*; **Tamil**: *Milagai*; **Telugu**: *Mirapakayi*.

CHILLIES

Description and Distribution

Chillies are the dried ripe fruits of the species of genus *capsicum*. They are also called red peppers or capsicums and they constitute an important, well-known commercial crop used both as a condiment or culinary supplement and as a vegetable. It is virtually an indispensable item in the kitchen. Among the spices consumed per head in India, dried chilli contributes the major share. *C. annum* is a variable annual sub-shrub (originated in the American tropics) to which the flowers are born singly and the fruits are usually pendent, which provide us all the red peppers, cayenne, paprika and chillies, while a mild form with large inflated fruits constitutes the sweet pepper and is used as vegetable. Red peppers or chillies are cultivated mainly in tropical and subtropical countries, notably Africa, India, Japan, Mexico, Turkey and the USA, etc.

Almost all the varieties of low and medium pungency that are cultivated on field scale in India belong to *Capsicum annum* species. It is only the few perennial chilli varieties which are characterised by the small size of the pod and high pungency which are rarely cultivated on field scale (such as Bird chilli and Tabasco chilli) and belong to the other species *Capsicum fruitescens*. Chilli was not known to Indians about 410 years, ago, since this crop was first introduced into India by the Portuguese towards the end of the 15th century. Its cultivation became popular in the 17th century. Chilli is actually reported to be native to South America and its cultivation was known to the natives of Peru since prehistoric times.

Chillies are grown practically all over India. They occupy about 8,14,000 hectares with a production of about 8 lakh mt. Five states, namely, Andhra Pradesh, Maharahtra, Karnatka, Orissa and Tamil Nadu alone account for about 75% of the total area as well as production. The other states growing chillies commercially are Madhya Pradesh, Punjab and Bihar. The highest yield is in Jammu & Kashmir, Orissa, Tamil Nadu, Delhi, West Bengal, Punjab and Bihar.

Varieties

Commercially, chillies may be classified on the basis of their colour, size, pungency and the end-use to which they are put. According to B. Choudhuri, only four species are under cultivation in different parts of the world. However, out of these, the cultivation of two species, viz. C. *pendulam* and C. *pubescent* is mostly restricted to South and Central America. The other two species, viz. C. *annum* and C. *fruitescens* are commercially cultivated practically throughout the world. C. *annum* is the most commonly cultivated species and most of the chillies grown in India belong to this species.

Many varieties of chillies have been recorded in India, varying in shape, colour, size and pungency of fruits. As such, there appears to be scope for the selection and breeding of species suited to the hot wet tropics and different climates in India. Recently, successful attempts have been made at the IARI, New Delhi, to obtain induced chilli mutants containing high pungency or capsaicin content but low carotenoid pigments and are also high yielding. This will facilitate the extraction of capsaicin from such yellow or cream coloured chillies since otherwise, red pigments do interfere and delay its extraction.

The varieties of chillies are broadly divided into two groups as follows: and (i) The long pungent type, including the pickling type, used as a spice, and (ii) the bell shaped, non pungent or mild, and thick fleshed type, popularly known as *'Simla Mirch'* which is commonly used as a curried vegetable.

'Paprika' also belongs to the mild group *(C. annum)*.

The varieties vary in colour from red to yellow or white, in shape, from long and thin to round or oblong, and in size from 1 cm to as much as 30 cm in length. Good fruit length, shining red colour, high pungency and strong attachment of of calyx are the important quantity factors which determine the price of chillies. Commercially, there are various grades such as 'First Sort', 'Second Sort' and Mixtures, etc. or alternatively as *'Special' 'Medium'* and *'Fair'* grades as prescribed under Agmark.

Uses

As Food Flavourant : Dry chilli is extensively used as a spice in all types of curried dishes in India and abroad. Curry powder is made by grinding roasted dry chilli with other condiments such as coriander, cumin, turmeric and farinaceous matter, etc. It is also used for seasoning of egg, fish and meat preparations, sauces, *chutneys*, pickles, frankfurters, sausages, etc.

Bird chilli is used in making hot sauces such as chilli sauce and tabasco sauce. *'Mandram'* is a West Indies stomachic preparation made by adding cucumber, shallot, lime juice and Madeira wine to mashed fruits of bird chilli.

Medicinal Properties: Capsicum preparations are used as counter irritants in lumbago, neuralgia and rheumatic disorders. Taken internally, capsicum has a tonic and carminative action and is specially useful in atonic dyspepsia. It is, however, contraindicated in gastric catarrh. Taken inordinately, it may cause gastro-enterities. It is sometimes added to tannin or rose gargles for pharyngitis and sore throat. It is administered in the form of powder, tincture, linament, plaster, ointment, medicated wool, etc. In some of these preparations *'oleoresina capsici'* B.P.C., syn. Capsaicin, the alcohol soluble fraction of the ether extract of capsicum, is the active ingredient. Pharmacopoeial requirements are chiefly met by the highly pungent varieties of capsicum *(C. frutescens)* grown in Sierra Leone, Nyasaland and Zanzibar. Indian capsicum, known in trade as 'Bombay capsicum' is used as a substitute.

According to the latest researches conducted at Cancer Research Institute, Adyar, Chennai, green chillies are reported to retarch cancer due to the natural presence of an enzyme *'asperginase'* which is effective only when applied/used in the pure or isolated from.

7

CARAWAY

Bot. Name : *Carum carvi* Linn.
Syn. : *(1) Apium carvi* (L) Crantz
(2) Seseli carvi (L) Lam et Dc.
Family : Umbelliferae
Indian Names : **Bengali**: *Jira or Zira*; **Kannada**: **Hindi**: *Shia Jira or Siya Zira*; *Shime Jeerige*; **Kashmiri**: *Gunyun*; **Malayalam**: *Shima Jirakam*; **Marathi**: *Wilayati Zirah*; **Punjabi**: *Zirasiah*; **Sanskrit**: *Sushavi*; **Sindhi:** *Kalu duru*; **Tamil**: *Shimai Shembu*; **Telugu**: *Sima Jirakaia*

Description and Distribution

Caraway, or *'Caraway seed'* of commerce, is the fruit of a biennial herb known botanically as *Carum Carvi*, Linn. It is native to North and Central Europe, and its extensively cultivated in Holland and Russia, Poland, Bulgaria, Rumania, Syria, Morocco and, to a small extent, in England. It has been introduced to the USA where it is grown as a garden crop. It grows wild in India in the north Himalayan regions. It is also cultivated in the plains as a cold season crop and in the hills of Kashmir and Kumaon at an altitude of 2,740 to 3,660 m as a summer crop.

The caraway plant usually has a fleshy root and a slender branched stem that attains a height of 0.5 to 0.6 m; the compound, pinnate leaves are divided into very narrow segments: the small white flowers are borne in flat compound umbels; the fruit, when ripe, splits into narrow, elongated carpels 4 to 6.5 mm long, curved, pointed at the ends, and with five longitudinal ridges on the surface. The dried fruit or seed is brown in colour, has a pleasant odour, aromatic flavour, warm and somewhat sharp taste (because of the presence of caravone). Seeds are hard and sharp to touch. They are free from stalk ends. Caraway seed is available whole or ground. The seeds, on steam on steam distillation, yield an aromatic essential oil (4-6%) which finds greater use in medicine than the seeds as such.

The spice is known in the market by the name of the country of origin, as, for instance English, Dutch, and Mogador seed. The Dutch seed is considered the best for distilling and about 10% of Holland's total caraway seed production is used for this purpose.

In India, the fruits are collected before ripening. Wellripened fruits may also be reaped in the early mornings when the plants are bathed in dew; otherwise many seeds fall during harvesting itself. The plants are dried and the fruits threshed out, cleaned and stored in bags. The yield is very variable. It may be as high as 1000 kg per acre on rich soils, but the average yield recorded in Holland is 300-800 kg per acre.

Composition

Caraway seed has the following composition-moisture : 4.5%; protein: 7.6%; fat: 8.8%; fibre: 25.2%; carbohydrates: 50.2%; ash: 3.7%; calcium: 1.0%; phosphorus: 0.11%; sodium: 0.02%; potassium: 1.9%; iron: 0.09%; vitamins (mg/ 100g): vit. C (ascorbic acid): 12.0; vit. A: 580 I.U.; calorific value (food energy): 465 per 100 g of spice.

Other samples of fruits were found to have the following composition: moisture, 11.5-15%; ash, 5.5-6.7%; water-soluble resin, 6.2-10.1%; crude fibre, 17.5-22.3%; and nitrogen, 5.9-6.4%.

Uses

As Food Flavourant: Caraway is widely used as a spice for culinary purposes and for flavouring bread, biscuits, cakes and cheese. It is also used in the manufacture of Kummel and as an ingredient of sausage seasoning and pickling spice.

It is a mild stomachic and carminative, occasionally used in flatulent colic and as adjuvant or corrective for medicines. However, its volatile oil is employed more often than the fruit itself.

Carvone isolated from caraway oil is used as anthelmintic in hook-worm disease. Caraway oil is used chiefly for flavouring purpose and in medicine as a carminative. It is also used to correct the nauseating and griping effects of medicines. For the treatmant of scabies, a solution containing 5 parts each of alcohol and oil of caraway in 75 parts of castor oil is recommended. Caraway seed oil is used in oral preparations for overcoming an unpleasant odour or taste.

For Scenting Soaps: When employed for the scenting of soaps, the soap gives the characteristic full note.

Decarvonised oil consists of limonene with traces of carvone and is sold in the market as light oil of caraway. It finds use in scenting cheap soaps. The characteristics of light oil are: Sp. gr: 0.848 and Opt. rot: 130^0.

An inferior oil, caraway chaff oil, is said to be distilled from the husks and stalks that remain after threshing. The dried, exhausted and pulverised caraway chaff contains 20-23.5% crude protein (of which 75-85% is digestible) and 14-16% fat. It can be used as a nutritious cattle-feed.

8

CARDAMOM

GREATER CARDAMOM & LESSER CARDAMOM

Cardamoms of commerce are the dried capsules of a small group of species or plants belonging to the family *Zingiberaceae,* which contain seeds possessing a pleasant characteristic aroma. All these cardamoms are broadly grouped into two categories:

(a) **Small Cardamoms** - popularly known as *Chhota Elaichi (Elettaria cardamomum)* or the true cardamom.

(b) **Large Cardamoms** - *Bara Elaichi (Aframomum* and *Amomum* species).

The former is commercially far more important than the latter as it constituties one of the most important species of the world. *Chhota Elaichi* actually constituted the second most important 'national spice' of India and was rightly known as the 'Queen of Spices', being next to black pepper, the 'King of Spice' which incidentally is also the world's most important spice as far as international trade is concerned.

However, after several years of careful deliberations by the member countires, the I.S.O. (the International Organisation for Standardisation) has officially recognised 9 species under 3 main groups,i.e. 4 species each under

Aframomum and *Amomum* genus and one *Elettaria cardamomum* as in the 3rd group shown below :

Botanical Names	Common English Names
I. Large Cardamom *(Aframomum species)*	
(i) *Aframomum augustifolium* (Sonn) K. Schum	Madagascar Cardamom
(ii) *Aframomum hannburyi* K. Schum	Cameroon Cardamom
(iii) *Aframomum korarima* (Pereira) Engler	Korarima Cardamom
(iv) *Aframomum melegueta* (Roscoe) K. Schum	Grains of Paradise or Guinea Grains
II. Greater Cardamom *(Amomum species)*	
(i) *Amomum aromaticum* Roxburgh	Bengal Cardamom
(ii) *Amomum kepulage* Sprague et Burkill; Syn. *Amomum cardamomum* Roxburgh	Round Cardamom or Chester Cardamom or Siam Cardamom
(iii) *Amomum krervanh* Pierre et Gagnipain	Cambodian Cardamom
(iv) *Amomum subalatum* Roxburgh	Greater Indian Cardamom or Nepal Cardamom
III Lesser Cardamom	
Elletaria cardamomum Maton	Small cardomam or *Chhoti llaichi* or 'True Cardamom'

I. Cardamom *(Aframomum species)*

(i & ii) Madagascar and Cameroon Cardamoms

According to Guenther, there is not much difference in these two species. The plants occur in West Africa, East Africa, in the Seychelles Islands and in Madagascar. The seeds possess an aromatic odour and flavour slightly resembling that of true cardamom seed, but much more cineole like and cajuput like.

Several oils have been described in literature. Their yield and composition are summarised below:

Physico-chemical Properties	East Africa	Cameroon	Geiger
Yield of oil	4.5%	2.33%	1.72%
Specific Gravity at 15⁰	0.9017	0.907	0.9030
Optical Rotation at 20⁰	-16⁰ 50'	-20⁰ 34'	-6⁰ 49'
Refractive Index at 20⁰	1.46911	-	-
Acid Number	0.4	-	-
Ester Number	4.2	-	-
Saponification Number	-	-	50
Saponification Number after Acetylation	-	-	107

Oils of this type are not produced on a commercial scale, chiefly because their odour is not sufficiently interesting and distinctive. It is used as a spice and also in medicine.

(iii) Korarima

Aframomum korarima is found growing in Thailand and some African countries. It is not grown in India. The dried ground spice obtained from Thailand on steam distillation for eight hours, yielded 3.5% of pale yellow volatile oil which had a flat cineolic odour.

The following compounds were found to be present in the oil (%): pinene (3.2), camphene (0.2), β-pinene (6.8), sabinene (6.7), myrcene (0.4), a phellandrene (0.3), α-terpinene (0.9), limonene (13.5). 1,8-cinecol (35.1), α-terpinene (2.6), p-cymene (3.9), terpinolene (0.4), terminen 4 ol (5.4), A terpineol (3.4) and geraniol (4.8). This spice and its oil are not produced commercially. It is used as a spice.

(iv) Grains of Paradise or Guinea Grains

Bot. Name: *Aframomum melegueta* (Roxb.) Schum, K.

It is cultivated to a small extent in Indian gardens. It is a native of Africa, where it is found growing wild. It was also introduced to the West Indies. It occurs on the west coast of Africa from Congo to Sierra Leone. Hence the name 'Pepper Coast' or 'Melegueta Coast' for this section of Africa. The shrubs furnish the 'grains of paradise'. It is a perennial herbaceous, reed like plant upto 1.80 m high with distinct leaf and flower stems, arising from short rhizomes. Leaves sessile or sub sessile, basically mostly glabrous or apically shortly pubescent, linear or linearlanceloate, with numerous close parallel veins, glossy green with a short and rounded or subcordate, about 18-22 cm long and 1.8-2.5 cm broad. Flowers sometimes upto 13 cm growing rather close to the ground, each consisting of a very short, bracteat peduncle and a single trumpet shaped flower, springing from a cluster of reddish, rounded and mucronate bracts; carolla with one erect lanceolate lobe, two narrow linear lobes white or pale violet, and a large horizontal spreading, fan shaped labellum (a petaloid staminode), white tinted with pink, with a red and yellow blotch at the base; only one fertile stamen. Fruits flattish, oblong or pearshaped berries with a presistent calyx, yellow, oblong or pear shaped berries with a persistent calyx, yellow, russet or scarlet and (according to most publications) not fluted but 3 valved; fruit size varying from 4-9 cm, diameter 2.5-3.5 cm; inside the rind, there is a sweet white edible pulp in which there are numerous gold, red brown (oliver), chestnut brown (potter) or dark brown seeds. Seeds about 3-4 mm, rather variable in form with a paler, beak shaped hilum on the granular outside (according to most publications) and a white kernel inside; seeds aromatic and pungent; number of seeds in the berry varying from about 60-100 in wild plants.

'Grains of Paradise' in many aspects, resemble the seeds of official cardamom. When rubbed between the fingers, they give off a faint aromatic odour; their taste is hot and peppery. African natives have always esteemed these grains as a most wholesome spice; in fact, newly captured Negroes were so dependent upon the spice that slaving ships had to carry ample supplies on board. In Europe and America, 'Grains of Paradise' are now seldom used, except in veterinary preparations, and for the flavouring of certain types of liqueurs and vinegars. Formerly, they were employed quite widely as a condiment or spice.

Composition

The seeds of the pepper are only feebly aromatic but have a most pungent and burning taste, caused by a small proportion of essential oil. Their pungency is due to paradol, a yellow oily substance, similar to gingerol, present in the fatty oil of the seeds (0.75%). The amount is said to vary from 0.3 to 0.75%. The oil, mainly in the two sub epidermic layers, is 'fainly yellowish, neutral, of agreeable odour, reminding one of the seeds, and of an aromactic, non acrid taste'. The specific gravity at 15.5 ^{0}C is 0.825.

On steam distillation, the grains yield from 0.3 to 0.7% of a yellowish or slightly brown volatile oil, with a spicy but not too characteristic odour and the following properties Sp. gr. at 15^0 :0.8970; Opt. rot: 3^{0}10'; Ref. index at 20^0:1 49116; Acid no: 2.7; Ester no: 41.2; Ester no. after Acetylation: 63.9; Solubility: not soluble in 90% alcohol. Soluble in 1 vol. of 95% alcohol; slightly turbid with more alcohol. When treated with a 3% solution of sodium hydroxide, about 16% of the oil went into solution. Nothing is known about the chemical composition of the oil. The oil is not produced on a commercial scale.

Uses

There have been many uses that varied over the centuries. It is very probable that there are still many be unknown uses, especially in native medicine. The uses may be considered under the headings of medicines, spices and perfumes. Employment as medicine has been strongly interwoven with magical uses too. It has been employed both for man as well as for animals. Further more, we must point out that not only the grains are used, the pulp of the fruits, the stem, the leaves and the roots are also sometimes employed, usually for medicinal purposes.

As a Flavourant: The most celebrated application as a spice in liquid is undoubtedly in the making of 'Hippocras', the famous spiced wine in vogue during the 14th and 15th centuries. It was employed with other spices, such as cinnamon and ginger. It is still used in beer, spirits and cordials, lemonades, vinegar and sauces. The spice gives a fiery pungency to all alcohols and a taste resembling ginger ale.

Melegueta Pepper is also used to season meat and game. In an interesting article by Bouquet and Kerharo, there is an extensive description of an extract used in after dinner coffee in North Africa in which extracts of Melegueta and other ingredients such as butter, honey, groundnuts and almonds, date seeds and nutmeg are mixed.

In Perfumery: Mention must also be made of perfume, in the manufacture of which the seed oil is currently employed.

In Human Medicine: In human medicine, there are many uses. Before the seeds are mature, the pulp is chewed as a stimulant. The stem is sometimes employed to make and extract used as a purgative in treating tape worm. An extract of the young leaves is valved as a styptic. Further information indicates the use of Melegueta Pepper in Liberia in a so called 'root bottle', in which the grains are mixed with rum or brandy and drunk as a sexual stimulant. Parts of the plant are often applied externally after pulping to relieve pain. The seeds are taken to cure dysentery; chewed together with cola nut, they are considered a sedative against toothache; to guard against rheumatism and migraine; to cure fevers, etc. The extract may be used as fish poison also.

In Veterinary Medicine : In many countries, the plant and particularly the pungent seeds are still valued in veterinary medicines too.

9

GREATER CARDAMOM

Bot. Name : *Amomum aromaticum* Roxb.
Indian Names : **Bengali, Hindi**: *Morang Elaichi*; **Marathi**: *Veldoda*.

Description and Distribution

This herb is 0.6-0.9 m high, indigenous to East Bengal (now Bangladesh) and Assam and distributed over surrounding areas. It is cultivated in the wetter districts of Bengal and Assam, at the foot of the Himalayas. The fruits are produced on pendant spikes. They are narrowly obovoid (3.75 cm) and 3 valved, with numerous seeds in each cell.

Greater Cardamom I-Golsey variety

(Courtesy: Deputy Director, Spices Board, Sikkim)

Uses

The seeds are used as a spice and are medicinal. They yield about 1-1.2% of oil; Sp. gr. 0.92; Opt. rot, 13 containing a large quantity of cineol. This oil does not possess the characteristic odour of cardamom. Cardamoms or 'Winged Bengal Cardamoms' contain an essential oil with a strongly camphoraccous and cineole like odour and taste. Steam distillation of the fruit yielded 1.12% of a volatile oil with these properties Sp. gr. at 15^0: 0.920; Opt. rot $12^0 41'$; solubility: clearly soluble in 1 and more volume of 80% alcohol.

The oil contained cineole, identified by the preparation of several derivatives. The odour of the oil differed markedly from that of true cardamom oil (from *Elettaria cardamomum* Maton). The oil offers no practical interest.

(ii) Round Cardamom

Bot. Name : *Amomum cardamomum* Roxb.

Description and Distribution

As was mentioned earlier, there are other members belonging to the family *Zingiberaceae* (and particularly the genus *Amomum*), the fruits of which resemble those of *Elettaria cardamomum*), the true cardamom. One of them is *Amomum cardamomum* L., the so called 'Siam', 'Round' or 'Cluster Cardamom', which grows in Siam, Java, Sumatra, Thailand and other parts of the East Indian archipelago. The fruits are now seldom encountered in Europe and America. At one time, the fruit was official in the French Codex.

Round or Siam cardamoms occur in small compact bunches; they are smaller than a cherry, roundish, somewhat ovate, and possess a strong camphoraceous and aromatic flavour, resembling that of true cardamoms (*Elettaria cardamomum* Maton).

Volatile Oil: Distilling the seed of *Amomum cardamomum* L. (Java), 2.4% of a semi solid liquid, m.p. 42^0, with an odour reminiscent of camphor and borneol, was obtained. The oil had these properties - Sp. gr. at 26^0 : 0.909; Opt. rot: $-0^0.20'$; Acid no: 0.8; Sap. no: 14; Cineole content (Resorcinol Method): 12%; Solubility: soluble in 1.2 vol. of 80% alcohol. Further, d-borneol, and d-camphor were indentified in the oil. The crystalline mass separating from the oil consisted of approximately equal parts of d borneol and d camphor. However, the oil of Amomum cardamomum is not produced on a commercial scale yet.

Uses

The seed is used as a condiment and ground rhizomes are used medicinally for cold.

(iii) Cambodian Cardamom

Little published information is readily available on this species of the genus Amomum which is not of much commercial importance.

(iv) Greater Indian Cardamom (Large Cardamom) or Nepal Cardamom

Bot. Name : *Amomum subulatum* Roxburgh.
Indian Names : **Bengali, Hindi, Punjabi** and **Urdu**: *Bara Elaichi*; **Malayalam** : *Perelam*; **Sanskrit**: *Brihadaela*; **Tamil** : *Periya yelam*; **Talugu**: *Peddayelaki*.

Description and Distribution

This species is cultivated in swampy places along the sides of mountain streams in Nepal, Bengal, Sikkim and Assam (eastern Himalayas) and forms one of the important cash crops of the eastern region of India. Sikkim has the largest area and the highest production. It is estimated that there are about 17,000 holdings under the crop in Sikkim, covering an area of about 22,000 hectares. In North Bengal/ Darjeeling and Dooars, the estimated area under crop is about 2,200 hectares. As against the large area under this cultivation, the output or yield per hectare is very poor.

Composition

Large cardamom had the following chemical composition: The fruit, on an average, comprised: 70% seeds and 30% skins. Moisture: 8.49% volatile oil: 2.8% v/w; protein: 6.0%; total ether extract: 5.31%; (non volatile ether extract: 2.32; volatile ether extract: 3.0%); crude fibre: 22.0%; starch: 43.21; alcohol extract: 7.02; total ash: 4.01%; water soluble ash: 0.90; ash insoluble in acid: 0.42. According to an expert, total ash in whole large cardamom and seeds varied from 5.49-6.56 and 3.45%-4.57%; acid insoluble ash 0.27-072% and 0.31-1.3% and volatile oil: 0.5-1.50% and 0.9-2.0% respectively.

Volatile Oil

Essential oil is obtained on steam distillation of the crushed seeds which yield 2.5% of dark-brown coloured mobile liquid having a characteristic smell of cineole with the following physical and chemical constants-Sp.gr.at 29 °C: 0.9142; Ref. index at 29 °C: 1.46000; Opt. rot. in chloroform: -18°3'; Acid value: 2.90%; Sap. value: 14.53; Saponification value after acetylation: 40.20; Cineole: 64.94%; Terpinene: 10.7%; Terpeniol: 7.15%; Sabinine: 6.6%; Terpinyl acetate:5.1%; Bisabolene: 3.6% and polymerised oil: 3.6%. According to another expert, the dried comminuted fruit was steam distilled for 8 hours yielding 2.5% of a pale yellow volatile oil which had a flat cineolic odour. This was analysed and the percentages of the compounds present were as follows :

α-pinene (2.0), β-pinene (2.4); sabinene (0.2), myrcene (0.3), A- terpinene (0.2), limonene (10.3), 1, 8 cineol (74.0), y terpinene (0.2), p-cymene (0.2), terpinen-4-ol (2.0), δ-terpineol (5.6) and nerolidol (1.0).

More research work has recently been done on the volatile oils at CFTRI, Mysore and RRL, Thiruvaranthapuram.

Uses

As Food Flavourant: Large cardamoms/seeds are mostly used as a flavouring agent in curries, curry powders and masalas manufactured in India. The seeds are also used in sweet dishes, cakes and pastries.

In Medicine: The seeds of *Amomum subulatum* have a sharp, good taste and are a tonic to the heart and liver; are astringent to the bowels, a hypnotic, an appetiser and cause belching. The outside covering is good for headache and for the teeth and heals stomatitis. The decoction of seeds is used as a gargle in affections of teeth and gums. In combination with the seeds of melons, it is used as a diuretic in cases of gravel of the kidneys. In certain disorders of the digestive

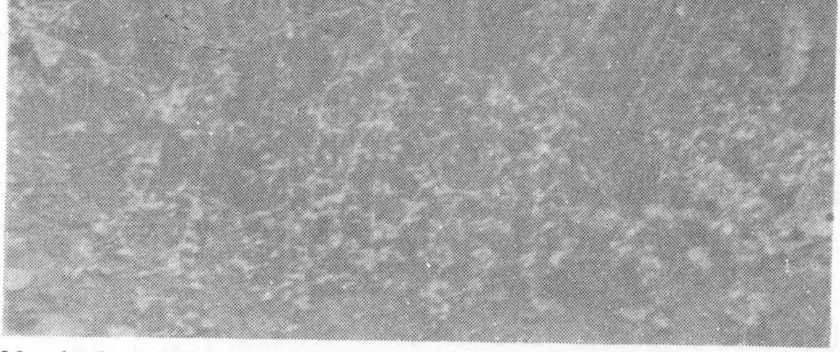

Very high yielding clone of green Cardamom (E.cardamomum)
(Courtesy: Director, Indian Cardamom Research Instt. Kerala)

system marked by scanty and viscid secretion from intestine, it promotes elimination of bile and is useful in congestion of the liver. The seeds are used in gonorrhoea and as an aphrodisiac: They have also been found useful in neuralgia in large doses (30 grains), in conjunction with quinine. The seeds are an antidote to either snake venom or scorpion venom. The seeds are also widely used in India as a spice or condiment, and in the preparation of sweetmeats.

In medicine, they are fragrant adjuncts to other stimulants, bitters and purgatives. An oil extracted from them is applied to eyelids to allay inflammation. It is aromatic, stimulant and stomachic.

The ripened fruits, considered to be a delicacy, are eaten raw by inhabitants of Sikkim and Darjeeling during September and October.

10

CASSIA

Cassia *(Jangli Dalchini)* and Cinnamon (Dalchini or Darchini) are very popular spices commonly used in the Indian diet. The name *Darchini* which has come to stay in Indian parlance, is actually a derivation from the Arabian term *Dar- al-chini*, meaning the wood (or bark) of China, one of the oldest and largest producers of China Cassia so well-known in commerce. Several reports indicate that cinnamon is one of the oldest spices known to mankind.

Cinnamon and cassia of commerce consist of layers of dried inner barks of branches of a number of species of evergreen tropical trees belonging to the same genus *Cinnamomum*, family *Lauraceae*. There appears to be considerable confusion about the nomenclature of these species. The same species is known by 6-10 different names in different producing countries. However, after careful prolonged delebrations discussions by the member countries under the aegis of I.S.O., the following spices have been officially recognised.

ISO Classification of Important Cassia Species

Popular Names	*Botanical Names*
(A) CASSLA	
(i) Cassia China or Cassia	*Cinnamomum aromaticum* C.G. Nees or C. Cassia (Syn.)
(ii) Batavia Cassia or Java	

Cassia or Cassia Vera or Padang Cinnamon	C. *burmannii* Blume
(iii) Saigon Cassia	C. *laureirii* Nees.
(B) CINNAMON	*Cinnamomum zeylanicum* Blume

So far as India is concerned, the most important aromatic barks which are in commercial use, are (i) the genuine or 'true cinnamon' (*C. zeylanicum*), (ii) *Karuva* or Jangli-Dalchini (C. *inners*); (iii) Tejpat or Tamal Patra or Indian Cassia Lignea (C. *tamala*); (iv) Tezpat or Ram Tazpat (C. *obtusifolium*). These are briefly described below:

(i) Jangli-Dalchini (*Cassia*)

Bot. Name : *Cinnamomum inners* Reinw.
Family : *Lauraceae*
Hindi : *Jangli Darchini*; **Kannada**: *Adavi lavangapatte*; **Marathi**: *Tikhi, Ranacha Dalchini*; **Tamil**: *Kuttukkaruvapatty*; **Telugu**: *Adavi lavangappatte.*

Description and Distribution

A large evergreen tropical tree reported to occur in the evergreen forests on the Western Ghats from Mysore and Coorg to annamalais and Kerala, etc. The method of preparation and curing is the same as described under cinnamon.

Uses

The end use of the bark is the same as that of cinnamon reported later.

The bark contains 0.5% volatile oil with the odour of cloves and musk. Its wood is light brown, fairly hard, shining. It machines well, takes on a good finish and hence can be used for the manufacture of light furniture.

(ii) Tejpat (Indian Cassia Lignea)

Bot. Name : *Cinnamomum tamala* Ness and Eberm
Family : *Lauraceae*
Indian Names : **Bengali, Hindi, Panjabi** & **Urdu**: *Tejpat*; **Gujarati**: *Tamalapatra*; **Marathi**: *Darchini*; **Sanskrit**: *Tamalaka (Tajpatra)*; **Tamil**: **Talishappattiri** and **Telugu**: *Talisapatri*.

Description and Distribution

A moderate-sized evergreen tree attaining a height upto 8 m and a girth of 1.4 m, distributed in tropical and sub-tropical Himalayas (915-2440m altitude), Khasi and Jaintia hills (915-1220 m altitude), and in eastern Bengal.

The species is the source of Tejpat leaves used extensively in northern India as a spice. The bark of the tree, known in trade as Indian Cassia Lignea, is collected from trees growing at the foot of the Sikkim Himalayas. There are regular plantations of C. *tamala* in Khasi and Jaintia Hills, Garo Hills, Mikir Hills, Manipur and Arunachal. Tejpat is grown mainly in the Jaintia Parganas of Sylhet district. Many plantations in this tract are self-sown; a few are planted. Although exact statistics are not available, the total area covered is approximately 600 acres, mostly in the north eastern region of India, distributed largely in the Himalayas at 250 to 700 m above sea level.

Leaves are ready for harvesting when trees are 10 years old and they continue to bear for a century. Leaves are collected every year from young vigorous plants and in alternate years from old and weak ones. Collections are made in dry weather from October to December till March. Continuous rain diminishes the aroma of the leaves. Small branches with leaves are dried in the sun for three or four days and tied up into bundles for marketing. Sometimes the leaves are separated and packed in cylindrical bamboo nets called *bora or gungra*. A tree yields 20-50 lb of dry leaves per year.

Leaf Oil

The leaves yield about 2% essential oil with the following characteristics: Sp. gr. 1.025; (α) D, 16° 37'; nD 20°, 1.526. It is soluble in 1.2 vol. of 70% alcohol. The oil contains 80-85% eugenol while imported oil contains 75-80%. The oil resembles cinnamon leaf oil and also contains d-phellandrene.

Bark oil

The essential oil from bark is pale yellow, and contains 70-85% cinnamic aldehyne. The trade in cassia has declined appreciably with the advent of synthetic cinnamic aldehyde. The oil is often adulterated with cheap terpenes.

Uses

The leaves are used mainly as a spice mostly in *Biryani* and Veg. *Pulao*. In Kashmir, they are used as a substitute for pan or betel leaves. It takes in Indian cookery the place of bay leaves in Europe. It is used as a clarifier in dyeing with myrobalans or kalala.

The leaves of C. *tamala* are carminative and are used in colic and diarrhoea. The bark is aromatic. It is coarser than the bark of cinnamon (C. *zeylanicum*) and is one of the common adulterants of true cinnamon.

(iii) Tezpat

Bot. Name : *Cinnamomum obstifolium* Ness
Family : *Lauraceae*
Indian Names : **Assamese** : *Patichanda*; **Bengali**: *Kinton, Ram Tezrat or Tezpat* **Kumaon**: *Phatgoli*; **Nepal**: *Barasingoli*.

Description and Distribution

A large robust tree occurring in the central and outer eastern Himalayas, Bangladesh, Assam and Andaman Islands.

Uses

The wood (wt. 38-44 lb/cft) is reddish grey, moderately hard and shining. It is generally used in Assam for making charcoal. The timber is said to be suitable for tea boxes and planking. The leaves, also known as Tejpat, are aromatic and are put to the same uses as those of C. *tamala*. The bark especially that of the root, collected in Marataban, resembles Sri Lanka cinnamon. It is used in dyspepsia and liver complaints in Nepal.

(iv) Cassia or Cassia China

Bot. Name	:	*Cinnamomum cassia* Blume or *C. aromaticum*
Family	:	*Lauraceae*

Description and Distribution

This commercially important product originates from C. *cassia* cultivated in the provinces of Kwajgsi, Kweichow and Kwangtung in China. The bark is the regular 'Cassia lingena' of commerce. Because of its brittleness, much of the bark is fractured, thus yielding the 'broken' grades. The main grades are (a) Whole Quills or China Rolls, (b) Selected brokens or Canton Roll, and (c) Extra selected brokens. Otherwise, the more popular four grades are; '*thin*', *medium*', '*thick*' and '*broken*'. Trees growing at higher altitudes (180-300 m) yield better quality bark with higher volatile oil content. Trees growing at lower altitudes (90-150 m) yield a relatively thick, coarse bark, somewhat deficient in flavour, containing 1.0 to 1.2% of volatile oil.

The cassia tree is larger than that of cinnamon, with more oblong-obtuse leaves having short thick stalks, blunt lobes to the perianth and a fruit smaller than that of Ceylon cinnamon. The pale yellow flowers, which are borne in panicles, are pollinated mostly by flies, and the seed is dispersed by birds which swallow the pulpy black fruit as soon as it is ripe. These fruits when dried before maturity constitute the well known 'Cassia buds', known in India as *kala Nagkesar*. The bark has been known from the earliest times.

Though this species of cassia is not grown in India, considerable quantities of it are imported into the country as mentined earlier. Hence, it is of interest to know more about it. Cassia trees are grown in China on artificially terraced hillsides at altitudes ranging from 90 to 305 m above sea level.

Preparation/Curing of Cassia Bark

When the trees about six years old, the first cut of bark is obtained. The season for working commences in March and continues till the end of May, after which the bark loses its aroma. The branches, which are about 2.5 cm. thick, being cut to within a few cm of the ground, are carried to houses and shades in the vicinity of the plantations, all the twigs and leaves being cleared off. A large bladed knife, with the cutting edge like the end of a budding knife, is used to make two longitudinal slits and three or four cuts, 50 cm apart, round the circumference through the bark. The bark is then loosened by passing underneath it a slightly curved hornknife, with the two edges slightly sharpened. Pieces of bark 40 cm long and half the circumference are thus obtained.

The bark, after its removal and while it is still moist with sap, is then laid with the convex side downwards. A small plane is then used to remove the epidermis, which is also removed by scraping. After this operation, the bark is left to dry for about twenty four hours, and then tied up in bundles of about 45 cm diameter and sent to market towns.

Composition

The composition of cassia varies from species to species, region to region *vis a vis* agro climatic factors. The following is the range of variation in different cassias: moisture: 6-5-11.9%; volatile oil: 0.5-5.1%; cold alcohol extract: 4.6-16.7%; fixed oil:0-2.1%; carbohydrates: 6.9-32.0%; crude fibre: 12.0-28.8%; protein:3.1-3.4%; total ash: 1.9-8.2%; acid insoluble ash: 0.02-0.42%.

The important constituent of commercial importance is the volatile oil which finds numerous uses in various culinary preparation, perfumery and cosmetics as well as in pharmaceutical/medical preparations.

Cassia Oil

Cassia oil is distilled in a country still by the water distillation process. The material used for distillation is the inferior or broken bark, leaves, flowers and peduncles, the major component being leaves (70%) and twigs and inferior bark (30%). The oil is somewhat similar to the cinnamon oil, but pleasant to a lesser degree. Cassia oil differs from cinnamon oil in that only one type of oil is produced from the various parts of the tree. Cinnamic aldehyde is the main constituent of cassia oil, i.e, at least 80%. It goes upto 93% as reported below :

Variations in yield and quality of cassia oil obtained from different plant components of C. *cassia* are given below :

Source: Cassia Plant part	*Yield of Cassia oil (%)*	*Sp. gravity at 15°/15°C*	*Cinnamic aldehyde. (%)*
Leaves	0.54	1.056	93.0
Branches	0.20	1.045	90.0
Cassia buds	1.90	1.026	80.4
Pedicels	1.70	1.046	92.0
Mixture of leaves, stalks and twigs	0.77	1.055	93.0

Adulteration in Cassia Oil

Pure cassia oil is very rarely exported from China. It is generlly adulterated with a mixture of rosin and kerosene and sometimes even with synthetic cinnamic aldehyde or a mixture of this aldehyde and benzyl acetate. In addition to these adulterants, cassia oil almost invariably contains lead, as a result of the action between the free cinnamic acid in the oil and container in which the oil is usually packed. It is, therefore, necessary that the cassia oil intended for use in foods or pharmaceutical preparation be rectified by distillation.

11

CELERY SEED

Bot. Name : *Apium graveolens* Line. var. *Chanu Celery*
Family : *Umbelliferae*
Indian Names : **Bengali**: *Bandhuri, Chanu*; **Gujarati**: *Bodiajmoda*; **Hindi**: *Shalari, Ajmud*; **Marathi**: *Ajmoda*; **Punjabi**: *Kernauli*; **Sanskrit**: *Ajamoda*; **Tamil**: *Ajmada*.

Description and Distribution

Celery seed is the dried ripe fruit of the umbelliferous herb, usually 60 to 180 cm high, erect, with conspicuously jointed stems bearing well-developed leaves on long expanded petioles. The rigid fruit is small, 1 to 1.5 mm long and 1 mm in diameter, contains a small seed, united or separated pericarp–some with stalk ends, brown in colour and somewhat bitter in taste. The epicarp is intercepted with oil ducts. It is widely used as a spice. The native habitat of celery extends from Sweden to Egypt, Algeria and Ethiopia, and in Asia, to India, Caucasus and Baluchistan. It is also claimed to be first mentioned as a cultivated food plant in France in 1623! Of course, celery is cultivated both for salad and seed raising in the north west Himalayas, Punjab, U.P., and France and the USA. In the Amritsar district of Punjab alone, about 300 acres had been put under this crop in the *rabi* season.

Thus, celery seed is one of the very important seed spices of India. During recent years, its export figures have further gone up. Indian celery seed is exported mostly to the UK and the USA, and to a lesser extent, to continental countries like France, Italy, the Netherlands. West Germany, as well as to Australia and New Zealand.

In colder climates and on the hills, celery is a biennial crop and produces seeds only in the second year, but in the plains, it becomes an annual and produces seeds in the very first year. It is a moisture loving plant, requiring a cool climate.

Celery seed is available both as whole and ground. It is subject to adulteration by addition of exhausted or spent seeds (from which oleoresin or oil has been extracted), excess stems, chaff, earth, etc. The ground celery is sometimes adulterated with farinaceous products, linseed meal, worthless vegetable seeds or weed seeds, etc.

Composition

Moisture; 5.1%; protein: 18.1%; fat (ether extract): 22.8%; crude fibre: 2.9%; carbohydrates: 40.9%; total ash: 10.2%; calcium: 1.8%; phosphorus: 0.55%; iron:0.45%; sodium:0.17%; potassium: 1.4%; vitamins (mg/100g): vit-B (thiamine): 0.41; vit.B (riboflavin): 0.49; niacin: 4.4; vit. C (ascorbic acid): 17.2; vit A: 650 I.U.; calorific value (food energy): 450 calories/100g.

According to another source, the variation in important quality characteristics is as follows–moisture: 5-11%; volatile oil: 1.5-3.00; (average 2.4%); non volatile ether extract: 5.8-14.2% (average 9.4%); cold water extract: 5.9-12.6%, (average 8.4%); total ash: 6.9-11.0% (average: 8.8%); ash insoluble in acid: 0.5-4.0% (average 2.5%).

Fresh celery leaves and stalk have the following typical composition respectively-moisture:81.3, 93.5% protein: 6.0, 0.8%; fat: 0.6, 0.1%; fibre: 1.4, 1.2%; carbohydrates: 8.6,

3.5%; mineral matter: 2.1, 0.9%; calcium: 0.23, 0.3%; phosphorus: 0.14, 0.4%; iron: 0.06, 0.05%; vit. A: 5,800,7,500 I.U. vit. B: trace; vit. C; 62, 6 mg/100g; calorific value: 64, 18, calories per 100g.

From the foregoing, it is apparent that leaves are more nutritious than stalk, particularly from the view point of protein and vitamins A and C.

Volatile Oil

The celery fruits yield 2-3% of a pale yellow volatile oil with a persistent odour, characteristic of the plant. In trade, this is known as celery seed oil and and is much valued both as a fixative and as an ingredient of novel perfumes. The oil has the following constants-Sp.gr.: 0.850-0.875; Ref. index: 1.478-1.484; Opt. rot: +65°-82°; Acid value upto 5 ester val: 15-40. The principal constituents are: d=limonene: 60%; d-selinene:10% sedanonic acid anhydride: 0.5% and sedanolide: 2.5-3%. The last two are responsible for the aroma of the oil. The volatile oil from the green leaves (0.1%) is of no commercial importance.

Uses

As a Food Flavourant: The dried ripe fruits (celery seeds) are used as spice. Leaves and stalks are used as salads in soups and as a pre-dinner appetiser.

In Medicine : They are stimuland and tonic, used in asthma and for liver diseases. Essential oil contracts gravid and virginal uterus. As a domestic medicine, seeds are used as nervine sedative and tonic. A domestic remedy for rheumatism is a 1-in-20 decoction. Celery seeds are the main ingredient of celery tonics.

Fatty Oil : The fruits also yield 17% of a fatty oil-*oil of celery*. This is used as an antispasmodic and nerve stimulant.

It has been successfully employed in rheumatoid arthritis and probably acts as an intestinal antiseptic. The root is considered alternative and diuretic and is given in anasarca and colic. Celery seed serves as a bird food also.

In Perfumery: The commercial use of celery seed oil is as a fixative, as an important ingredient in novel perfumes, in medicine and in the flavouring of different kinds of foods-canned soups, meats, sausages and particularly in the flavouring of the popular celery salts, celery tonics and culinary sauces. Celery seeds oil is one of the most valuable flavouring agent as it imparts a warm, aromatic and pleasing flavour to food products.

12

CINNAMON

Bot. Name : *Cinnamomum zeylanicum* Blume
Family : *Lauraceae*
Indian Names : **Bengali**, **Gujarati**, **Marathi**, **Oriya**, **Punjabi** and **Urdu**: *Dalchini*; **Hindi**: *Darchini*; **Kannada**, **Malayalam**: *Lavangpattai*; **Sanskrit**: *Darushila*; **Tamil**: *Sanna lavangapattai*.

Description and Distribution

Cinnamon is one of the most important tree spices of India. Like its cousin cassia, cinnamon consists of layers of dried pieces of the inner bark of branches and young shoots from the evergreen tree *Cinnamomum zeylanicum* which is obtained when the cork and the cortical parenchyma are removed from the 'whole bark'. The thickness of the bark ranges from 0.2 to 1.0 mm. Pure cinnamon is free from any admixture with cassia which is considered inferior to the former in appearance, flavour and odour. As stated earlier, cassia is the commonest substitute of cinnamon. While it may be possible morphologically to distinguish one from the other in the whole form, it is difficult to identify them in the powder form.

The quanlity of cinnamon depends, among other factors, on the region where it is grown. Sri Lankan cinnamon, and cinnamon from the Seychelles Island are considered to be among the best. In India, it is grown on the west coast. At

Anjarakkandi, Cannanore district, Kerala, there is a 248-acre Randa Tarra cinnamon plantation one of the biggest and perhaps the oldest plantation in Asia. It also grows on the Western Ghats from south Kanara southwards at low altitudes.

Composition

Moisture: 9.9%; protein: 4.6%; fat (ether extract): 2.2%; fibre: 20.3%; carbohydrates: 59.5%; total ash: 3.5%; calcium: 1.6%; phosphorus: 0.05%; iron: 0.004%; sodium: 0.01%; potassium: 0.4%; vitamins (mg/100g): vit: B_1: 0.14; vit. B_2: 0.21; niacin: 1.9; vit. C:39.8; vit. A: 175 I.U. per 100g; calorific value (food energy); 355 per 100g.

Composition varies according to the quality and region. According to many experts, the following range of variation may be seen–moisture: 5.4 11.4%; volatile oil: 0.3 2.8%; fixed oil: 0.3 1.9%; fibre: 25.6–30.5%; carbohydrates: 16.6–22.6%; protein: 3.0–4.5%; total ash: 3.4–6.0%; ash insoluble in acid: 0.02–0.6%.

Healthy Cinnamon Plant

Of these, the most important component is the volatile oil of commerce which finds numerous uses as discussed below. Besides, volatile oil is also prepared from cinnamon leaves, fruits and roots as a by-product which too finds use in the trades.

Uses

Cinnamon is a very useful tree. Every part of the tree–bark, wood, leaves, buds, flowers, fruits and roots–finds some use.

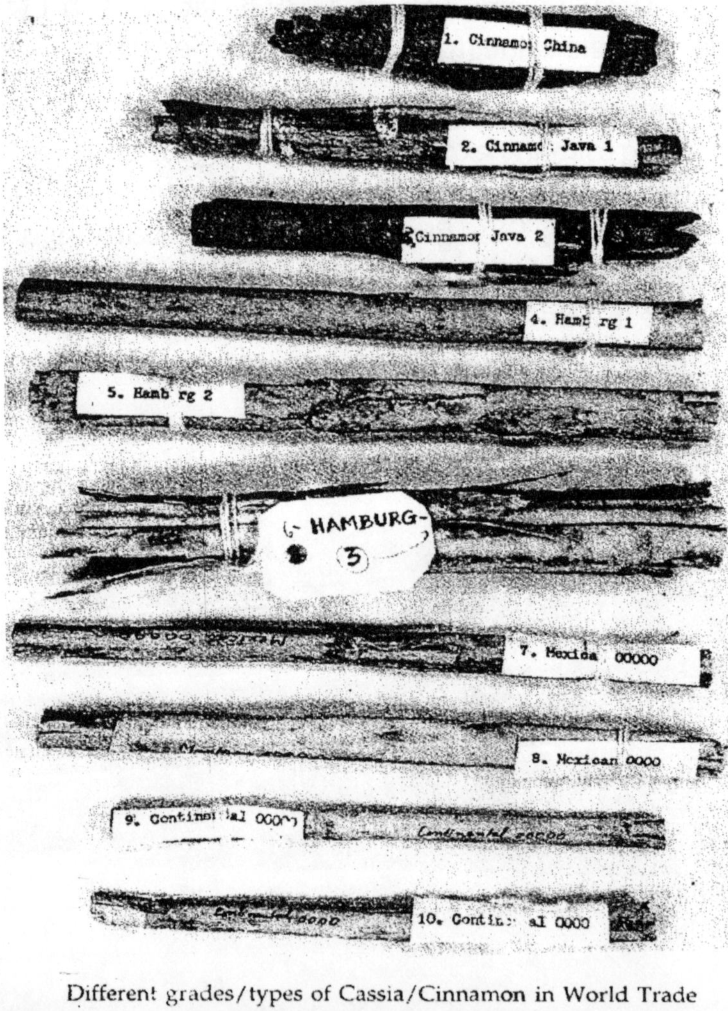

Different grades/types of Cassia/Cinnamon in World Trade

13

CLOVE

Bot. Name : *Eugenia caryophyllus* (Spregal) Bullock et Harrison
Syn. : *Syzygium aromaticum* (Merrill *et* Perry)
Family : *Myrtaceae*
Indian Names : **Bengali**: *Lawang*; **Gujarati**: *Lavang*; **Hindi**: *Laung*; **Kannada**: *Lavanga*; **Malayalam**: *Grambu*; **Marathi**: *Luvang*; **Oriya**: *Labang*; **Punjabi**:*Laung*; **Sanskrit**: *Lavanga*; **Tamil**: *Kirambu*, *Lavangam*; **Telugu**: *Lavangalu*.

Description and Distribution

The clove a commerce is the air dried, unopened flower bud obtained from a handsome, medium sized, evergreen, straight-trunked tree that grows in Kerala and Tamil Nadu, to a height of 10.7-12 m. It is also imported to some extent.

The term 'clove' is derived from the French word 'clov' and the English word 'clout', both meaning 'nail'–from the likeness of the flower bud of the clove tree to a broad headed nail.

Clove is one of the most ancient and valuable spices of the Orient, known as far back as the first century before Christ.

The cultivation of clove is largely confined to South India and an area of about 200 acres is estimated to be under this crop the main growing regions being the Nilgiris, Tenkasi hills and Kanyakumari districts in Tamil Nadu state, and Kottayam and Quilon districts in Kerala state. The long pre bearing age, lack of scientific knowledge of the culture of the crop, and want of reliable planting material seem to have stood in the way of its large scale cultivation and economic utilisation of cloves.

Preparation of Cloves

The fully grown, but unopened buds, are picked green and dried in the sun till they become dark brown, to form the clove of commerce. The buds have a slightly cylindrical base and are surrounded by the plump ball like unopened corolla which is surrounded by the four toothed calyx. If the bud is left unpicked, the flower develops after fertilisation into a fleshy, purplish and one seeded oval fruit known as 'Mother of Clove'. The fruit is about 2.5 cm long and 1.25 cm wide. The seed is oblong, rather soft in texture and grooved on one side. The leaves, unripe fruit and broken clove, including the stalk are all aromatic and yield an essential oil.

The air dried cloves are graded according to their appearance and level of impurity present. About 8,000-10,000 cloves weigh one kg or 8-10 cloves weigh just 1 g. Good quality cloves should be brownish black in colour, with full and plump crown, somewhat rough to touch, without wrinkles and should not contain more than 12% moisture and 2-3% foreign matter (induding 'Khoker', headless' and 'mother cloves', clove stems, etc. briefly descri bed below). Yellowish wrinkled cloves are immature and yield volatile oil poorer in eugenol content the main constituent. They should have fine aroma and flavour, be free from mould and should readily exude oil when their stem is pressed with the finger nail–a layman's test before purchase. This is to make sure at the time of purchase of this valuable spice that one is not cheated with 'exhausted' cloves, i.e., cloves from which essential oil has been removed partially or wholly. Such exhausted cloves do not exude oil when pressed with the nail.

Composition

The composition of cloves varies somewhat according to the agro climatic conditions under which it is grown, processed and stored. A typical analysis reveals the following–moisture: 5.4%; protein: 6.3%; volatile oil: 13.2%; non volatile ether extract (fat): 15.5%; crude fibre: 11.1%; carbohydrates: 57.7%; mineral matter: 5.0%; ash insoluble in HCI: 0.24%; calcium: 0.7%; phosphorus: 0.11%; iron: 0.01%; sodium: 0.25%; potassium: 1.2%; vitamins (mg/100g): vit B_1: 0.11%; vit B_2: 0.04; niacin: 1.5; vit C: 80.9 and vit. A: 175 I.U.; calorific value (food energy): 430 calories/100g.

The clove buds, stem and leaves, on steam distillation yield essential oils '15-17%, 4.5-5.5% and 1-2% respectively. Their comparative composition and quality are briefly as follows :

Based on a systematic analysis of 43 samples of cloves (whole and powder) for important physico chemical parameters and their histograms, two quality grades for whole cloves and one grade for clove powder have been suggested under Agmark.

Uses

As Food Flavourant: Clove is very aromatic, has a fine flavour and imparts warming qualities. In all Indian homes, it is used as a culinary spice as the flavour blends well with both sweet and savoury dishes. Cloves, both whole and ground, are used in baked goods, cakes, confectionery, chocolate, puddings, desserts, sweets, syrups, preserves, etc. Clove is used for flavouring curries, gravies, pickles, ketchup and sauces, spice mixture, and pickling spice. It is highly valued in medicine as carminative, aromatic and stimulant. It is also used in flatulence and dyspepsia. Clove has stimulating properties and is one of the ingredients of betelnut chew. In Java, clove is used in the preparation of a special brand of cigarette for smoking.

Clove Oil: The essential oil which is obtained by distilling clove with water or steam has even more uses. It is used in medicine as an aid to digestion and for its antiseptic and antibiotic properties in toothache. Externally, it has a counter-irritant action. It is an ingredient of many toothpastes and mouth washes. The oil has many industrial applications and is extensively employed in perfumes, in scenting soaps and as clearing agents in histological work. The chief constituent of the oil, eugenol, is extracted and used as an imitation carnation in perfumes, and for the formation of artificial vanilla

14

CORIANDER

Bot. Name : *Coridandrum sativum* Linn.
Family : *Umbelliferae*
Indian Name : **Bengali**: *Dhane, Dhania*; **Gujarati**: *Kothmiri, Lidhana*; **Hindi**: *Dhania or Dhanya*; **Kannada**: *Kothambri, Kothamiri bija*; **Kashmiri**: *Daaniwal, Kothambalari*; **Malayalam**: *Kothumpalari bija*; **Marathi**: *Dhana*; **Oriya**: *Dhania*; **Punjabi**: *Dhania*; **Sanskrit**: *Dhanyaka*; **Tamil**: *Kothumalli*; **Telugu**: *Dhaniyalu*

Description and Distribution

Coriander seed and fresh coriander *(dhania)* leaves are two well known to need any introduction or description in India, particularly to the housewife, as coriander is used almost daily in scores of curries, etc. Coriander is actually the housewife's secret of tasty dishes. It is a native of Mediterranean region. India, Morocco, the Commonwealth of Independent States, Hungary, Poland, Rumania, Czechoslovakia, Guatemala, Mexico and the USA are the important countries where coriander is commercially grown.

In India, coriander is cultivated in practically all the states and constitutes an important subsidiary crop in the black cotton soils of Deccan and South India (Andhra Pradesh, Maharashtra, Tamil Nadu), and the rich silt loams of North India (Punjab; Rajasthan, U.P., Himachal Pradesh, Assam, M.P. etc). In Andhra Pradesh and Tamil Nadu, over one lakh acres are under coriander cultivation. Similarly, it is grown on a fairly large scale in Punjab and other neighbouring states like Haryana & Rajasthan.

Practically all the parts of the plant, that is, tender stem, the leaves, flowers and the fruits have a pleasant aromatic odour or fragrance. The coriander leaves also constitute one of the richest sources of vitamin C (250 mg/100g) and vitamin A (5,200 I.U./100g). Its use as a condiment in curries, and particularly as fresh leaves for garnishing of curries and other dishes, and in chutney as an appetiser, should be encouraged.

Composition

Composition of coriander seeds varies, depending upon its country of origin and the agro climatic conditions under which grown, harvested, dried and stored. The following typical analysis gives a fair idea of its composition - moisture: 6.3%; protein: 1.3%; volatile oil: 0.3%; non volatile ether extract: 22%; total ether extract (fat): 19.6%; crude fibre: 31.5%; carbohydrates; 24.0%; mineral matter (total ash): 5.3%; acid insoluble ash; 0.20%; calcium: 0.08%; iron: reduce 0.006%; phosphorus: 0.44%; sodium: 0.02%; potassium: 1.2%; vitamins (mg/100g): vit. B_1: 0.26; vit. B_2: 0.23; niacin: 3.2; vit. C: 12.0; vit. A: 175 I.U./100g. Coriander seed contains volatile oil, fixed oil, tannis, cellulose, pentosans and pigments.

Coriander leaves (fresh) have the following composition - moisture: 87.9%; protein: 3.3% fat: 0.6%; carbohydrates: 6.5%; mineral matter (total ash): 1.7%; calcium: 0.14%; phosphorus: 0.06%; iron: 0.01%; vit. A: 10,460 I.U./100g; niacin: 0.8 mg/100g; vit. B_2: 60 mg/ 100g; vit. C: 135 mg/ 100g.

The aromatic odour and taste of coriander fruits (seeds) is due to an essential oil. The amount of oil varies considerably according to the source of the fruits, Indian coriander being rather poor in oil content (0.4 to 0.8%). The fruits from European countries are usually rich in oil and samples from test plots in Norway have yielded as much as 1.4-1.7% oil and up to 2% in Russian coriander. The low oil content of Indian coriander is stated to be due to the loss of a portion of the volatile oil during the drying of fruits, too much splitting of fruits, and faulty harvesting procedure of the already inferior variety of coriander.

Indian coriander is not generally preferred for the distillation of essential oil by some Western countries. This is because the Indian seeds are low in essential oil and not uniform in colour and grade. Hence, there is urgent need to evolve new suitable high yielding, firm (like Russian varietries, not easily breakable), and disease resistant varieties, rich in essential oil, adaptable to the various agro climatic regions of the country. This is necessary to increase the country's output to meet the internal and external demands. Co-operation and co-ordination between governments, research institutions and farmers are very essential to achieve this objective. By increasing our production, maintaining the seed quality, and thereby keeping our price of coriander on par with that of our competitors in the international market, and by popularising the various uses of coriander listed below, India's export could possibly be increased further.

Uses

As Food Flavourant. The fresh stem, leaves and fruits of coriander have a pleasant aromatic odour. The entire plant, when young, is used in preparing chutneys and sauces, and the leaves are used for flavouring curries and soups. The fruits (seeds) are extensively employed as condiment in the preparation of curry powder, pickling spices, sausages and seasonings. They are used for flavouring pastry, cookies, buns, cakes, and tobacco products. In the USA and Europe, coriander is employed for flavouring liquor, particularly gin. Coriander seeds are generally used after roasting. Coriander has a mild, distinctive, fragrant odour and pleasant aromatic taste, reminiscent of a combination of lemon peel and sage. It is probably one of the first spices to be used by mankind, having been known as early as 5000 B.C., and is one of the important ingredients in the manufacture of the following food flavouring (i) Bakery products, (ii) imitation flavour, (iii) pork, frankfurter, meat fish and salads, (iv) soda and syrups, (v) gelatin dessert and pudding, (vi) candy, preserves, (vii) liquors.

In Medicine: Coriander seeds are considered to be carminative, diuretic, tonic, stomachic, antibilious, refrigerant and aphrodisiac. They are used chiefly to conceal the odour of other medicines and to correct the griping qualities of rhubarb and senna. The seeds are chewed to correct foul breath. They are also considered to lessen the intoxicating effects of spirituous liquors. An infusion of the seeds combination with cardamom and caraway seeds is useful in flatulence, indigestion, vomiting and intestinal disorders.

15

CUMIN SEED

Bot. Name : *Cuminum cyminum* Linn.
Family : *Umbelliferae*
Indian Names : **Bengali** and **Punjabi**: *Safaid Jira or Zeera*; **Gujarati**: *Jiru or Jeeru*; **Hindi**: *Zira;* **Kannada**; *Jeerige*; **Kashmiri**: *Zyur*; **Malayalam**: *Jeerakam*; **Marathi**: *Jeregire*; **Oriya**: *Jira, Jeera*; **Sanskrit**: *Jiraka, Jira*; **Sindhi**: *Zero*; **Tamil**: *Ziragum or jeeragum*; **Telugu**: *Jidakara, Jikaka.*

Description and Distribution

Cumin or *Safaid Zeera* comprises the dried yellowish to light greyish brown seeds of a small slender annual herb of the coriander family, believed to be native of Egypt and Syria, Turkestan and the Eastern Mediterranean region. It grows to a height of 30-45 cm and produces a stem with many branches bearing long, finely divided, deep green leaves and small flowers, white or rose in colour, borne in umbels.

The aromatic seed like fruit, commonly known as 'seed' is elongated, oval, approximately, 6 mm long and light yellowish brown in colour, somewhat similar to caraway seed but slightly longer. The odour is peculiar, strong and heavy, pleasant to some and rather disagreeabie to others, while flavour is warm, slightly bitter and somewhat disagreeable.

Cumin is one of the oldest spices, known since Bibilical times. Today, the plant is grown extensively in Iran, India,

Morocco, China, Southern Russia, Indonesia, Japan and Turkey. Iran is the major world exporter of the cumin seed known as 'green cumin'. In India, cumin is cultivated in almost all the states (except Assam, Kerala, and Bengal), notably in U.P., Punjab, Rajasthan, Gujarat and Tamil Nadu in about 77,164 hectares average producing about 35,410 mt of cumin seeds.

Surprising enough, we also imported 300 mt of cumin (excluding black cumin) from abroad, valued at about Rs. 73.60 lakhs. This should be discouraged and instead, India, being now one of the major producers of cumin seed, can definitely lead other producing countries and also stop the drain of foreign exhange, provided high yielding and disease resistant varieties, rich in essential oil content, are evolved to suit various agroclimatic regions of the seed quality, we can bring our price of cumin on par with those of our world competitors. By further popularising the used of cumin, India's export could be possibly increased substantially.

Composition

The physico-chemical composition of cumin seeds is as follows moisture: 6.2%; protein: 17.7%; fat:23.8%; crude fibre: 9.1%; carbohydrates: 35.5% mineral matter: 7.7%; calcium: 0.9%; phosphorus: 0.45%; iron: 0.48%; sodium: 0.16%; potassium: 2.1%; vitamins (mg/100g): vit. B_1:0.73; vit. B_2: 0.38; niacin: 2.5; vit. C: 17.2; vit. A: 175 I.U./100g; calorific value: (food energy): 460 calories/100g.

From the commerical quality viewpoint, a summary of analysis of 30 samples of Indian cumin is: mositure: 6 to 10 (av. 7.7%); volatile oil content: 2.5 to 3.6 (av. 3.1%); cold water extract: 14.9 to 20.4 (av. 17.5%); total ash: 6.9 to 7.6 (mean 7.3%); acid insoluble ash: 0.2 to 0.8 (av. 0.4%). The exhausted cumin seeds and powder had 0.2-1.2% volatile oil content and very low cold water in adulteration of the genuine stuff by unscrupulous merchants.

Volatile Oil

The dried fruit is crushed and soon thereafter, it is steam distilled to yield 2.5 to 4.5% of valuable volatile oil, colourless or pale yellow, turning dark on keeping. The yeild of the oil depends upon the quality and age of the seed; the older seeds contain less oil. The range of variations in physico-chemical properties of the oil produced in India and other countries is summarised as follows Sp. gr. at 25°C: 0.8923-0.9246 (mean 0.8969); Opt. rot. at 20°C: +3 to +6°30 (mean +3°56); Ref. index at 20°C: 1.4945-1.5060 (mean 1.4968); aldehyde content: 32-42% (average 36.30%).

The chief constituent of the oils is cuminaldehyde (20-40%) and is used in perfumery.

Uses

As Food Flavourant : Cumin seeds have an aromatic odour and a spicy and somewhat bitter taste. They are largely used as condiment and form an essential ingredient in all mixed spices and curry powder for flavouring soups, pickles and for seasoning breads and cakes. They are also candied. In Holland and Switzerland, cumin is used to season some kinds of cheese, while in France and Germany, it is used to flavour bread, cakes and pastries. Cumin makes an excellent seasoning of soups and stews, for which it is widely used throughout Latin America. It is also employed in native dishes of Central and South America.

In Medicine: Cumin seeds have long been considered stimulant, carminative, stomachic, astringent and useful in diarrhoea and dyspepsia. They are now chiefly used in veterinary medicine.

Uses of Volatile Oil: The volatile cumin seed oil is employed advantageously instead of the seed in many types of flavouring compounds, especially in curries and culinary preparations of oriental character. Because of its powerful odour and flavour, the oil must be used sparingly and most carefully. The oil is used in perfumery and for flavouring liquors and cordials. It is also used as a carminative. The residue left after the extraction of volatile oil contains 17.2% protein and 3% fat. It can be used as cattle fodder.

Use of Fatty Oil: The fixed oil could also find use in the oil, fat and soap industries.

Because of the growing popularity of cumin, the demand for Iranian and Indain cumin seed is always on the increase as seen from the export trend during the past six to seven years. This happy trend must be maintained.

16

CUMIN BLACK

Bot. Name : *Nigella sativa* Linn.
Family : *Umbelliferae*
Indian Names : **Bengali**: *Kalijira*; **Hindi**, **Punjabi** and **Urdu**: *Kalunji, Kala jire*; **Malayalam**: *Karunshiragam*; **Marathi**: *Kalanjira*; **Sanskrit**: *Krishna jiraka*; **Tamil**: *Karun jiragam* **Telugu**: *Nulajilakara*.

Description and Distribution

Black cumin is the dried seed like fruit of a small herb about 45 cm in height and a native of the Levant (eastern Mediterranean region). It is said to be cultivated or occasionally found as a weed of cultivation in Punjab, Himachal Pradesh, Bihar and Assam. Leaves 2.5-3.0 cm long, cut into linear lanceolate segments; flowers pale blue; seeds trigonous, black regulose tubercular.

Cumin block or *Kala zira* is a promising aromatic and medicinal perennial herb found in the dry temperate region (1850 to 3100 m above mean sea level) and has recently been domesticated from its wild habitat. Because it is an important item of ayurvedic medicines and a rare condiment, it is in great demand and has thus become a paying cash crop of the dry temperate areas of Himachal Pradesh.

Composition

Analysis of black cumin reveals–total ash 3.8%-5.3%;

ash insolin-acid: 0.0%-0.5%; volatile oil: 0.5%-1.6%; ether extract (crude oil): 35.6%-41.6% alcoholic acidity as oleic acid (FFA): 3.4%-6.3%. crude fibre: 7.94%; total carbohydrates:31.94%. Patassium, phosphorus, sodium and iron are present in low levels.

Volatile Oil

The seeds give on steam distillation, a yellowish brown volatile oil with an unpleasant odour. The oil has the followoing characteristics–Sp.gr.at 15°: 0.875-0.886; Ref. index (20°): 1.4836-1.4844: Opt. rot. 20°: +1.43 to +2.86; Acid value: upto 1.9; ester value: 1.0 to 31.6; ester (after acatylation): 15-73; soluble in 2.0 to 4.5 or more volumes of alcohol.

Essential Oil

The essential oil contains carvone (45%-60%), *d*-limonene and cymene. A carbonyl compound, nigellone, which protects guinea pigs against histamine–induced broncho spasm, has been isolated from the oil. Preliminary clinical trials indicate its possible therapeutic use in some conditions of cough and bronchial asthma.

Uses

In Medicine: The seeds of *N. sativa* are considered carminative, stimulant, diuretic, emenagogue, galactogogue, and are used in the treatment of mild cases of puerperal fever. They are externally applied for skin eruptions. They are also used against scorpion sting. Alcoholic extracts of the seed show antibacterial activity against *Micrococcus pyogenes var. aureus* and *Escherichia coli*.

They can be used as a stabilising agent for edible fats.

Seeds are scattered between folds of linen or woollen clothes to preserve them against insect attack.

17

FENNEL

Bot. Name : *Foeniculum vulgare* Mill.
Syn. : *Foeniculum officinale* All.
Family : *Umbelliferae*
Indian Names : **Bengali**: *Pan Muhiri, Mauri*; **Gujarati**: *Variari*; **Hindi**: *Saunf, Sonp*; **Kannada**: *Badi sopu*; **Malayalam**: *Perumjeerakam*; **Marathi**: *Badi Shep*; **Punjabi**: *Saunf*; **Sanskrit**: *Madhurika*; **Tamil**: *Shombei*; **Telugu**: *Sopu, Padda jilakare*.

Description and Distribution

The dried, ripe fruit (seed) of cultivated varieties of *Foeniculum vulgare* Mill., fam. *Umbelliferae*, which is a biennial or perennial, aromatic, stout, glabrous herb, 1.5-1.8 m high, cultivated in Mediterranean countries, in Romania and in India. The seed is small, oblong, ellipsoidal or cylindrical, 6-7 mm long, straight or slightly curved, and of greenish yellow or yellowish brown colour: Mescocarp is 5 ridged; it possesses an agreeable, sweet aroma resembling aniseed.

Fennel is cultivated mostly as a garden or homeyard crop throughout India at all altitudes up to 1,825 m. It requires a fairly mild climate and is cultivated as a cold weather crop in parts of N.India. It does not succeed so well in S. India except at high elevations. It is cultivated in Maharashtra, Gujarat and Belgaum and Dharwar districts in Karnataka, to a small extent in a few western districts of U.P., in small plots in the irrigated areas of Jalandhar, Amritsar, Gurdaspur, Ludhiana, Ferozepur districts of the Punjab, Karnal district in Haryana and in small patches in Kotah, and Udaipur in Rajasthan.

Varieties :

Vareties and races differing in size, odour and taste of the fruits exist among wild and cultivated fennels, but they are hardly distinguishable from one another: they are regarded as races, varieties or sub species of *F. vulgare*. The varieties which yield commercially important volatile oils are referred generally to the sub species *Capillaceum* and placed under two distinct varieties, (i) var. *vulgare* (Mill.) Thellung (cultivated or wild, yielding Bitter Fennel Oil) and (ii) var. *dulce* (Mill.) Thellung (cultivated, yielding Sweet or Roman or Florence Fennel Oil). Var. *vulgare* is cultivated chicfly in Russia, Hungary, Germany, France, Italy, India, Japan, Argentina and USA. The cultivation of var. *dulce* is confined to France, Italy and Macedonia in southern Europe. Indian fennel is sometimes regarded as a distinct variety, var *panmorium* (syn. *F. panmorium*).

Fennel fruits (seeds as they are known in commerce) are classified for trade purpose according to their place of origin. Some of the well known types in India are Bombay, Bihar and U.P. fennels; seeds from Lucknow are considered to be the best and are priced higher than those from other areas. Commercial samples vary considerably in quality, depending upon the variety or race to which they belong and the care bestowed in harvesting and storing the fruits. They often contain sand, stem tissue, stalks and other umbelliferous seeds. They are sometimes adulterated with exhausted or partially exhausted fruits or with undeveloped or mould attacked fruits. There is also some confusion between the seeds of fennel and those of anise *(Pimpinella anisum* Linn.*)*.

though typical samples of each have distincitve features and flavours.

Fennal fruits produced in India are largely consumed within the country. The chief importing countries are Pakistan, Sri Lanka, Burma, Malaysia, Straits Settlements, Kenya, Sweden, UK, France and USA.

Composition

Moisture: 6.30%; protein: 9.5%; fat: 10%; crude fibre: 18.5%; carbohydrates: 42.3%; mineral matter: 13.4%; calcium: 1.3%; phosphorus: 0.48%; iron: 0.01%; sodium: 0.9%; potassium: 1.7%; vitamins (mg/100g)–vit. B_1: 9.41; vit. B_2: 0.36; niacin: 6.0; vit. C: 12.0; vit. A: 1,040 I.U./100g; calorific value (food energy): 370 calories per 100g.

Volatile Oil

On steam distillation of crushed fennel seed, volatile oil (0.7-6.0%) is obtained. The percentage of oil varies considerably, being the lowest in fruits of Indian origin (0.7-1.2%) and highest in fruits from Eastern Europe (4.6%). The essential oil of fennel seed is a colourless or pale yellow liquid with a characteristic taste and odour. Two types of oil are recognised in commerce–sweet fennel oil from the fruits of var. *dulce* and bitter fennel oil from the fruits of var. *vulgare*. The taste and odour of sweet fennel oil are superior to those of bitter oil.

The characteristics of Indian fennel seed oil are: Sp. gr. at 15°: 0.9744-0.9767; Opt. rot.: 11° 42'-16" 54'; Ref. index: 1.5355-1.5363. The constants of Indian fennel of oil lie within the limits of commercial fennel oils. The composition of the oil varies widely according to the variety or race from which the oil has been distilled and according to the region or origin. Indian fennel oil contains over 70% anethole and 6%

fenchone. It posssesses a sweet taste.

The main constituent of the oil from the fruits of cultivated F. *vulgare* is anethole. Oils of good quality contain 50-70% anethole.

The oil of Sweet or Roman fennel fruits contains: anethole, d-phellandrene and d limonene. The high percentage of anethole (upto 90%) and the absence of fenchone are responsible for its delicate sweet odour and flavour. Terpeneless fennel oil is obtained by removing terpenes from sweet fennel oil.

The volatile oil distilled from the above ground parts of wild growing bitter funnel plants, has the following constants– Sp. gr. c 15°c: 0.873-0.925; (a)+40°0' to + 68°0; n20°: 1.484-1.508; soluble in 0.5-1 vol. of 90% alcohol, sometimes with opalescence. It contains little, if any, anethole, the chief ingredient being d-α-phellandrene. The oil has not found any commercial application.

Uses

As Food Flavourant: The plant is pleasantly aromatic and is used as a pot herb. The leaves are used in fish sauce and for garnishing; leaf stalks are used in salad. Thickened leaf stalks of Florence fennel are blanched and used as vegetable.

Dried fruits of fennel have a fragrant odour and a pleasant aromatic taste. In India and the neighbouring countries, they are used as a masticatory or for chewing alone or in *paans*. They are used for flavouring soups, meat dishes and sauces, bread rolls, pastries and confectionery, liquors, and in the manufacture of pickles.

In Medicine: The fruits are aromatic, stimulant and carminative. They are official in the pharmacopoeias of all countries and are considered useful in diseases of the chest, spleen and kidney. They are employed also as a corrective for less pleasant drugs particularly senna and rhubarb. Fennel is a constituent of liquorice powder and of preparations for allaying griping. An infusion prepared with 8-12 g of fruits in 500 cc of boiling water is employed as an enema for infants for the expulsion of flatus. A hot infusion of the fruits is used in indigenous medicine to increase lacteal secretion and to stimulate sweating.

The leaves are reported to have diuretic properties. The roots are regarded as purgative; they have an aromatic odour and taste.

Fennel Oil in Medicine: During World War II, fennel oil was utilised in place of anise oil as a source of anethole. It is aromatic and is mildly carminative. It is useful in infantile colic and flatulence. It checks griping in purgatives and is considered a good vermicide against hookworm in doses of 60 minims. It is employed as a corrective for medicinal preparations with less pleasant flavour and odour and enters into the composition of 'Fennel Water' used medicinally as a vehicle for drugs. It is not much used in perfumery, though occasionally employed in scenting soaps.

Other Uses: The residus left after the distillation of essential oil from the fruits is used as a feed for cattle. It contains 14–22% proteins and 12-18.5% fat.

18

FENUGREEK

Bot. Name : *Trigonella foenum–graecum* Linn.
Family : *Leguminosae*
Indian Names : **Bengali**, **Gujarati**, **Hindi**, **Marathi**, **Oriya**, **Punjabi**, **Sanskirit** and **Urdu**: *Methi*; **Kannada**: *Menthya*; **Malayalam**: *Ventayan, Uluva*; **Tamil**: *Vendayam or Venthiyam*; **Telugu**: *Mentulu or Menthulu*.

Description and Distribution

Fenugreek is the dried ripe fruit of an annual herb, native of south-eastern Europe and West Asia and now cultivated in Indian, Argentina, Egypt and Mediterranean countries (southern France, Morocco and Lebanon). The seed is small and yellowish brown in colour. It has a pleasantly bitter taste and a peculiar odour and flavour of its own.

The seed is produced as a spice, as a vegetable for human consumption, as forage for cattle and, to some extent, for medicinal purposes. This robust herb has light green leaves, is 30 to 60 cm tall, and produces slender beaked pods 10 to 15 cm long. Each pod contains 10 to 20 small hard yellowish brown seeds, which are smooth and oblong, about 3 mm long; each is grooved across one corner, giving it a hooked appearance.

India is one of the major producers and exporters of fenugreek.

This spice occupies third place in area and fourth in production among all minor spices grown in this country. India being the world's major producer of the major spices, can also overtake other countries producing and exporting fenugreek provided we evolve high yielding and disease resistant varieties suited to our various agro climatic regions. It is very essential to carry out scientific and technological research on this important seed spice of our country.

Composition

Moisture: 6.3%; protein: 9.5%; fat: 10.0%; crude fibre: 18.5%; carbohydrates: 42.3%; ash: 13.4%; calcium: 1.3%; phosphorus: 0.48%; iron: 0.011%; sodium: 0.09%; potassium: 1.7%; vitamins–vit. A: 1,040 I.U./100g; vit. B_1: 0.41 mg/100: vit. B_2: 0.36; vit. C: 12.0 and niacin: 6.0 mg/ 100g; calorific value (food energy): 370 calories /100g.

Accoding to another source, fenugreek seed also contains gums (23.06%): mucilage (28.00%).

At CFTRI, Mysore, recent systematic analysis of 24 samples of fenugreek drawn from different regions showed the following variations–moisture: 7-11% (av. 8.7%); crude protein: 27.7-38.6% (av. 31.6%); mineral matter (total ash): 3.35-6.80% (av.4.9%); acid insoluble ash: 0.2-2.3% (av.1.0%); pet. ether extract: 5.2-8.2% (av.6.3%); alcohol extract: 16.6-24.8%); (av.20.4%); hot water extract: 29-39.7%) (av. 34.0%). Thus, alcohol is able to extract about twice the quantity of oleoresin as that with pet. ether. Fenugreek seeds are a very good source of protein.

In a nutshell, fenugreek seed contains many substances like protein, starch, sugars, mucilage, mineral matter, volatile oil, fixed oil, vitamins and enzymes. Seeds are rich in essential amino acids.

Fenugreek leaves and stems are also rich in calcium, iron, carotene (vit. A) and ascorbic acid. Although fresh leaves contain only 3-5% protein, on dry weight basis, they are comparable to pulses.

Volatile Oil

The volatile oil content of fenugreek is very small, less than 0.02%. It is brown in colour and slightly odorous. Its specific gravity is stated to be 0.871 at 15.5 C. Very little is known of its chemical composition. It is not of any commercial importance.

Uses

As Food or Food Flavourant: Fenugreek has been used both as a food or food additive as well as in medicine. Fresh tender pods, leaves and shoots which are rich in iron, calcium, protein, vitamin A and vitamin C, are eaten as curried vegetable since ancient times in India, Egypt, etc. As a spice, fenugreek seed also adds to the nutritive value and flavour of foods. Because of this, fenugreek is of considerable importance in those countries in the Middle and Far East where meathess diets are customary for cultural and religious reasons.

In Egypt and Ethiopia, fenugreek is a popular ingredient of bread, known to the Arabs as 'hulba', and in Ethiopia going by the Amharic name 'abish'. In Greece, the seeds, boiled or raw, are eaten with honey. In the United States, it is used in the manufacture of chutneys and in various spice blends, but its most important culinary use is as a source of fenugreek extract, the principal flavouring ingredient of imitation maple syrup. It is used in recipes like hearty Vegetable. Been Soup and Fenugreek Beef Stew. In the north, fenugreek seeds from an important ingredient in "mango pickle in oil". The most popular pickle & urban population.

Fenugreek is mainly of interest as one of the principal odorous constituents of curry powder.

In Medicine

Medicine papyri from ancient Egyption tombs reveal that it was used both to reduce fevers and also as a food. According to the belief of the ancients, fenugreek stimulates the digestive process as well as the metabolism in general. The seeds are used in colic flatulence, dysentery, diarrhoea, dyspepsia with loss of appetite, chronic cough, dropsy, enlargement of liver and spleen, rickets, gout, and disbetes. The seeds are used as carminative, tonic, aphrodisiac; and infusion given to small pox patients as a cooling drink; roasted and then infused, used in sweets served to ladies during the post natal period.

Although the use of most spices in medicine has declined substantially in recent years, fenugreek is an important exception to the rule. Recent studies in England indicated that fenugreek seeds substantially contain the steroidal substance diosgenin which is used as a starting material in the synthesis of sex hormones and oral contraceptives. Diosgenin is at present obtained mainly from the tubers of certain species of Dioscorea grown in Mexico and Central America. This is a long, duration and costly crop whereas fenugreek is a short duration and non expensive crop. If plant breeders are successful in developing fenugreek varieties with a high content of diosgenin, this little known spice could make a two fold economic contribution to a solution of the world's population problems by assisting in birth control and at the same time providing additional food. Also, the seed is used by Indian women for its power to promote lactation.

19

GARLIC

Bot. Name : *Allium sativum* Linn.
Family : *Lilliaceae*
Indian Names : **Assamese**: *Naharu*; **Bengali**: *Rashum*; **Gujarati**: *Lason*, **Hindi**: *Lasum, Lassan, Lahsun*; **Kannada**: *Bellulli*; **Kashmiri**: *Ruhan*; **Malayalam**: *Vellulli*; **Marathi**: *Lusoon*; **Oriya**: *Rasuna*; **Punjabi**: *Lassan, Lasum*; **Sanskrit**: *Lashuna*; **Tamil**: *Ullipundu, Vellaippundu'* **Telugu**: *Velluri*; **Urdu**: *Lessun, Lashun*.

Description and Distribution

Garlic or *Lassan* needs no introduction since it has long been recognised all over the world as a valuable condiment for foods, and a popular remedy or medicine for various ailments and physiological disorders.

Garlic has since long been cultivated practically throughout India as an important minor spice or condiment crop.

It is desirable that a central co-ordinating agency/ department be set up for collecting, collating and projection of annual progress in production. There is ample scope for exports and for increasing the area under garlic which is such a valuable crop.

It is a hardy, bulbous perennial with narrow flat leaves, and bears small white flowers and bulbils. The bulb consists of 6–30 smaller bulblets called 'cloves' and is surrounded by a thin white, or pinkish papery sheath. Garlic has a stronger flavour than onion or its other allies. Recovery of cloves is 86-96% (average 93.7%).

Garlic grows under much the same conditions as onion, except that it favours a richer soil and a higher elevation (900-1200 m). A well drained, moderately clayey loam is best suited for its cultivation. It requires a cool, moist period during growth and a relatively dry period during the maturing of crop. It takes longer (4-5 months) than onion to mature, and is consequently grown as a late season irrigated crop. In South India, it is rotated with ragi (*Eleusine coracana*), chillies, maize, potatoes and beans.

Two Garlic Crops a year

The scientists have also found in experimental farms that garlic too can be produced in *kharif*. Planting of garlic by the last week of August gave the highest yield and the biggest size of bulbs.

Varieties

No distinct varieties of garlic are recognised by the trade in North India but two distinct types, namely *Fowari* and *Rajalle Gaddi* with slightly bigger bulbs are grown in the Bellary district of South India. Breeding for production of new varieties with large bulbs of white colour, uniform shape and size, bold and compact cloves, high yield and resistance to diseases and pests, is under way at the Punjab Agricultural University, Ludhiana.

During the course of the development of a patented process at CFTRI, Mysore, for the economic manufacture of garlic powder from Indian garlic, the author had the unique opportunity of testing garlic grown in important states of India and observed that Jamnager garlic was the biggest and the best, giving the highest recovery of dehydrated peeled garlic and garlic powder of good pungency and antibacterial activity.

The crop is ready for harvesting when the tops turn, yellowish or brownish, and show sigs of drying up, usually about a month or so after the emergence of seed stalks. The bulbs are lifted, freed from earth and the leaves tied at the top. The bulbs are cured for three to four days in the shade before storing them in a well ventilated room. Tops are removed before marketing the produce. Thoroughly cured garlic bulbs keep fairly well in ordinary well ventilated room/ store.

Composition

Fresh peeled garlic cloves (bulblets) have the following composition moisture: 62.8%; protein: 6.3%; fat: 0.1%; mineral matter: 1.0%; fibre: 0.8%; carbohydrates: 29.0%; calcium: 0.03%; phosphorus: 0.31%; iron (Fe): 0.001%; calorific value (food energy): 142 calories/100 g; vit.A:0, nicotinic acid: 0.4 mg/100g; vit. C: 13 mg/ 100 g.

Garlic Powder (Dehydrated garlic) has the following nutritive value–moisture: 5.2%; protein: 17.5%; fat: 0.6%; mineral matter: 3.2%; fibre: 1.9%; carbohydrates: 71.4%; calcium: 0.1%; phosphorus: 0.42%; iron (cs): 0.004%; sodium: 0.01%; potassium: 1.1%; vit. A: 175 I.U./100; vit. B_1: 0.68; vit. B_2: 0.08; niacin: 0.7%; vic. C: 12.0 mg/100g; calorific value (food energy): 380 calories/ 100g.

The author and his assicates have published a series of 12 R&D papers on garlic powder according to which the following additional information is available. Antibacterial acitivity: 15-31 mm (by cup plate method): allyl sulphide:0.57 to 2.70%; total sulphur: 594-834 mg/100g; volatile oil: 0.04 0.1%; alcohol extract: 7.22%; non-volatile extract: 6.20%;

volatile ether extract: 0.10%; starch: nil; total ash: 3.46%, water soluble ash: 3.4%; acid insoluble ash: nil; total bacterial load: 50 x 10^4/g. We also succeeded in preparing an odourless garlic powder by inactivating the enzyme *'allinase'*. It had almost the same composition as that of garlic powder except in respect of allicin, the pungent principle, which could be regenerated at will by either incorporation of fresh enzyme or fresh crushed garlic in small quantity.

Garlic Salt is prepared by mixing rapidly garlic powder: 20 parts; refined pulverised salt: 78 parts; and anti caking agent (usually calcium stearate or equivalent): 2 parts: total, 100 parts. Accordingly, the composition will be proportion to the .garlic powder used. However, the major points of difference would be: total ash: 82.32%; water soluble ash: 78.43%; ash insoluble in acid: 1.04%. The higher ash and water soluble ash values are due to the added 78% common salt and higher acid insoluble ash due to the added calcium stearate (anti caking agen.)

Garlic Powder

The author and his associates have developed a patented echnique at CFTRI, which, apart from being very economica. yieids a powder of better colour, flavour and pharmaceutical value or antibacterial activity. It has the following advantages: (1) About 20% of the fresh crop is wasted due to repiration, transpiration and micro biological spoilage due to lack of proper, storage and transport facilities. Thus, if the surplus crop could be conveniently and economically channelled into the production of garlic powder by this improved technique, a considerable national waste could be avoided. Incidentally, this will also assist in regularising the market rates, particularly in tl e glut season. (2) All undersized or culled but healthy bulbs, which normally fetch a very low price in the market, could be conveniently utilised in the manufacture of garlic powder with advantage. (3) Given the necessary publicity, garlic powder should prove very handy to the housewife for day-to-day use both as condiment and as folk medicine. (4) It could also save her the botheration of peeling garlic everyday and thus save time and late our. (5) A cheap garlic powder of good overall quality could be most welcome to the food industry in the country for flavouring several food products. (6) Garlic powder converted into suitable tablets or packed into capsules should find a ready market in this country, in the face of costly synthetic tablets claiming anti–bacterial activity. (7) It also has bright future possibilities for export purposes.

Uses

As Food Flavourant & in Medicine: Garlic has since long been recognised all over the world as a valuable condiment for foods, and a popular remedy for various ailments and physiological disorders. According to the Unani and Ayurvedic systems as practised in India, garlic is carminative and is a gastric stimulant, and thus aids in digestion and absorption of food. It is also given in flatulence. In modern allopathy, it is being used in a number of patented medicines and other preparations. Besides, garlic is also anthelmintic and antiseptic. The active principle in garlic is an antibiotic–allicin, which is an enymatic clevage product from its precursor, 'allin' naturally present in garlic.

The antibacterial action of garlic had been noticed from early days, its healing capacity and effectiveness against cholera having been recorded as early as 1758. Besides, its antibacterial action against *Eberthella typhosa*, *Escherichiacoli*, Acid fast bacilli, *Aerobacter aerogenes*, *Stephylococcus aureus* and *Shigella sonnei*, various gram positive and gram negative organisms in dilutions as low as 1:85,000 to 1:125,000 and its ineffectiveness against L. *caseii* and *S. faecalis* have been experimentally demonstrated. Further, 1 mg of allicin has been reported to correspond to 15 Oxford units of penicillin. Preparation of several odourless garlic preparations has also been reported.

Garlic as Condiment: Garlic is used practically all over the world for flavouring various dishes. In America, about 50% of the entire output of fresh garlic is dehydrated and salad dressings, tomato products and in several meat preparations. Further, raw garlic can be used in the manufacture of garlic powder, garlic salt, garlic vinegar, garlic cheese croutons, garlicked potato chips, garlic bread, garlicked meat tit bits and garlicked bacon, etc., which have been boosted in the American market. Recently, spray dried garlic products have also been put in to the market, though liquid garlic preparations have also been available for some years.

In Italy, Europe, and particularly in Latin American countries, spectacular popularity of garlic is shown by the methods by which it is boosted by the garlic growers.

In India and other Asian and Middle East countries, it is already being used in several food preparations notably in chutneys, pickles, curry powders, curried vegetables, meat preparations, tomato ketchup and the like. Of late, there has been considerable demand by the food industries in this country for garlic powder as a condiment.

Garlic Oil as an Insecticide an Antilritoic : Recently, studies conducted at the Bhabha Atomic Research Centre, Mumbai, on differential toxicity of garlic oil to housefly and khapra beetle indicated that adults as well as the larvae of both the species respond to the vapours of garlic oil by exhibiting hyper excitability, ataxia, salivation and excretion, the usual signs of poisoning when treated similarly with insecticide. The larvicidal prinicples of garlic have been isolated and identified as 'diallyl disulphide' and diallyl trisulphide' which are fatal at 5 parts per million to larvae of *Culex pipiens quinquefasciatus* Say.

Oil of garlic has lately come to be appreciated as a valuable flavouring agent, for use in all kinds of meat preparations, soups, canned foods and sauces.

According to an American patent, the residue of garlic, obtained by alcoholic extraction and distillation, contains a bacteriostatic and bactericidal substance identified as 'allyl disulfide oxide'.

On steam distillation of crushed garlic at atmospheric pressure, the major odour producing principle, allicin, is decomposed down to diallyl disulphide and other disulphides. That explains why the volatile oil of garlic consists chiefly of disulphides. However, allicin can be isolated by steam distillation at reduced pressure. It may also be clarified that the mother precursor allin does not possess bactericidal properties. It is only allicin produced as a result of enzymic cleavage of allin which is bactericidal.

The inhalation of garlic oil or garlic juice has been recommended in cases of pulmonary tuberculosis, rheumatism, sterlity and impotence.

Garlic juice is used for various ailmants of the stomach. as a rubefacient in skin diseases, and as ear drops in earache. The juice diluted with water can be used against duodenal ulcers. In cambodia, the leaves are used in the treatment of asthma.

Because of its highly curative properties, it has been described as derived from *Amrita* or *Ambrosia*. The later prejudice against the use of garlic in India, particularly among the Brahmins, appears to have originated from its popularity with the foreign invaders. The prejudice became so intense that not only socio religious writers like Manu deprecated its use, but also the authors of medicine like Kashyapa disparaged it. The recent scientific evidence about its several highly curative properties clearly shows that the old prejuidice was not justified. It is one of the cheapest and most efficient folk medicines in the hands of the housewife and the layman alike for day to day use which should be encouraged.

Recent scientific texts on rabbits proved that garlic inhibited, to a certain degree, the development of extremely severe forms of experimental hypercholestrinaemia. In an acute experiment on 75 cats, garlic fractions displayed a considerable hypotensive effect. In dogs, with experimental hypertension, garlic reduced their systolic arterial tension to values nearly as high as the normal ones.

Clinical application of garlic in 114 human patients with clear cut hypertension and atherosclerosis, markedly improved their complaints and in the overwhelming majority, provoked a drop of their systolic arterial tension by 8 to 33 mm and their diastolic by 4 to 20 mm of mercury. Some bio-chemical taste improved as well.

In small doses, garlic intensified the tonus of the intestinal muscles, thus increasing peristaltic movements, while in large doses, it inhibited them.

In experiments on animals and human workers exposed to chronic lead intoxication, garlic has been found to be an efficacious preventive and curative drug against saturnism.

In Cancer: Influence of garlic antibiotic on malignant tumours of humans as well as animals has been found to be useful. Transplanted tumours of Jensen sarcoma in rats regressed, and in some cases, completely disappeared after the injection of 1-3mg of allicin, given either intramuscularly or directly into the tumour. However, all types of tumours do not respond equally well.

20

GINGER

Bot. Names : *Zingiber officinale* Linn.
Family : *Zingiberaceae*
Indian Names : **Bengali**: *Ada*; **Gujarati**: *Adu*; **Hindi**: *Adrak*; **Kannada**: *Shunti, Ardraka*; **Malayalam**: *Inji*; **Marathi**: *Ale*; **Oriya**: *Ada*; **Punjabi**: *Adrak*; **Sanskrit**: *Ardraka*; **Tamil**: *Inji*; **Telugu**: *Allam*; **Urdu**: *Adrak or Adhrak*.

Description and Distribution

Ginger of commerce or *'Adrak'* is the dried underground stem or rhizome of the Zingiberous herbaceous plant, Z. *officinale*, which constitutes one of the five most important major spice of India, standing third or fourth, competing with chillies, depending upon fluctuations in world market prices and world demand and supply position. During the past three years, 8,000-13,000 mt of dried ginger of different grades, worth Rs. 5-20 crores annually were exported to fifty countries. In fact, India still enjoys the unique position of being the largest producer and exporter of ginger in the world. India's production alone constitutes about 50% of the total world production of ginger. Besides, Indian ginger or Cochin ginger is also considered one of the best in the world.

Ginger, like cinnamon, clove and pepper, is one of the most important and oldest spices. It consists of the prepared and sundried rhizomes known in trade as 'hands' or 'races' which are either with the outer brownish cortical layers intact ('coated' or 'unscraped'), or with outer peel or coating partially or completely removed (i.e. 'uncoated' or 'scraped' or 'decorticated' ginger.) To improve their appearance, some grades of ginger are bleached by various means, e.g. by liming, etc.

According to available historical records, ginger was certainly known to and highly esteemed by the ancient Greeks and Romans who obtained this spice from Arabian traders via the Red Sea. It was obtained into Germany and France in the 9th century and to England in the 10th century. Since the ginger rhizome can be easily transported in a living state for considerable distances, the plant has been introduced to many tropical and sub tropical countries. It is now cultivated in several parts of the world, the most important producing regions being India, Jamaica, Sierra Leone and Nigeria (West Africa), southern China, Japan, Taiwan and Australia. Of these, Jamaica and India produce the best quality ginger, followed by the West African variety. Chinese ginger is usually not exported as a dried spice, but preserved in sugar syrup or converted into 'ginger candy'. It has low pungency, but lacks the characteristic ginger aroma. Ginger produced in other countries (Malayasia, Indonesia etc.) is not of much commercial importance yet.

Ginger ranked fourth in value among all the spices exported from India during 1990-91 being next to pepper, chillies and turmeric.

The major bottlenecks in boosting up further exports of ginger are (i) its higher fibre content than that of its main competitor, Jamaican Ginger, in world markets, and (ii) its higher cost of production. Both these problems can be overcome by developing higher yielding, disease resistant, exotic varieties of lower fibre content but richer in volatile oil and oleoresin content. Nearly 26 varieties of ginger are under study at Agricultural Research Station, Ambalavayal in Kerala, and elsewhere.

Ginger requires a warm and humid climate. It is cultivated from almost sea level to an altitude of 1500 m, either under heavy rainfall conditions of 150-300 cm or under irrigation. The crop can thrive well in sandy or clayey loam or lateritic loam soils.

Composition

Dry Ginger has the following composition moisture: 6.9%; protein: 8.6%; fat: 6.4%; fibre: 5.9%; carbohydrates: 66.5%; ash: 5.7%; calcium: 0.1%; phosphorus: 0.15%; iron (Fe): 0.011%; sodium: 0.03%; potassium: 1.4%; vit. A: 175 I.U./ 100g; vit B_1: 0.05mg/100g; vit B_2: 0.13; niacin: 1.9%; vit C: 12.0mg/100g and calorific value (food energy): 380 calories/ 100g;

It may be added that the composition of ginger varies with type or variety, region, agro climatic conditions, methods of curing, drying, packaging and storage. Therefore, there are seven different trade types of ginger, namely, (i) Jamaican ginger, (ii) Indian ginger, (iii) West African or Nigerian ginger, (iv) Sierra Leone ginger, (v) Japanese ginger, (vi) Rio de Janeiro ginger, and (vii) China ginger. The Indian ginger is further classified as (i) Malabar ginger (Kerala): (a) Cochin ginger (b) Calicut ginger or Wyanad ginger, (ii) Assamese ginger (iii) Himachal ginger. For export purposes, Cochin and Calicut gingers are graded according to the number of fingers contained in the rhizome. There are three export qualities, B,C,D, consisting of three fingers, two fingers, and pieces, respectively. Then there are 'bleached' or 'coated' ginger and 'uncoated', peeled or decorticated 'scraped' ginger and 'unscraped' ginger, their prices depending upon their respective quality as per Agmark specifications.

Chemical analysis of 26 varieties of ginger grown in India was conducted at CFTRI, Mysore, which showed the following range of variations in important qualities moisture: 8.5–16.5% (av. 10.85%); volatile oil: 1.0-2.7% (av. 1.8%); oleoresin (acetone extract): 3.9-9.3% (av. 6.5%); water extract: 14.4-25.8% (av. 19.6%); cold alcohol extract 3.5-9.31% (av.6.0%); starch : 40.4-59.0% (av.53%); crude fibre: 4.8-9.80% (av.7.17%); crude protein: 10.3 to 15.0% (av. 12.4%); total ash: 5.1-9.3% (av. 6.64%) water soluble ash: 3.9-8.84% (av. 5.48%); acid insoluble ash: 0.0-0.59% (av. 0.14%) and alkalinity of ash: 25.7-79.0 (av. 48.1) ml. of 0.1N HCl per 100g of unpeeled ginger.

'Mysore', 'Manantody' and 'Ernad Manjari' varieties were found to be rich in volatile oil content. 'Assam' and

Freshly harvested Ginger
(Courtesy: Spices Board)

'Manantody' were rich in oleoresin (acetone extract). 'Thinladuim', 'Jorhat' and 'Assam' were fibrous. 'Nadia', 'Vengara' and 'Narasapatam' were highest in starch content.

The expert and his associates developed an integrated process for the economic recovery of volatile oil from peel, oleoresin and starch from the spent residue. Varieties rich in volatile oil, oleoresin, and starch should make the venture more successful.

Volatile Oil

On steam distillation, dried, cracked and comminuted ginger yields 1.0 to 3.0% (av.2.0%) of pale yellow, viscid oil. The oil possesses the aromati odour but not the pungent falvour ('bite') of the spice. Of course, the odour of the oil is quite lasting.

The physico chemical characteristics of the oil vary depending upon the variety, age or period of storage and method of extraction, etc. They range as follows–Sp. gr. at 15°C: 0.876-0.887; Opt. rot: 30° to 44° 20', occasionally as–low as 23°58; Ref. index at 20°C: 1,4876 to 1,4917; Acid no: 1.1-3.7; Sap. no: 0.9–11.2 (upto 20.6).

It is more economical and convenient to recover oil or oleoresin from dried ginger than from fresh ginger. However, fresh scrapings of ginger are quite rich in oil and should be immediately used for steam distillation, otherwise, 60-80% of the volatile oil is lost overnight, as experienced by the author in his detailed studies on the development of useful products from ginger, including volatile oil, oleoresin and edible products from the exhausted or 'spent' ginger.

Ginger Oleoresin

Is obtained by extraction of powdered dried ginger with suitable organce solvents like alcohol, acetone or any other efficient solvent. Unlike volatile oil, it contains both the volatile oil and the non volatile pungent principles for which ginger is so highly esteemed. Concentration of the acetone extract under vacuum and on complete removal of even traces of the solvent used, yields the so–called oleoresin of ginger. The quantitative composition of the oleoresin depends upon the solvent used. Ginger oleoresin (commercially known as 'Gingerin') generally contains the following compounds; gingerol, zingerone, shorgaol, volatile oil, resins phenols, etc. Ginger oleoresin is manufactured on a commercial scale in India and abroad and is in great demand by the various food industries.

Uses

In Food Preparations: The aroma of ginger is pleasant and spicy and its flavour penetrating, slightly biting due to antiseptic or pungent compounds present in it, which make it indispensable in the manufacture of number of food products like ginger bread, contectionery, ginger ale, curry powders, certain curried meats, table sauces, in pickling and in the manufacture of certain soft drinks like cordials, ginger cocktail, carbonated dirnks, bitters, etc. Ginger is also used for the manufacture or ginger oil, oleoresin, essences, tinctures, etc.

Ginger Candy/ Preserve: Ginger preserve and ginger candy prepared from green or fresh ginger are quite a favourite of many and find great demend.

Ginger Plantation

Recovery of Starch and Soft Drinks from Spent Ginger: The anthor developed a number of useful products from spent or exhausted ginger (after the recovery of volatile oil) such as vitaminised effervescent ginger powder, vitaminised ginger powder, plain effervescent ginger powder. Likewise, the anthor suggested the recovery of starch from ginger residue left after the recovery of oleoresin. The integrated process for recovery of oleoresin, protein and starch recommended by the author is worth commercial exploitation.

Alcoholic Beverages: A numbers of alcoholic beverages are prepared from ginger in foreign countries, such as ginger brandy, ginger wine, ginger beer and ginger ales, etc.

In Medicine: According to the Ayurvedic medical system, ginger is considered to be carminative, stimulant and given in dyspepsia and flatulent colic. It is also prescribed as an adjunct to many tonic and stimulating remedies. It also has aphrodisiac values, besides its use in tinctures and as a flavourant.

Use of Ginger Oil

As Flavourant: Ginger oil is primarily used as a food flavourant in soft drinks like ginger ale, bitters, cordials and liquors, as a spice in bakery products, confactionery, pickles, sauces and preserves, etc.

Pharmaceutical Uses: The pharmaceutical uses are carminative, rubefacient, stimulant, in alcoholic gastritis, dyspepsia, flatulent colic, etc. Veterinary uses of ginger are as stimulant and carminative, in indigestion of horses, and cattle, in spasmodic colic of horses, and to prevent the griping by purgatives.

Uses in perfumery: The oil of ginger finds limited use in perfumery, where it imparts a unique individual note to compositions of the oriental type.

21

NUTMEG

Bot. Names : *Myristica fragrans* Hout.
Family : *Myristicaceae*
Indian Names : **Bengali**, **Gujarati**, **Hindi**: **Marathi**, **Punjabi** and **Urdu;** *Jaiphal*; **Kannada**: *Jayikai*; **Kashmiri**: *Zaaphal*; **Malayalam**: *Jathikka*; **Oriya**: *Jaiphala*; **Sanskrit**: *Jatiphala*; **Tamil**: *Jathikai*; **Telugu**: *Jajikai*.

Description and Distribution

As already described under mace, nutmeg is the dried seed (kernel) of the peach–like ripe fruit of *Myristica fragrans* the evergreen tree, native of Moluccas and cultivated in Indonesia, West Indies, etc. Indonesia is one of the largest world suppliers of nutmeg. In India, nutmeg is grown on a small scale in Tamil Nadu (Nilgiris etc.) Kerala, Karantaka, Assam and other states, but it is not enough to meet the country's own requirements.

East Indian nuts have the finest aroma. They are ovoid, approximately 2.25 to 2.75 cm long, 1.75 to 2.25 cm in diameter, and longitudinally wrinkled. The colour is grayish brown, with the furrows sometimes white because of liming.

Composition

Comparative analysis of the nutmeg gave the following values–moisture: 14.3%; protein: 7.5%; ether extract: 36.4%; carbohydrates: 28.5%; fibre: 11.6%; and mineral matter:

1.7%; calcium:0.12%; phosphorus: 0.24%; iron: 4.6 mg/ 100g; Nutmeg also contains a volatile oil (6-16%); starch 14.6 24.2+); pentosans (2.25%); furfural (1.5%) and pectin (0.5-0.6+). It is only a fair source of vitamins.

The principal constituents are a fixed oil, a volatile oil and starch. The flavour and therapeutic action are due to the volatile oil.

Quality Grades

The following classifications have been adopted in the nutmeg trade :

1. Whole, Sound Nutmegs

a. Large
b. Medium
c. Small

These range from 65 to 110 nuts per pound, the greatest demand being for 80 nuts pound. These nuts are of interest to the spice trade but usually too highly priced for oil distillation.

2. Sound Shrivels: These are employed for grinding but are usually too expensive for oil distillation.

3. Rejections: Considerably lower priced; this grade can be used for oil distillation.

4. Broken and Wormy: This is the cheapest grade, large quantities of which are shipped yearly to Europe, especially to Hamburg, for oil distillations. This quality grade comprises all broken and loosened up nutmegs which seem to contain much less fatty oil then the sound nuts. For this reason, it is very suitable for distilling. The US customs regulations forbid importation of this grade except for oil distillation. The USA and UK import mainly sound nutmegs; Germany (Hamburg) imports both the highest and the lowest grades, the latter only for distilling: France buys only broken and wormy nutmegs.

Volatile Oil : The comparative physico chemical properties of oil of nutmeg from different countries are summarized below.

Properties	*East Indian*	*West Indian*	*Travancore, Kerala*	*I.P.*
Specific Gravity	0.880-0.913 (at 25/25°)	0.859-0.865 (at 25/25°)	0.890 (at 30°)	0.882-0.910 (at 25°)
Refractive Index	1.408-1.486 (at 20°)	1.4429-1.4446 (at 20°)	1.4445 -	1.4110-1.482 (at 25°)
Optical Rotation	+7.9°to +22.16°	+25.8°to +35.8°	-	+10°to 45°
Acid value	-	-	0.12	-
Easter value (after acetylation)	-	-	46.27	-
Solubility in 90% alcohol	1-2.5 vol. & more	2-3 vol & more	-	3 vol.
Evaporation Residue%	0.3-2.1	0.2-0.8	-	*max.* 3.0

The percentage of volatile oil in nutmeg varies from 6 to 16%, according to the origin and quality of the spice. A sample from Travancore gave 10.2% volatile oil. Wormy nutmegs give a much higher yield than sound ones; in the former, most of the fixed oil, present in the endosperm which tends to retain the volatile oil during distillation, would have been devoured by worms, while the strongly aromatic oil in the inner layer of perisperm remains intact.

Commercial oil is derived from broken and wormy nutmegs. The material is comminuted, pressed to remove fixed oil, and immediately subjected to steam distilation. Loss of volatile oil from ground nutmegs is relatively rapid (about 80% in 2 months). Cohobation of distilled waters may be necessary for the recovery of the total oil.

Oil of nutmeg is a mobile, almost colourless or pale yellow liquid with a characteristic odour. On ageing, it partly resinifies and becomes viscous. The aroma of East Indian oil is much more pronounced and more characteristic of the spice than that of West Indian oil. The latter have lower specific gravity and refractive index and higher optical rotation.

Nutmeg Butter

Nutmeg contains 38-43% of ether extractable material which, in addition to glycerides, contains a volatile oil (6-13%), a small quantity of resin, and a substantial proportion of unsaponifiable material.

Commercial Nutmeg Butter, a highly aromatic fat, is obtained from undersized, damaged or worm eaten kernels which are unfit for sale as spice. The material is ground and cooked or steamed before pressing. A yield of 24-30% is reported. The fat may be obtained by solvent extraction but this process is not usually employed.

Nutmeg butter is a soft solid at (m.p. 38-51°), yellow or yellowish red in colour, with the odour and taste of nutmeg. The analytical characteristics of the method of preparation and the proportion of volatile oil and resin present. The recorded ranges of values are as follows: % Sp. gr. 20°C: 0.945-0.960; Ref. index: 1.46662-1.4604; iod. val: 33-65; acid val. : 10-25; sap. val.: 154:190; and unsapn. matter (containing myristicin): 8-18%.

Leaves

The leaves of M. fragrans yield on water distillation, 0.41-0.62% of a light brown volatile oil (Sp. gr., at 20°C: 0.8642; Ref. index: 1.474; Ester val.: 8.44) with a pleasing spicy odour. Steam distillation of dried leaves (from East Indies) gave 1.56% of a colourless volatile oil. (Sp. gr. at 20 C: 0.8772; Opt. rot.: 3.5; Ref. index: 1.4742) containing α-pinene (80%) and myristicin (10%).

Uses

In Medicine: Both nutmeg and mace are used as condiment and in medicine. In eastern countries, they are used more as a drug than as condiment. Nutmeg is stimulant, carminative, astringent and aphrodisiac; it is used in tonics and electuaries and forms a constituent of preparations prescribed for dysentery, stomachache, flatulence, nausea, vomiting malaria, rheumatism, sciatica and early stages of leprosy. Excessive doses have a narcotic effect; symptoms of delirium and epileptic convulsions appear after 1-6 hours. Mace is similarly used. It is also chewed for masking foul breath.

Oil of nutmeg or mace is employed for flavouring food products and liquor. It is used for scenting soaps, tobacco and dental creams, and also in perfumery. It is mildly counter-irritant and used in liniments and hair lotions. It has been recommended for the treatment of inflammations of bladder and urinary tract. The oil is somewhat toxic owing to the presence of myristicin and should be used with caution.

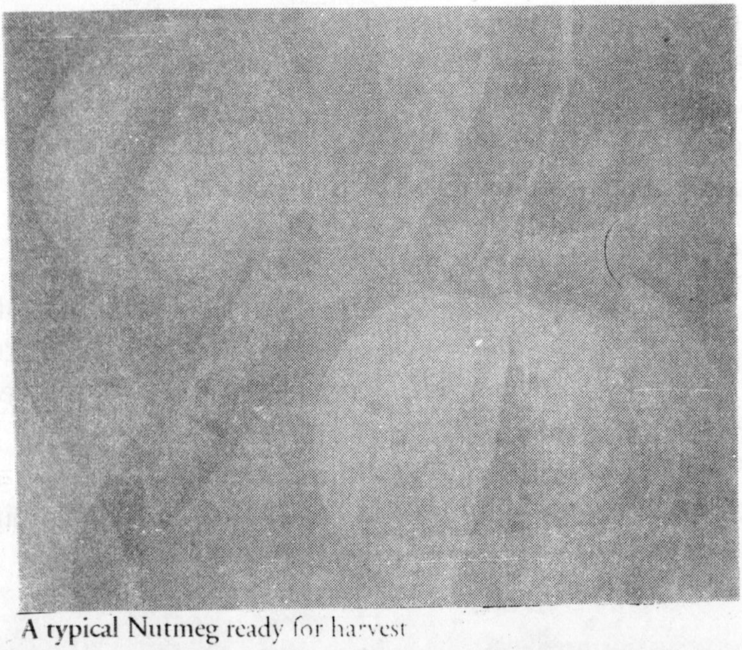

A typical Nutmeg ready for harvest

22

PEPPER - BLACK, WHITE AND GREEN

Bot. Name : (i) Black pepper: *Piper nigrum* Linn.
(ii) Green Pepper: *P. nigrum* Linn.
(iii) White Pepper: *P. nigrum* Linn.

Family : Piperaceae

Indian Names : **Bengali**: *Kala marich, Golmarich*; **Gujarati**: *Kala Mari, Kalomirch*; **Hindi**: *Kali Mirch*; **Kannada**: *Kare Menasu*; **Kashmiri**: *Marutis*; **Malayalam**: *Kurumulaku, Nallamulaku*; **Marathi**: *Mire, Kali Mirch*; **Oriya**: *Gol maricha*; **Tamil**: *Milagu*; **Telugu**: *Miriyalu*; **Urdu**: *Kali Mirch or Siah Mirch*.

Description and Distribution

Black Pepper or Kali Mirch is known to one and all due to its day-to-day use as one of the most popular spices. Black pepper is rightly considered the 'King of Spices' as judged from the volume of international trade, being the highest among all the spices known.

It is one of the most ancient crops cultivated in India and has probably originated in the hills of south-western India where it is met with in the wild state in the rain forests-from North Kanara to Kanyakumari. It is also cultivated in Indonesia, Malaysia, Sri Lanka, Brazil, Thailand and other tropical countries.

Types/Varieties

There are many varieties/types of black pepper known in the world trade. They take their names from the localities where grown or from the parts through which they are exported, e.g. Tellichery, Malabar, Alleppey (Kerala), Lampong, Saigon, Penang and Singapore. These peppers differ slightly in their physical and chemical charactertistics, colour, size, shape, flavour and bite. Tellichery and Alleppey peppers are large, attractive, dark reddish brown to black, very aromatic and among the best varieties, as also the Malabar Garbled' (MG_1) which alone accounts for nearly 90% of the total exports from India. Lampong and Singapore pepper ar smaller, more shrivelled but almost equally pungent.

There are nearly 24 varities/types of black pepper grown in India and their indentification is rather dificult, since some of them go by different names in different regions. There is considerable scope for evolving crosses of hybrids combining important quality attributes like high yield, hardiness, disease resistance, long spikes with good fruits (berries) compactly set all over. Some good crosses have been recently evolved at the Pepper Research Station, Panniyur (Kerala), notably hybird Panniyur-I which has been found to be quite promising.

Yield/Revery of Dried Pepper

Generally 100 kg of fresh berries yield about 26-39 kg of black pepper of commerce. Of course, the yield of pepper varies widely in different producing areas depending upon several factors such as elevation, temperature, distribution of rainfall, soil fertility, cultural practices, type or variety of pepper, and age of the pepper vine, etc. In India, the yield varies from 110 to 335 kg per hectare (av. 251 kg/ha).

Composition

Analysis of 23 types of black pepper from Kerala, South and North Kanara, Coorg and Assam gave the following ranges of values moisture; 8.7-14.1%; total nitrogen: 1.55-2.60%; nitrogen in non-volatile ether extract: 2.70-4.22%; volatile ether extract: 0.3-4.2%; starch (by acid hydrolysis): 28.0-49.0%; crude fibre: 8.7-18.0%; crude piperine: 2.8-9.0%; piperine (spectrophotometrically): 1.7-7.4%; total ash: 3.9-5.7%; and acid insol. ash (sand): 0.03-0.55%; The Kerala types, particularly Kottanadan, Kumbhakodi and Kuthiravali, are fairly high in crude piperine, while the North Kanara types show low values for piperine. Assam types are characterised by a low moisture content, high ether and alcohol extractives and consistently high values for total nitrogen and piperine. Thus numerous types of Indian black pepper are characterised by variations in size, colour, flavour

Green Pepper spikes of an improved variety— (P. nigrum)

and physico chemical properties. The bulk density of pepper varies with the type of pepper. Examination of 82 samples, belonging to different locatities, showed that their bulk density ranged between 426 and 850 g/litre, the Tellicherry and Baliapatnam types showing the highest values.

Starch is the predominant consitituent of pepper. It accounts for 34.8% in black pepper, 56.5% in white pepper and 63.2% in decorticated white pepper. Pepper starch consists of minute polygonal granules resembling those of rice, but much smaller (diam: 0.5-5μ). The hilum is visible only under high power magnification.

Protein of pepper has not been fully investigated. A considerable portion of nitrogen in pepper exists in a non proteinous form (such as alkaloids). Of the 12% of water soluble nitrogen, non protein nitrogen constitutes about 82% and of this, more than half is made up of simple amino acids which can be readily utilised by the human system.

Uses

In Medicine: Pepper is used for a variety of purposes. The ancient Aryans considered it as a powerful remedy for various disorders of the anatomical system and prescribed it as an effective cure for dyspepsia, malaria, delirium, tremors, hemorrhoids, etc. The Egyptians used it for embalming. The Asians are said to have used it as an aphrodisiac. Dutch and French house wives use it as an insect repellant and moth killer! However, its value as an essential preservative for meats and other perishable foods has been known for centuries. It is, therefore, largely used by meat packers and in canning, pickling, baking, confectionery and preparation of beverages. One of the principle values of pepper is its ability to correct the seasoning of dishes. Just before the end of cooking, a final dash of pepper can be used effectively to adjust the flavour.

Piperine, the bite factor of pepper, has no market physiological action and is no longer used in medicine. However, it possesses some feeble anti periodic property. Piperine has been used to impart a pungent taste to brandy. It has also been tried as an insecticide. It is stated to be more toxic to houseflies than pyrethrum, and a mixture of 0.05 per cent piperine and 0.01 per cent pyrethrins is more toxic than 0.10 per cent pyrethrins alone.

23

TAMARIND

Bot. Name : *Tamarindus indica* Linn.
Family : *Leguminosae*
Indian Names : **Assamese**: *Ttali*; **Bengali** and **Gujarati**: *Ambli*; **Hindi, Punjabi, Urdu**: *Imli*; **Kannada**: *Amli; Huli*; **Malayalam**: *Puli*; **Marathi**: *Chinch, Chincha*; **Oriya**: *Teetuli, Konia, Konya*; **Sanskrit**: *Amli, Abdika*; **Tamil**: *Puli*; **Telugu**: *Chinthappandu–Chinta, Amlika*.

Description and Distribution

The ripe fruit (pod) of the tree *(Tamarindus indica)* is used as condiment, or more precisely, as an 'acidulant', like *amchur* (dried slices of raw green mango or its powder) or *anardana* (the dried sour pomegranate seeds) or kokam fruit *(Garcinia indica)*. Tamarind fruit or tamarind pulp is quite popular all over India, particularly in southern India where tamarind constitutes an essential ingredient of *sambars, rasams,* chutneys and curries.

India is the only country which produces a commercial crop of tramarind. It is chiefly grown in Madhya Pradesh, Andhra Pradesh, Tamil Nadu and Karnataka states.

Composition

Tamarind pulp

The ripe fruit, on an average, comprises about 55% tamarind pulp, 33% seeds and about 12% fibre. A typical sample of tamarind pulp showed the following–moisture: 18.2%; free acid (tartaric): 9.8%; combined acid: 6.7%; total sugars as invert: 38.2%; protein: 2.8%; pectin: 2.8%; cellulosive residue (fibre): 19.4%; mineral matter: 2.8%; calcium: 0.17%; phosphorus: 0.11%; iron: 0.011%; calorific value: 283 calories per 100g; vit. A: 100 I.U/100g; niacin: 0.2 mg/100g.

Of the reducing sugars present, 70% is glucose and 30% is fruit sugar (i.e. fructose). Only a trace of sucrose or cane sugar is present. The pectin present in pulp is of good quality having a jelly grade of 180-200.

Tamarind Juice Concentrate

The CFTRI, Mysore, has developed a process for the manufacture of tamarind concentrate which is free from fibre, seeds, foreign matter, etc. and is very hygienic. Of late, there has been a growing demand for it from abroad. It is almost of jam consistency. It is easily dispensible in hot water at the time of its use.

Tamarind seed consists of 30% testa (outer skin) and 70% endosperm. The testa contains 40% of water solubles, 80% of which is tannin and colouring matter. The composition of the seed kernel is–moisture: 8.1%; protein: 17%; fat: 7%; crude fibre: 5.6%; non fibre carbohydrates: 65%; other components: 5.4%; and mineral matter: 2.8%.

The only factors in tamarind pulp and kernel having food value are carbohydrates and protein. They also have small amounts of vitamins, carotene, vit. B and nicotinic acid.

Uses

As Food Flavour: Practically all the parts of tamarind tree have one use or the other. Ripe fruit or tamarind pulp has an important role in numerous culinary preparations in the country, notably Sambar, Rasam, curries, chutneys, etc. which are quite popular in the southern parts of India.

An integrated process has been developed at CFTRI, Mysore, for the manufacture of pectin, tartarates and alcohol from tamarind pulp. Likewise tamarind juice concentrate is also becoming popular in the country as well as abroad.

In Medicine: According to the Ayurvedic system, the ripe fruit is appetising, laxative, warning, tonic to the heart, anthelmintic, cures *vata* and *kapha,* heals wounds and fractures. The ripe fruit is also regarded as a controding and digestive and useful in diseases caused by deranged bile, such as burning of the body and intoxication from liquors or dhatura. A gargle of tamarind water is recommended in sore throat.

Tamarind tree in full bloom with tamarind pods

24

TURMERIC

Bot. Name : *Curcuma longa* Linn.
Syn. : *Cucuma domestica* Val.
Family : *Zingiberaceae*
Indian Names : **Bengali**: *Halud, Haldi, Pitras*; **Gujarati**: *Haldhar, Haldi*; **Hindi**: *Haldi*; **Kannada**: *Arishina*; **Konkani**: *Halad*; **Malayalam**: *Manjal*; **Marathi**: *Halede, Halad*; **Oriya**: *Haldi*; **Punjabi**: *Haldar, Haldhar, Haldi*; **Sanskrit**: *Haladi, Haridra, Harita*; **Tamil**: *Manjal*; **Telugu**: *Pasupu*; **Urdu**: *Haladi*.

Description and Distribution

The spice, turmeric or *haldi*, consists of the dried, boiled, cleaned and polished rhizomes (the underground swollen stem of the plant) of *Curcuma longa*. Turmeric is too well known to need any further description. It suffices to say that turmeric is one of the most important and ancient spices of India, cultivated virtually throughout the length and breadth of the country.

It is used extensively daily by all classes of people in the preparation of tasty curried dishes. Turmeric not only adds its typical flavour but its colour also, thereby helping to bring out the best in curried dishes. Besides, it is also used as dye in certain cotton textiles, in medicine and in cosmetics. Further, it is also regarded by the Hindus as something 'sacred' for use in ceremonial and religious functions.

Turmeric, a herbaceous perennial, 60-90 cm high, with a short stem and tufted leaves, a native of India or China, is now a commercial crop of the tropics. It is cultivated extensively in India, Sri Lanka, parts of China, Pakistan, Haiti, Jamaica, Peru, Bangladesh, El-Salvador, Thailand, Taiwan and Indo-China. India, is by *far, the largest producer of turmeric in the world.* It is estimated officially that about 80% of the world production of turmeric is from India alone. Besides, in India, turmeric occupies about 6% of the total area under spices and condiments. The main turmeric growing areas are Andhra Pradesh, Maharashtra, Orissa, Tamil Nadu, Karnataka and Kerala. About 3.5 lakh mt of cured turmeric are produced annually, of which 92% is consumed within the country and it is the remaining 8% which brings us foreign exchange ranging from Rs. 15 to 55 crores annually, depending upon the prevailing price demand of supply.

Harvesting and Processing (Curing) of Turmeric
Curing of raw turmeric rhizomes freshly dug out of earth is essential both for the development of the attractive yellow colour (mostly due to the curcumin pigment) and the characteristic aroma. Without the curing process, turmeric lacks both.

For optimum recovery of dry turmeric, it is beneficial to harvest the rhizomes at about 37 weeks maturity, but for economic retrieval of the value added products like oleoresin/ dye, etc., rhizomes harvested at 29 weeks maturity give the best results.

The fingers and bulbs are boiled separately in water for 1/2 to 3/4 hour until until froth and white fumes (with characteristic aroma) appear. They are then drained and dried in the sun for 10-15 days until they become dry and hard. At this stage, the fingers produce a metallic sound, when broken by hand. They are then cleaned and polished mechanically in a drum rotated by hand or by power.

Earlier, cowdung used to be added to boiling water to make it alkaline and after removal, the fingers used to be artifically coloured with lead chromate (chemichrome) which is a cumulative poison. CFTRI, Mysore has developed a simpler, more hygienic and more efficient technique of curing and colouring of turmeric. According to this technique, the rhizomes are boiled in lime water or sod. bicarbonate solution. A water solution con-taining 20g sod. bisulphite and 20g hydrochloric acid per 100 lbs of tubers is recommended in place of chemichrome to give them the desired yellow tint. The new process has been demonstrated to the turmeric growers and merchants in A.P. and Tamil Nadu.

Varieties

Under the genus *Curcuma* to which turmeric belongs, botanists have so far recognised 30 varieties. Of these, C. *longa* is economically *the most important*, accounting for about 96.4% of the total area under turmeric and the remaining 3.6% of the total area are cultivated under C. *aromatica*, which is mostly grown in small areas in East and West Godavari districts of Andhra Pradesh and Tanjavoor and South Arcot districts of Tamil nadu.

Composition

Turmeric has the following composition–moisture 5.8%; protein: 8.6%; fat: 8.9%; carbohydrates: 63.0%; fibre: 6.9%; mineral matter: 6.8%; calcium: 0.2%; phosphorus: 0.26%; iron: 0.05%; sodium: 0.01%; potassium: 2.5%; vit. A: 175 I.U./100g; vit B_1: 0.09mg/100g; vit: $B_2$0.19; vit. C: 49.8 and niacin: 4.8mg/100g; calorific value or food energy: 390

calories per 100g.

Use

Of course, turmeric is largely consumed as a spice while only limited quantities are utilised for other purposes.

As Food Flavourant and Colournat: By far the largest quantity of turmeric is utolized in most of the Asiatic countries as a food adjunct in many vegetable, meat and fish preparations. It is used to flavour and at the same time to colour butter, cheese, margarine, pickles, mustard and other foodstuffs.

It is also used to colour liquor, fruit drinks, cakes and table jellies. It is one of the principal ingredients of curry powder which is a blend of many spices, common salt and farinaceous matter.

Turmeric, by dint of its aromatic oil content, flavours food stuffs, acts as an appetiser and aids digestion. A pinch of turmreic powder is often added to most of our savouries to impart simultaneously an agreeable flavour and colour and to improve the keeping quality.

As Dye : Earlier, in India, turmeric was largely used for dyeing wool, silk and cotton to impart a yellow shade, in an acid bath. It is still used for dyeing cotton. The dye is also employed as colouring material in pharmacy, confactionery, rice milling and food industries. Considerable quantities of turmeric are converted as *kumkum* used for *tilak*. Its use as a colouring material is reported in the paints and varnishes industry also.

Turmeric paper is an offical reagent in British pharmacopoea for testing alkalinity. A diluted tincture of turmeric is suitable for use as a fluorescence indicator even

Healthy Turmeric plants (Inset : Turmeric Fingers)

in brown and yellow solutions.

Turmeric is an antioxidant, due to the phenolic character of curcumin.

Medicinal Uses: In the Indian systems of medicine, turmeric occupies an important place, as an ingredient in the preparaiton of medicinal oils, ointments and poultice. It is a stomachic, carminative, tonic, blood purifier, vermicide and an antiseptic. It is indicated in case of diabetes and leprosy. Is is also prescribed as an anti periodic alternative. Boiled with warm milk and taken internally, or used as an inhalation from boiling water, or as a smoke through pipe in combination with omum, it relieves sore throat and common cold.

25

AJOWAN EXTRACTION FROM AJOWAN SEEDS

Ajowan oil, both pure and dethymolized, is employed as an antiseptic and aromatic carminative. It is occasionally used for performing disinfectant soaps and as an insecticide. The action of the oil and its uses are similar to those of thymol. The oil is reported to be useful as an expectorant in emphysema, bronchial pneumonia and some other respiratory ailments. Preliminary pharmacological studies of the oil indicated that it had a parasympathomimetic effect and produced contraction of the isolated ileum, tracheal chain, and bronchial musculature in guinea-pigs. It depressed the cardiac musculature in frogs and caused marked full in blood pressure in cats. On account of its low toxicity, further trials of the oil as an hypotensive agent are recommended. The drug also seems to possess some anti-diuretic effect.

PROCESS OF MANUFACTURING

Steps :-

1. Cleaning of Seeds.
2. Crushing of Seeds .
3. Feeding of Crushed seeds in distillation tank.
4. Steam distillation process is continued.
5. Collection of oil.

6. Testing of oil.
7. Bottling of oil.

The seeds are cleaned to remove the foreign matters, such as dust, soil sticks and other items.

Then seeds are crushed by passing through pulveriser to the extracted form. Then seeds are fed in the steam distillation tank. Where steam is fed through the fluidized seed beds to vaporize the volatile oil. The oil so vaporized is collected by cooling through condenser.

Detailed process of steam distillation is as follows.

In this method, the plant material is supported on grid and saturated steam in injected through the charge be means of open or perforated coils placed below the grid.

Most aromatic plant materials are distilled by steam distillation. It has been noted earlier that steam does not penetrate the cell membranes and the essential oil is vaporized only after diffusing out as an aqueous solution through the cell membrances. Therefore, presence of a certain amount of moisture in the steam is necessary to distil out the complete oil.

Steam distillation process is superior to the other two processes in regard to cost, rate of distillation and capacity of production. Since high pressure steam causes considerable decomposition, distillation is best started with steam of low pressure, followed by steam of higher pressure towards the end of operation when the oil content of the charge has decreased considerably, and when chiefly high boiling constituents of the essential oil remain in the still.

Steam Distillation at Reduced Pressure

This method is used when volatile oil is likely to decompose at high pressure, especially for oils containing esters. However, it should be noted that in case of distillation at reduced pressure the ratio of oil to water in the distillate is less than when some products are distilled at atmosphere pressure, because any lowering in the external pressure reduce the vapour pressure of all high boiling compounds relatively much more than that of water. Besides, at reduced pressure, because of lowering in temperature, effective log mean temperature between water and vapours will reduce and considerable oil losses may be expected by evaporation.

In order to achieve high rate of distillation at reduced pressure the empty space above the liquid in the vacuum still should be kept sufficiently large to permit the still content to boil without foaming into the condenser (this is particularly so in respect of hydro distillation). Besides, the condenser surface must be larger, estimated to be 4 to 5 times than that required for distillation at atmosphere pressure, because of high volumetric rates and low temperature difference.

Distillation at high Pressure

Pressure in the still can be increased by inserting a throtting valve in the vapour line connecting the still and condenser. Steam distillation at high pressure is useful for certain purpose, for instance, for the hydrolysis of ester if so desired. There is another advantage, i.e. relative to steam pressure, the vapour pressure of higher boiling oil constituents increases more as the temperature rises resulting in better oil to water ratio in the distillate. However, from this viewpoint distillation with superheated steam is better because it vaporizes more oil without necessitating the high pressure of the former method, but hydrodiffusion in this case has to be maintained by injecting wet steam, intermittently to obtain good yield.

Superheated Steam Distillation

In this method saturated steam may be superheated within the still by means of closed coils or jacket or outside the still in boiler. Usually the stills employed for distillation by superheated steam are constructed high with small diameter, well insulated and provided with jacket. This method is mostly used for distilling all high boiling and chemically stable compounds and with the plants containing high moisture (60-80%), because hydrodiffusion is automatically maintained by the presence of water in the plant material.

The operation can be carried out with superheated steam at reduced pressure as well. By this method, it is possible to regulate the temperature of the oil vapours at will. According to degree of superheat, rise in vapour temperature will result which means a more favourable ratio of oil in the distillate than is the case when oil is merely steam distilled at reduced pressure without superheating. Injection of wet steam intermittently is necessary to maintain hydrodiffusion conditions.

Equipment

The equipment required for carrying out distillation of plant materials depends upon the size of the operation and the type of distillation to be used. But, however, in industrial practice, the following items are necessary.

1. Still,
2. Condenser,
3. Separator,
4. Steam generator,
5. Labour saving devices.

1. Still- This serves primarily as a container for the plant material where steam contacts the plant material and vaporizes the essential oil from the plant material. It is usually cylindrical, vertical tank equipped with a removable cover which can be clamped upon the cylindrical section. On or near the top of the cylindrical section a pipe is attached for leading the vapours to the condenser. Nearby the bottom, there is a grid or false bottom on which the material rests and live steam is introduced through a steam line, usually a perforated coil below false bottom.

The cylindrical section is slightly tapered to facilitate easy discharging of material manually or mechanically. The bottom of the still is provided with a drain valve so that any water condensing within the charge can be drawn off in the course of distillation.

Insulation - The still, including the top should be well insulated to conserve heat. If insulation is neglected, excessive steam condensation occurs resulting in bumping of particles, higher steam consumption, prolonged distillation and inferior yield of oil. Usually all heated sections including steam lines are well insulated.

2. Condenser - This serves to convert the steam and accompanying oil vapours into liquid. This requires the removal of an amount of heat equivalent to the heat of vaporization of the vapours plus steam and cooling the distillate to near ambient temperatures.

Condenser design is important, the most efficient type being the multitubular condenser. It is compact, does not develop back pressure and permits higher distillation rate than the single coil or pipe condenser as U valves are much higher. Another point of importance in favour of shell and tube condenser is that when a distillation is carried out by cohobation, the condenser being compact, enables the distillates to be returned easily to the still from the oil separator without recourse to a high still head connection to the condenser.

3. Oil Separator - Its function is to achieve a quick and complete separation of the condensed water. Volatile oil and water are mutually insoluble. Because of the difference in their specific gravities two liquids form two separate layers. Since the total volume of water is removed continuously. Various types of designs for separator are in practice and are designed on the basis of specific gravities and averages flow rates.

PLANT ECONOMICS

Rated Plant Capacity = 12.00 Kgs./Day

LAND & BUILDING

Land Area 350 Sq. Mt. = Rs. 5,05,000.00

PLANT & MACHINERY

1. Pulverizer
2. Solvent Extraction System with Complete Accessories Volumetric
3. Vacuum distillation system
4. Condenser S.S. Tube
5. Miscellaneous pipes fittings pumps, valves, etc.
6. Laboratory testing equipments
7. Bottle filling and sealing Machine
8. Baby Boiler

FIXED CAPITAL

1.	Land & Building	Rs.	5,05,000.00
2.	Plant & Machinery	Rs.	9,35,000.00
3.	Other Fixed Assets	Rs.	1,65,000.00
	Total	Rs.	16,05,000.00

RAW MATERIALS

1. Ajowan Seed
2. Solvents n-Hexane
3. Packaging Bottle, Materials

TOTAL WORKING CAPITAL/MONTH

1.	Raw Materials	Rs.	1,14,500.00
2.	Salary & Wages	Rs.	21,875.00
3.	Utilities & Overheads	Rs.	29,900.00
	Total	Rs.	1,66,275.00

TOTAL CAPITAL INVESTMENT

Total Fixed Capital	Rs.	16,05,000.00
Total Working Capital for 3 Months	Rs.	4,98,825.00
Total	Rs.	21,03,825.00

TURN OVER/ANNUM

Ajowan Oil 3600 Kgs.
Ajowan Cake for spice 87,000 Kg. Rs. 30,30,000.00

PROFIT SALES RATIO = Profit/Sales x 100 = 12.87%

RATE OF RETURN = Operating profit/T.C.I x 100= 18.54%

BREAK EVEN POINT (B.E.P) = 69.61%

26

ASAFOETIDA (HING)

Uses & Application

As Flavourant:

Asafoetida is extensively used in India for flavouring curries, sauces and pickles in conjunction with onion and garlic. In Iran (Persia) the natives rub asafoetida on warmed plates prior to placing meat or them. Besides, the large cabbage-like tops of the plants are relished raw by the natives.

In Medicine:

Medicinally, it stimulates the intestinal and respiratory tracts and the nervous system. It is useful in asthma, whooping cough and chronic bronchitis. It is used as an enema for intestinal flatulence. It is also administered in hysterical and epileptic affections and in cholera. Asafoetida is often employed in veterinary medicine. It is very useful remedy for relieving spasms and in indigestion and colic. It is applied externally on the stomach to stimulate the intestines.

Recent studies have shown that:

1. Asafoetida oil has antibiotic properties and inhibits growth of mircobes,

2. Asafoetida has sedative properties and its possible use in heart disease has been suggested.

In the Ayurvedic system of medicine, the well-known recipe called 'Hingashtaka' contains asafoetida as one of the important ingredients. However, the important question still remains as to whether such a reputation which asafoetida enjoys as a medicine is scientifically well-found. If so, the precise mode of its action is yet to be understood clearly. Likewise, there is also need for rigorous implementation of purity standards as well as for the development of rapid and reliable analytical methods for the detection of adulteration. According to the Prevention of Food Adulteration Act (PDA), asafoetida (Hing or Hingra) shall not contain any colophony resin, galbonum resin, ammoniacum resin or any other resin, but it is generally felt that these standards so not fully reflect the true quality of asafoetida. The estimation of the odoriferous principles may be a truer measure of odour and hence the quality of asafoetida. There is need off intensification of researches in this direction. Further, knowing that there is considerable internal demand for asafoetida in India, particularly for medicinal and culinary purposes, there is need to encourage its cultivation in suitable areas in the inner Himalayas in order to be self-sufficient and thereby to avoid the heavy drain of valuable foreign exchange from India.

PROCESS OF MANUFACTURE

Description and Distribution

Asafoetida or Asafoetida is the dried latex or gum oleoresin exuded from the living rhizome or rootstock or taproot of several species of Ferula, three of which grow in India, mainly in Kashmir. These are the perennial herbs belonging to the genus Ferula which are the sources of the doeogum resins used as condiment as well as in medicine. The species are distributed from the Mediterranean region to Central Asia. The more important ferula oleogum resins imported into India, chiefly from Iran and Afghanistan, are :

(a) Asafoetida,
(b) Galbanum and
(c) Sumbal.

Of these, asafoetida is the most important. A part of the imported resin is re-exported from India to various countries. The trade name asafoetida is based on the scientific name of a related species, 'Ferula asafoetida'. Nearly a crore of rupees worth of asafoetida is being imported annually into India. The gross value of the sales, especially of the compounded asafoetida, as consumed in South India is probably many times more. Surprisingly enough, very few of the consumers are aware of what the substances is, to what extent it is pure and whether it could be produced in India to the extent of our becoming at least self-sufficient.

The Ferula plants from which the asafoetida of commerce is extracted, have massive taproots or carrot - shaped roots, 12.5 to 15 cm in diameter at the crown when they are 4 - 5 years old. In March - April just before the plants flower, the upper part of the living rhizome / root is laid bare and the stem cut off close to the crown. The exposed surface is covered by a dome - shaped structure made of twigs and earth. A milky juice exudes from the cut surface. After some days, the exudate is scraped off and a fresh slice of the root cut when more latex exudes; some times the resin is removed along with the slice.

The collection of the resin and the slicing of the root are repeated until exudation ceases (about 3 months after the first out). The resin is sometimes collected from successive incisions made at the junction of the stem of rhizome and taproots. With these incisions, some plants have been reported to yield about 1 Kg. or more of gum-resin.

Asafoetida is acrid and bitter in taste and emits a strong, disagreeable, pungent, alliaceous odour due to the presence of sulphur compounds therein. Hence its common name abroad, *"Devil's dung"*.

PLANT ECONOMICS

Rated Plant Capacity = 6.67 Kgs./Day

LAND & BUILDING

Land area 5000 Sq.Mt. = 36,00,000.00

PLANT & MACHINERY

1. Farming implements
2. Tools
3. Miscellaneous Utensils etc.

FIXED CAPITAL

1.	Land & Building	Rs.	36,00,000.00
2.	Plant & Machinery	Rs.	2,10,000.00
3.	Other Fixed Assets	Rs.	85,000.00
	Total	Rs.	38,95,000.00

RAW MATERIALS

1. Manures
2. Seeds
3. Miscellaneous

TOTAL WORKING CAPITAL/MONTH

1.	Raw Materials	Rs.	12,000.00
2.	Salary & Wages	Rs.	50,000.00
3.	Utilities & Overheads	Rs.	30,500.00
	Total	Rs.	92,500.00

TOTAL CAPITAL INVESTMENT

Total Fixed Capital	Rs.	38,95,000.00
Total Working Capital for 3 Months	Rs.	2,77,500.00
Total	Rs.	41,72,500.00

TURN OVER/ANNUM

By sale of 2000 Kg of Hing/annum Rs. 40,00,000.00

PROFIT SALES RATIO = Profit/Sales x 100 = 46.47%

RATE OF RETURN = Operating profit/T.C.I x 100= 45.03%

BREAK EVEN POINT (B.E.P) = 42.27%

27

BLACK PEPPER

Uses & Application

Utilization:- Pepper fruits are used mainly after drying as black pepper or after processing into white pepper. In parts of Kerala, fresh green pepper is sometimes used for preparing pickles. Black and white pepper are among the major condiments employed for seasoning freshly cooked and prepared foods. In U.S.A. & other western countries they are used mainly for preserving meat. Over half of the American consumption of pepper is reported to go into the meat industry for curing and preservation of meat. The whole fruits are added to pickles, certain types of sausages, etc. but the bulk of the product is generally ground before use. Black pepper is mostly mostly used for its characteristic delicate penetrating aroma and pungent, biting taste. White pepper has a similar flavour, but is less pungent. On grinding, white pepper yields a product with low ash and fibre contents and very little pungency. In Borneo, white pepper enters into the composition of the brew employed for growing yeasts.

Pepper owes its characteristic pungency and aroma to its oleoresin which can be obtained by extracting the crushed, not fully ripe fruits with volatile solvents. It is a dark or brownish green heterogeneous mass and is widely used in Europe and U.S.A. for flavouring foods.

In modern European medicine, black pepper is rarely

prescribed, except indirectly, as an ingredient of some combined preparations. In modern Indian medicine, it is much employed as an aromatic stimulant in cholera, weakness following fevers, vertigo,k coma, etc., as a stomachic in dyspepsia and flatulence, as an antiperiodic in malarial fever and as an alterative in paraplegia and arthritic diseases. Externally, it is valued for its rubefacient properties and as a local application for relaxed sore throat, piles and some skin diseases.

Pepper retards the development of rancidity in oils and fats, frozen ground pork, beef and lard. This activity has been attributed to the presence of tocopherols in the oleoresin.

Analysis of Trade Grades and By Products of Pepper:-

Table: Analysis of Trade Grades and By-Products of Pepper

	Moisture %	Total N %	Nitrogen in Non-volatile etherextr.	Non-volatile etherextr. %	Volatile etherextr. %	Alcohol extr. %	Starch %	Total ash %	Crude Piperine %
Trade grades Tellicherry black pepper, garbled special bold	9.57	2.00	3.16	6.17	1.24	7.46	47.25	4.55	4.04
Tellicherry black pepper, garbled F.A.Q.	9.8	1.98	3.55	7.00	1.02	8.28	45.00	4.35	5.06
Malabar black pepper, garbled F.A.Q.	11.20	1.85	3.49	8.53	2.32	9.88	43.65	4.83	6.08
Malabar black pepper, ungarbled	10.30	1.89	3.58	9.87	1.74	11.52	40.95	4.93	7.26
Malayan black pepper	12.74	1.84	3.92	7.67	1.02	8.42	48.15	3.60	6.11
Malayan White pepper	10.27	1.76	3.72	8.09	0.03	8.72	59.40	1.06	6.10
Indian white pepper	10.60	2.01	3.83	7.35	0.51	7.22	56.25	2.79	5.72
Trade wastes & by products Pepper stems and inflorescence stalks	9.15	1.94	2.72	4.21	0.48	6.18	16.94	9.37	2.31
Pepper rejections	11.31	2.15	3.38	12.44	2.00	13.36	21.15	8.02	8.58
Varagu (unfertilized buds)	9.30	2.19	1.51	2.34	0.28	4.26	14.40	13.07	0.70

BLACK PEPPER CULTIVATION

In India, Pepper is cultivated mostly as a mixed crop in homestead gardens. Under this system, the vines are trained on to existing trees like jack, mango, coconut or arecanut. The number of vines grown in this way is small, generally not more than 100. But the vines receive intensive care and continue to be productive up to 60 or even 100 years. The vines are also grown as an inter or subsidiary crop along with other plantation crops like coffee, cardamom, arecanut, coconut and orange. This practice is more common in North Kanara, Coorg and parts of Kerala. As a pure crop, pepper is grown on a plantation scale only in small areas in the sub-montane tracts and lower altitudes in South Kanara, Malabar, Wynaad na Travancore. It is stated that a plantation of more than 4 hectares (10 acres) is not economical.

In India, pepper is grown mainly in Kerala, Madras and Mysore and to a very small extent in Assam. In Kerala, pepper is grown in all the nine districts, the major ones being Cannanore, Calicut, Kottayam and Trivandrum districts. In Madras, it is grown to a small extent in the Nilgiri and Kanniyakumari districts. Among the districts of Mysore State, the important areas in North and South Kanara.

Climate and Soil:- The pepper plant is a climbing vine found growing up to an altitude of 1,500 m., but thrives best at about 500 m. It is usually raised on established supports. Pepper requires a warm and humid climate. It thrives in places where the annual rainfall is well over 200 cm. and in any case not less than 125 cm. On the eastern slopes of the Nilgiris, which receive hardly 120 cm. of rain, pepper is being grown fairly successfully on a small scale as an inter-crop in tea and coffee plantations. Similarly in some parts of Tirunelveli district, pepper is grown in the shade of tea, coffee and cardamom plantations. Pepper plants are pollinated by rain-water and consequently satisfactory yields are obtained when frequent showers of rain occur during blossoming period. In the important pepper growing areas, the maximum temperature during the hot weather seldom exceeds 40° and the lowest temperature may be about 10°. In parts of South India, Assam and in the Darjeeling district of West Bengal, pepper is found to tolerate even lower temperature.

Pepper thrives best on virgin soil rich in humus and other plant nutrients. Naturally well-drained, red laterite soils or alluvial soils rich in humus seem to be highly suitable for this crop. Soils 1.2 to 1.5 m. in depth with granite rock underneath, and intermixed with boulders are considered ideal for this crop. The soil should not dry up during the dry months as to kill the vines or get flooded during the rains. In kerala, major part of the pepper cultivation is on laterite or sandy loam along the alluvial banks of rivers. Compared to the soils of Indonesia, which are mostly volcanic the soils of pepper tracts in India are poor and consequently yield less. In order to improve production, cultivation of pepper should be encouraged in those areas where soil is more suitable. From this viewpoint, area in Mysore State are reported be better than Kerala.

Preparation of Land:- As pepper is a climbing vine, supports or standards have to be provided for the plants to grow on. The standards usually preferred are quick growing trees, which not only provide support, but also shade. While in India, living trees are mainly used as supports or standards, in Indonesia, Malaya and other South-East Asian countries, dead woods are used, since in these areas shade in not a big problem and also the equatorial climate with almost daily rainfall makes it unnecessary. Some of the trees preferred as standards are Erythrina variegata var. indica, Garuga pinnata, Oroxylum indicum, spondias pinnata, Ceiba pentandra, and Greuilea robusta. Occasionally wooden poles and stone or concrete pillars have been used as standards, though this practice is rare. Bamboo or wooden poles are used as temporary standards, till the permanent ones grow sufficiently.

For raising shade or standard trees, pits are dug at 2.5-3.0 m. apart and standard raised either by cuttings or as seedlings. Planting is done in April-May during the early rains so that these standards grow sufficiently to allow pepper vines to be planted in July-September. When planted as a mixed crop in coconut, arecanut, tea or coffee plantations, the main crop or the shade trees serve as standards besides providing the shade.

Propagation:- The pepper vine can be propagated either vegetatively or by seeds, Vegetative propagation is universally adopted, because raising of plants through seed is slow, uncertain and the seedling progeny takes a much longer period to attain maturity and does not always behave true to the parent. However, it is believed that the plants raised from seeds live longer, and give heavier crops in later years than plants raised vegetatively. For raising seedlings, selected, well ripened fruits are soaked in water for 2-3 days, the outer skin removed, the seeds dried in shade and sown in nursery beds. They are transplanted when they have developed 4-5 leaves. Experiments recently conducted in Panniyur have shown that sowing fruits with the coats give quicker germination that without them.

Methods of vegetative propagation vary in different places. There are two types of vegetative shoots preferred for planting, viz. the runners which are usually confined to the bottom portion of the vines, and the terminal shoots towards the top region. The runners form the most common material for propagation. Selection of shoots for the propagation is usually done in October, when the vines are in full crop and their cropping behaviour and other features are easily decided. The healthiest shoots among the ones found in a clump are selected, and they are kept coiled up on forks, in order to prevent them from coming in contact with soil and rooting prematurely. These shoots are separated from the parent vine, cut into lengths of four or five nodes and planted either in the field or are rooted in baskets and then planted in the field as rooted cuttings. The usual practice is to plant cuttings in a nursery towards the end of October and transplant them in the field during the next rainy season (July). Experiments at the Pepper Research Station, Panniyur, have shown that it is best to raise rooted cuttings in special bamboo baskets, 25-30 cm. in length and 10.0-12.5 cm. in diameter. A couple of cutting with four nodes each are planted in each basket and the basket kept under thatched roof or a pandal, and regularly watered until the cuttings strike roots. It is estimated that 750-1,000 vines are planted per hectare.

In some areas, particularly in North Kanara, the terminal shoots of the top fruiting branches are preferred. Plants raised from such cuttings are said to yield even in the second year of planting and produce a satisfactory crop from the fourth year onwards while vines raised from runner shoots give satisfactory yield even in the second year of planting and produce a satisfactory yields only from the sixth or seventh year. The former, however, are short-lived as compared to the latter, their longevity being about 15 years. Further, the removal of the fruiting branch from the top of the vine is reported to lead to a reduction the crop. In spite of this, the practice is prevalent to an appreciable scale, particularly in countries like Indonesia, Cambodia, Malaya, etc.

Propagation by layering is adopted on a small scale by

some growers in Malabar and South Kanara, where selected runner shoots from vines of known performance are layered in bamboo baskets 15-20 cm. in diameter. Within four to six weeks the shoots strike root, and are then carefully separated and planted. Raising pepper vines by single node cuttings instead of the usual 4-5 nodes, has been tried at the Pepper Research Station, Panniyur. Cuttings consisting of a single node with 5 cm. of stem above and below the node have been found to be economical.

Propagating pepper vines by grafting has been tried, particularly for exploiting the possibilities of using as rootstock, varieties and species known for resistance to diseases. Successful grafts by inarching or side grafting have obtained with some of the wild species and varieties of pepper and also with betel vine.

Planting:- The planting of the pepper vine is done either in July or august. The pits for planting are made preferably on the north and north-eastern sides of the standard so that the severe western sun is avoided. Pits about 45 cm. deep are dug in a semicircular form below and around the standard and these are filled about one half with good jungle soil. In the case of unrooted cuttings, 3-7 cuttings are planted in each pit. If all the cuttings strike root, two are retained and the remaining ones removed to fill in blanks where necessary. In the case of rooted cuttings generally a couple of cuttings are planted without disturbing the roots, the soil firmly pressed and heaped up a little to prevent water from collecting around. The pepper vine makes rapid growth and at the end of the first year may be 1.0-1.5 m. long. As the vines grow they have to be tied to the standard usually at intervals of 30 cm. Tying is done regularly during the first 3-4 years, but when once the vines establish themselves on the standards this may be discontinued.

Manuring:- Pepper is an exhausting crop and the soil needs high level of nitrogenous manuring. In India, where pepper is grown mostly in homestead gardens, not much of manuring is done except what is given to some of the trees serving as standards. Recent experiments in Kerala have shown that an application of a fertilizer mixture made up of ammonium sulphate, rock phosphate and potassium chloride in the proportion 6:9:12 nearly doubles the yield. Additional application of cowdung and green manure will result in still better yields.

Post-planting operations:- Widely different practices are adopted once the vines are established and well grown. In Malabar and South Kanara, diggings and weedings are done, once during south-west monsoon and again after north-east monsoon, to conserve soil moisture, and prevent weed growth and surface run off. In some areas contour bunding and terracing are done to prevent soil erosion. In Malaya, pruning is often practice to promote branching during the first few years; in some places the vines are lowered as in the case of P betel and buried in the ground in order to induce more vigorous growth and ensure larger crop.

Diseases & Pests:- The wilt and pollu are the two important diseases of pepper. The wilt is characterized by the death and decay of the roots, yellowing and shedding of the leaves and the ultimate drying up of the plant. It is widely prevalent in areas where the plant is raised in poor, shallow or ill-drined soils and in exposed situations, particularly in summer. The rotting of the root is attributed to the fungus phytophthora and a number of ungicides have been tried to control the fungus. Other control methods include buring the affected plants, applying slaked lime near the surface roots, soon after the first monsoon showers, and keeping the soil well drained and clean. Attempts have also been made to evolve and select wilt-resistant types suited to the various areas and to graft susceptible types on to rootstocks of resistant types.

The flea beetle, **Longitarsus nigripennis** Motsch., lays eggs inside the fruits, where they hatch in about a week and the grubs finally eat away the kernel leaving only a light hollow shell. Spraying with 0.25 percent DDT has been found efficacious; other insecticides found effective are Lindane, Dieldrin and Malathio.

Processed black pepper in storage is rarely attacked by pests. But when the moisture exceeds 12-13 percent, book lice or Psocids, cereal mites, grain beetles, cigarette beetles and drug-store beetles occasionally make their entry. They are best avoided by thoroughly drying the pepper before storing it. Fumigation of dry pepper with Chlorosol has been found effective.

Harvesting and Yield :- The pepper vine starts bearing from the third year of its growth. An adult vine yields annually C.0.5 kg. dried fruits under Indian conditions. The yield goes on increasing as the vines get older up to about the tenth year. In well cared gardens, tenth to twenty-fifth year may be reckoned as the best period; after the thirtieth year, the yield begins to decline, though in homestead gardens vines as old as 100 years continue to be productive. Usually there are two crops in a year, one in August-September and the other in March-April. On the west coast, the flowering commences in June-July soon after the commencement of the south-west monsoon. Sometimes the pre-monsoon showers also initiate flowering. The harvest season of pepper extends from the middle of December to the middle of March in the coastal areas. On the foot-hills of the ghats and in colder regions like Assam, the harvests are considerably delayed and extend up to April. The lower the temperature and higher the elevation, the later is the cropping period. When the fruits are ready for harvest, the whole spikes ar removed from the vines with the aid of a ladder. They are dried in the sun for 3-4 days, and the fruits separated form the stalks by beating the dried spikes with a stick or by trampling under foot. When completely dry, the outer skin of the fruits becomes black and wrinkled. It is estimated that 100 kg. of green pepper roungly yield 33 kg. of dried pepper.

The yield of pepper varies widely in the different producing areas depending on the elevation, temperature, distribution of rainfall, soil fertility, cultural practices, types grown and the age of the pepper bushes. Timely rainfall and proper climatic conditions during flowering, fruit setting and fruit development are important factors affecting yield.

The yield of pepper per vine varies from place to place and from type to type. The type **Balamcotta** on an average yields 1.0-1.5 kg. in Kottayam, 1 kg. in Chirakkal, and 1 kg. in Mysore, though in Mysore its maximum yield has been found to be 3.0-3.5 kg. Another good yielder is **Karimcotta** which on an average gives 1.0-1.25 kg. dried pepper.

In Malaya, pepper vines yield about 1-2 kg. dried pepper per vine in the first year of harvest and the yield up gradually to about 4 kg. per vine by the seventh year and then declines. In India, the average yield of commercial black pepper has been found to vary from 110 to 335 kg. per hectare.

For preparing black pepper, the freshly harvested spikes are spread on mats or concrete floors and dried in the sun for about a week with frequent turning over to prevent infection by mildew. Spikes which have dropped prematurely from the vines are also used. During drying, the green or red fruits gradually change in colour to dark brown or almost black and their skin becomes tough and wrinkled.

PLANT ECONOMICS

Rated Plant Capacity = 2000.00 Kgs./Day

LAND & BUILDING

Land Area 10 Bigha = Rs. 6,00,000.00

PLANT & MACHINERY

1. Water Pump
2. Agricultural implements, tools & others.
3. Wooden Bamboo
4. Water Tank (PVC Syntex),

FIXED CAPITAL

1.	Land & Building	Rs.	6,00,000.00
2.	Plant & Machinery	Rs.	1,35,000.00
3.	Other Fixed Assets	Rs.	41,250.00
	Total	Rs.	7,76,250.00

RAW MATERIALS

1. Manures
2. Fertiliser
3. DDT and Pesticides.

TOTAL WORKING CAPITAL/ANNUM

1.	Raw Material	Rs.	3,000.00
2.	Salary & Wages	Rs.	11,500.00
3.	Utilities & Overheads	Rs.	4,800.00
	Total	Rs.	19,300.00

TOTAL CAPITAL INVESTMENT

Total Fixed Capital		Rs.	7,76,250.00
Total Working Capital For 3 Months		Rs.	4,825.00
	Total	Rs.	7,81,075.00

TURN OVER/ANNUM

By sale of Black Pepper for 15 Years, total 30000 Kgs of Black Pepper	Rs.	15,00,000.00

Gross Profit in 15 Years = Rs. 4,29,420

28

CHILLI POWDER

Uses & Application

Dry chilli is extensively used as a spice in India . Curry powder is made by grinding roasted dry chilli with other condiments such as coriander, cumin and turmeric.

Capsicum preparations are used as counter-irritants in lumbago, neuralgia and rheumatic disorders. Taken internally Capsicum has a tonic, and carminative action and is specially useful in atonic dyspepsia.

PROCESS OF MANUFACTURE

The process of manufacture of chilli powder is simple, because it involves only some mechanical operations. No chemical reactions and so no need of automatically controlled chemical reactors and skilled operators for that. Select the combination of the chilli powder to be manufactured. It is not possible to a manufacturer to make all type of chilli powders but better to concentrate on a few variety of chilli powder. Here we have mentioned the important combination of chilli powders at the end of this section. However the process of manufacture is the same for all type of chilli powders.

The manufacturing process involves the following steps :

1) Washing and drying.

2) Grinding.
3) Packing.

1) Washing and drying

Most probably the spices will be clean and dry. Drying is necessary because even traices of moisture will affect the efficiency of the grinding machine and quality of the powder. So before feeding to the grinding machine the spices should be very dry. Usually sub drying is adopted.

GRINDING

The spices are ground. We must have a cooling arrangement for grinder. It is because sufficient amount of heat is produced during grinding operation.

The grinding is done on Impact Pulverizer.

Principles of Operations:

The standard pulverizer consists of an encased main rotor carrying swing hammers, fineners regulator and Exhaust fan. Raw materials from the feed hopper enters the roll feeder and, as the feeder pockets rotate, spills into grinding chamber to be reduced by impact with rotating hammers and sides of the chamber. The air steam flowing through the pulverizer carries the ground material towards the outlet, the oversize particles being rejected but the fineness regulators and returned for further grinding. classified material is then conveyed through the fan and into the cyclone for separation from the air system. Clean air is returned to the inlet of the pulverizer for recirculation. The small quantity of air entering the feder with the raw material is usually exhausted directly to a dust collector worth an almost negligible quantity of dust.

The Impact Pulverizer has a cast iron beater chamber, fan chamber and regulator chamber fitted with adjustable whizzers for varying the fineness of the ground products, the whole being mounted on a cast iron bedplate.

Renewable pulverizing hammers are mounted on the main shaft of shock resisting steel which is supported in two dust-tight housing fitted with heavy duty rolled bearing. The beater chamber is fitted with renewable liners.

The roll feeder is super imposed on the pulverizer and is operated by means of a rochet and pawl mechanism driven through a reduction gear from the main beater shaft.

In the beater chamber a pocket is arranged for the purpose of removing foreign material such as tramp iron which might be unintentionally introduced with the feed into the pulverizer.

Besides impact pulverizer there is other type of grinding machine available.

3) Packing

After the chilli powder is manufactured , it is packed in polythene bags of requisite quantity. The polythene bags are then packed in card-board boxes, which are then covered by polythene covering and then transferred to the store provided for the finished product. From that godown products sent to the market.

PLANT ECONOMICS

Rated Plant Capacity = 550.00 Kgs./Day

LAND & BUILDING

Land Area 450 Sq. Mt. = Rs. 4,62,500.00

PLANT & MACHINERY

1. Pulverizer
2. Drying Chamber (Continuous Type)

3. Automatic Packing Machine

FIXED CAPITAL

1.	Land & Building	Rs.	4,62,500.00
2.	Plant & Machinery	Rs.	1,15,000.00
3.	Other Fixed Assets	Rs.	60,000.00
	Total	Rs.	6,37,500.00

RAW MATERIALS

1. Spices (Chilli)
2. Polythene Bags
3. Card Board Boxes
4. Polythene Covering

TOTAL WORKING CAPITAL/MONTH

1.	Raw Material	Rs.	6,57,750.00
2.	Salary & Wages	Rs.	25,560.00
3.	Utilities & Overheads	Rs.	24,000.00
	Total	Rs.	7,07,310.00

TOTAL CAPITAL INVESTMENT

Total Fixed Capital	Rs.	6,37,500.00
Total Working Capital For 3 Months	Rs.	21,21,930.00
Total	Rs.	27,59,430.00

TURN OVER/ANNUM

By Sale of 165 Ton. of Chilli Powder Rs. 1,07,25,000.00

PROFIT SALES RATIO = Profit/Sales x 100 = 16.09%

RATE OF RETURN = Operating profit/T.C.I x 100 = 62.53%

BREAK EVEN POINT (B.E.P) = 30.29%

29

DRYING OF RED CHILLIES, HALDI, DHANIA, PEA AND GREEN PEAS

Uses & Application

The uses of the product is generally in food making i.e. in vegetable making and other uses of the product are categorized as follows :-

Red Chilli

Dry chilli is extensively used as a spices in India. Curry powder is made by grinding roasted dry chilli with other condiments such as coriander, cumin and tumeric-Capsicum Preparation are used as counter-irritants in lumbago, neuralgia and rheumatic disorders. Taken internally capsicum has a tonic , and carminative action and is specially useful in atonic dyspepsia.

Pharmaceutical requirements are chiefly met by the highly pungent varieties of capsicum grown in sierra Leone Nyasaland and Zanribar. Indian capsicum known in trade as Mumbai Capsicum in used as substitute.

Haldi (Turmeric)

It is an auspicious article in all religious observances in Hindu households. It is a normal constituent of condiments, curry powders and prepared mustards. It is also used for dyeing wool, silk and unmordanted to which it imports a yellow shade in an acid bath. Inspite of its poor light fastness it is still used for dyeing cotton, sometimes in combination with other natural dyes like indigo and satllower to impart different shades. It is used in colouring matter in pharmacy, confectionery and food industry.

In Indian systems of medicine, turmeric is used to some extent as a stomechic, tonic and blood purifier.

Dhania

The fruits are considered carminative, diuretic, tonic, stomachic antibilious, refrigerant and aphrodisiac. they are used chiefly to conceal the odour of other medicines and to correct the qualities of shubarb and senna (U.S.D, 329) they are considered also to lessen the intoxicating effects of spirituous liquors.

Peas

Pea is esteemed primarily for the nutritional value of its seeds. Peas are consumed both in the fresh form as vegetable and in the dried form as pulse, while in America and Europe considerable quantities are used for such processing the dried seeds of the field peas constitute the chief article of commerce. In India, it is often split, like other pulses into dal or in some places used for making roasted or parched pea.

Green Peas

It is used as vegetable, the green plant as well as the pods and grains and the hay are valued as folder. As a green folder, in mixture with oates, pea is said to be very favorable for milk production, having a high nutritive value.

MANUFACTURING PROCESS

Here manufacturing process is given below to the drying and powdering of Red Chilli, Haldi, Dhania, Peas and green Peas :-

1. Selection and grading

The best quality of the product are selected and graded from the raw. The worst quality are abstracted and the best quality has send to the further processing.

2. Washing

The materials should be thoroughly washed with water and in some cases thoroughly scrubbed while washing so remove soil and other extraneous matter.

3. Peeling

It is necessary to peel some of the matter before further processing. So peeling is done by peeling machine or manually.

4. Drying

It is done to get the dry product. It is done either by sun drying or by Mechanical equipments. e.g. Tray drier, belt drier etc.

5. Grinding

Grinding is done by grinding machine for the different meshes as required for the individual product.

6. Packing and storage

Packing is the most vital step for the success of the dehydration Industries. The dried and powdered product be quite dry and should be packed in moisture proof contains.

Tin containers are most suitable for it. But new a days it

is replacing by plastic packing.

Dehydration of the Product

The drying of individual product are given as follow :-

Lal Mirch (Chilli) Only the ripe chillies are used for processing. In India, they are mostly sun dried. Sometimes chillies are given steam treatment for 5 minutes before spreading for drying. This helps retention of calyx and gives fast colour to the finished product. The retention of caly prevents the seeds from falling out, chilli are although usually sun dried, tray dries may also be used, temperature should not exceed 50-60°C. Dried chilli have 8 to 10% moisture, and keep well. Tray 0 loading of 5 kg raw chillies/m^2 of tray area is considered good. Dry chillies are packed in jute bags.

Turmeric (Haldi) The turmeric rhizomes are removed from soil and washed thoroughly. There are then boiled in big iron vats using the available fuel at the place, till soft. The pieces are dried in sun till they give metallic sound when broken. Then they are given polish and coloured with turmeric solution. Mother shizomes and fingers are cured separately. They are stored in jute bags or ground in hammer mill and then packed as usual.

Coriander The plants are pulled out by the roots and after drying, the fruits are threshed out. They are further dried in sun, winnowed and stored in bags.

Peas Only tender peas are dehydrated. They are blanched for 1-2 minutes in boiling water and dried at a temperature not exceeding 145°F.

Green Peas Peas for dehydration should be even less mature than for canning. The temdeometer reading may range from 85 to 95. Green pods are brought to the plant. The peas are then removed from pods. It may be noted that peas deteriorate rapidly after removal from the pod, primarily because of unavoidable mechanical housing, these are then graded.

The peas are thoroughly washed with water, sorted to eliminate pod pieces, stem and dehydrated peas. Blanching may be accomplished minute the blanched peas are then slit the Machine which make a 1/8" slit in each pea.

Slitted peas are then dehydrated in tray-tunnel dryers, cabinet dryers continuous belt dryer or belt trough dryer. In a two stage tunnel dryer temperature of about 80-85°C for the initial stage and 70°C for the second stage are recommended. In high circulation continuous belt dryers temperatures from 90-95°C may be used during the early part of the drying cycle. When 8% moisture level is achieved peas are removed from the dries. The centers of the peas dry slowly, hence they should be dried.

Until crisp to moisture content below 5% in bin dryer using dry air at about 50°C. The Product is then packed in moisture proof pouches and bags.

PLANT ECONOMICS

Rated Plant Capacity = 1157.00 Kgs./Day

LAND & BUILDING

Land Area 800 Sq. Mt. = 8,40,000.00

PLANT & MACHINERY

1. Tunnel dryers with fan & Trays.
2. Peeling Machine
3. Screen grading machine with various type of screen
4. Washing Machine
5. Blanching Machine S.S.

6. Grinding Machine
7. Trollies, Trays etc.
8. Preparation table
9. Weighing Machine
10. Laboratories equipment
11. Packing filling machine automatic
12. Miscellaneous

FIXED CAPITAL

1.	Land & Building	Rs.	8,40,000.00
2.	Plant & Machinery	Rs.	10,10,000.00
3.	Other Fixed Assets	Rs.	1,90,000.00
	Total	Rs.	20,40,000.00

RAW MATERIALS

1. Red Chilli
2. Haldi (Turmeric)
3. Dhania (Coriander)
4. Peas
5. Green Peas

TOTAL WORKING CAPITAL/ANNUM

1.	Raw Materials	Rs.	18,50,000.00
2.	Salary & Wages	Rs.	5,14,500.00
3.	Utilities & Overheads	Rs.	3,55,000.00
	Total	Rs.	27,19,500.00

TOTAL CAPITAL INVESTMENT

Total Fixed Capital	Rs.	20,40,000.00
Total Working Capital for 3 Months	Rs.	6,79,875.00
Total	Rs.	27,19,875.00

TURN OVER/ANNUM

By Selling of 60 MT of Dried Chilli
62 M.T. of Dried Turmeric (Haldi)
75 MT. of Dried Coriander (Dhania)
75 MT. of Dried Peas
75 MT. of Dried Green Peas Rs. 48,34,500.00

PROFIT SALES RATIO = Profit/Sales x 100 = 25.20%

RATE OF RETURN = Operating profit/T.C.I x 100 = 44.79%

BREAK EVEN POINT (B.E.P) = 50.54%

30

DRY GINGER FROM GREEN GINGER

Ginger one of the oldest and most important spices, consists of the prepared and semi-dried rehizones of zinziber officinale Hoscoe belonging to family zingiber areas. The rehizones known in the trade as hands or race reach the spice trade either with the outer cortical layer intact (coated of unscrapped ginger) or the outer cost partially or completely removed (uncoated or scraped ginger). The remove their appearances, some singer of particular grades are bleached also by various means one among which is called lime giving rise to process lining.

Uses & Application

Ginger is good to give flavour and pungency to numerous foods including pies, cookies cakes, biscuits, Ginger bread, puddings and beverages,

Breaked ginger is an ingredient of whole mixed pickling spice & ground ginger is a constituent of curry powder, mince meatspice, pastry spice and other. Ground spice flavourly & seasoning mixtures.

Ginger Ale requires a heavy tonnage annually. Ginger tea is regarded as a carminative to ease an ailing stomach and is used for this purpose through out the world. Ginger is used for producing Ginger oil & oleoresin.

PROCESS OF MANUFACTURE

This depends upon the product being chosen pupping in view of the consumer,

GINGER NOT DIVESTED OF CORK

This is known as unscraped ginger and in this the rhizomes are cleaned with clean water to remove the external matter clinging to the green ginger. Then it is scalded in hot water at about 90°C for about 4 minutes after that it is removed to dried in sun.

Ginger Clivested of Cork :

This is known as scraped ginger. In this rhizomes are washed to remove any clinging external matter. Then they are scraped or peeled. The peeling is carefully performed to avoid cutting too deeply into the essential oil secreted in the tissues beneath the cork. This is then again washed in clean fresh water & then spread thinly and evenly on mats to dry slowly in the sun. The rhizomes should be spread on some frame work. It spread upon the ground there is always the danger of spotting, from the clampues of the earth. It required about 6 to 8 days for rhizomes to dry sufficiently for market.

At this stage moisture convent is between 7 to 12%. The ginger fermenls if there is a higher content of moisture. The process required great care as the rhizomes should not be fractured.

GRINDING

The dry ginger is then grinded in a grinder and screened to get the required ginger powder.

PROGRESS FLOW SHEET

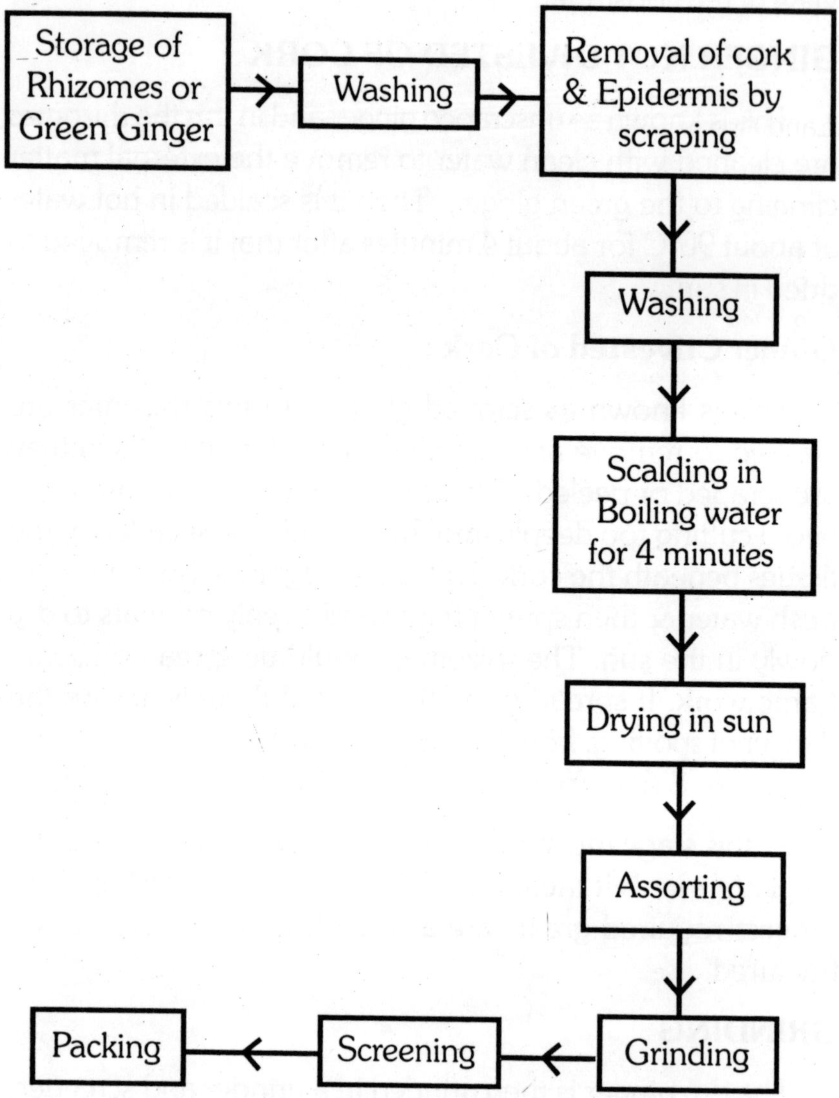

PLANT ECONOMICS

Rated Plant Capacity = 1.00 Ton/Day

LAND & BUILDING

Land Area 450 Sq. Mt. = Rs. 6,90,000.00

PLANT & MACHINERY

1. Tube well
2. Concrete structure for washing
3. Scalding drum heated with steam
4. Boiler for steam to heat dryer
5. Laboratory equipment
6. Drying trays with fences & supports of agriculture waste like leavosof Banana
7. Grinder

FIXED CAPITAL

1.	Land & Building	Rs.	6,90,000.00
2.	Plant & Machinery	Rs.	4,95,000.00
3.	Other Fixed Assets	Rs.	75,000.00
	Total	Rs.	12,60,000.00

RAW MATERIALS

1. Green Ginger

TOTAL WORKING CAPITAL/MONTH

1.	Raw Material	Rs.	12,60,000.00
2.	Salary & Wages	Rs.	51,250.00
3.	Utilities & Overheads	Rs.	1,10,600.00
	Total	Rs.	14,21,850.00

TOTAL CAPITAL INVESTMENT

Total Fixed Capital	Rs.	12,60,000.00
Total Working Capital For 3 Months	Rs.	42,65,550.00
Total	Rs.	55,25,550.00

TURN OVER/ANNUM

Sales of 300 Ton of Dry Ginger Rs. 2,25,00,000.00

PROFIT SALES RATIO = Profit/Sales x 100 = 17.98%

RATE OF RETURN = Operating profit/T.C.I x 100 = 73.20%

BREAK EVEN POINT (B.E.P) = 34.92%

31

DEHYDRATED ONIONS & ONION POWDER

The main advantages of dehydrated onions are that they are easy to store, being lighter in weight and smaller in bulk than fresh or other processed onions, they are cheap to pack compared with conned goods, they do not require refrigerated storage as do frozen onions and the contents of a container can be used some time after opening provided they are not dehydrated.

Uses of Dehydrated Onions

Dehydrated onions are used chiefly as a constituent in various food products i.e. they are sold to manufacturing concerns as an industrial raw material and demand for dehydrated onions is a function of the demand of these food products. However there is a demand for dehydrated onions for use as culinary onions, both by large catering concerns - institutions and industrial canteens; and for domestic use.

The other use of dehydrated onions is in the manufacture of dried soups-once virtually the sole outlet for these products, but now declining in relative importance as other applications including used in canned soups and stews, baby foods, fish meat and bakery products and more recently in dried 'ready-meals' have been developed.

So far as possible both merchants and users were consulted in the course. Since there are relatively few dried soup manufacturers, it was possible to contact a majority of the users in this class. Retail outlets obtain supplies largely from food manufacturers. The different market sectors account for varying proportions of demand for dehydrated onions. Dehydrated onion slices and pieces are sold to all four market sectors.

PROCESS OF MANUFACTURE

The onions are perishable commodity and cannot be stored for a long time after harvest at ordinary conditions, Dehydration is simple, effective and economical for preserving the onions during seasons of abundance and using then during off seasons.

Dehydration refers to removal of moisture from a product using heated air under controlled conditions. In additional to preservation aspect dehydration is important from many angles, such as weight and volume reduction, less cost in land being marketing etc.

It is desirable to set up small capacity processing dehydration plant near onion production pocket preferably in rural areas. In setting up the dehydration plant it must be remembered that regular supply of raw materials are ensured at moderate prices. The availability of cheap labour and low cost establishment of plant can further give impetus to expand other related agro-based industry in the region.

The important factors which determine the drying time are design of dehydrator, volume of air flow, high temperature, proportion of recirculated air, rate of input of wet product and the nature of the product being dried. In case of onion the relative humidity at the cool end and should be 20% to 25%.

Onions selected for quality and size are washed by water spraying or in rotary washers. The washing is repeated after peeling.

The equipment used for abrasion peeling consists of pairs of horizontal drums rotating in the same direction and lined with graded Carborundum. Water sprayers are used for loosening the dirt and assisting peeling. Peeling may affected steaming, radient heat or by heating oven gas flames and tumbling in washer.

Peeled onions are cut into cubes, strips, flapes or slices. Onions are usually dried in slices without scalding bhuched onions are immediately cooled by passing the trays containing the material through coolers in which refrigerated air is circulated. The material is then dried.

DEHYDRATION METHOD & DEHYDRATOR

Dehydration comprises sequence of operations pre-treatment, drying, compressing and packaging pre-treatment includes washing, pealing, trimming, strapping, shredding and blanching, followed then by actual dehydration of the product and finally the screening grading and packaging.

METHODS

1. Procurement of good tender quality onion.
2. Peeling of onion to remove the outer skin.
3. The onions are trimmed to remove upper and lower unused portion.
4. Then product onion is washed to remove any contact materials or soils, pesticides etc.
5. The ready onions are macerated to a fine slurry.
6. Some preservative is mixed properly at this stage.
7. The onion slurry is pumped through a spray dryer, operated under lower pressure or vacuum condition.
8. The moisture will be removed completely.

9. The product quality is checked.
10. The onion powder so produced will be packed in vacuum or in nitrogen flush system in a suitable desired container.

PLANT ECONOMICS

Rated Plant Capacity = 6.00 Ton/Day

LAND & BUILDING

Land Area 1 Acre = Rs. 59,65,000.00

FIXED CAPITAL

1.	Land & Building	Rs. 59,65,000.00
2.	Plant & Machinery	Rs. 2,80,00,000.00
3.	Other Fixed Assets	Rs. 74,00,000.00
	Total	Rs. 4,13,65,000.00

RAW MATERIALS

1. Onion (raw) of Suitable variety
2. Packaging material such as polyethylene packets, cartons or tin contains labels etc.
3. Miscellaneous Chemicals, Hydrogenated Groundnut oil etc.

TOTAL WORKING CAPITAL/MONTH

1.	Raw Material	Rs. 46,95,000.00
2.	Salary & Wages	Rs. 1,66,250.00
3.	Utilities & Overheads	Rs. 12,80,000.00
	Total	Rs. 61,41,250.00

TOTAL CAPITAL INVESTMENT

Total Fixed Capital		Rs. 4,13,65,000.00
Total Working Capital For 3 Months		Rs. 1,84,23,750.00
	Total	Rs. 5,97,88,750.00

TURN OVER/ANNUM

By sale of onion powder 1800 tons.
By sale of 675 ton. Skin dry cattle feed, Rs.12,68,10,000.00

PROFIT SALES RATIO = Profit/Sales x 100 = 27.33%
RATE OF RETURN = Operating profit/T.C.I x 100 = 57.97%
BREAK EVEN POINT (B.E.P) = 42.29%

32

GARLIC POWDER

Uses & Application

Garlic is most commonly used as a condiment and for flavouring and seasoning of food products such as soups, dals, pickles, etc It is also used for flavouring vinegar or oil for dressing. Incorporation of garlic in the diet at moderate levels is likely to shift the balance of the microflora in the intestines in favour of lactic organisms, which generally have a favourable effect on the absorption of minerals present in the diet.

Garlic has a pungent smell due to the presence of unsaturated sulphides. Several methods have been patented for the deodourization of garlic. An odour-free strain of garlic has been developed in Japan by continuous selection breeding. This strain tastes and smells like garlic until it is eaten, when for still unknown reasons, the odour disappears. This mutant strain of garlic does not revert to its original "smelly" strain even after six generations.

Garlic is endowed with several medicinal properties. It is stimulant, diaphoretic, expectorant, diuretic and tonic. It is rubefacient when applied externally. It is used as an anthelmintic and emmenagogue. The juice of garlic is used for various ailments of the stomach including amoebic dysentery. It is also used as an anti-tubercular drug, and in the treatment of epilepsy. It is reported to be anticholeric. Garlic reduces the blood sugar levels. It is an anti-fertility drug showing oxytocic activity.

MANUFACTURING PROCESS

The manufacturing process of garlic powder requires the following operations.

1. Washing
2. Peeling
3. Sulphitation
4. Packaging

WASHING

The fresh garlic as obtained from the vegetable market includes many contaminants like soil, leaves of other vegetables etc. It is very essential to wash the garlic purchased from the market before proceeding to any other process. The washing operation is performed by water spraying or in rotary washers.

PEELING

The outer leaves of garlic after washing are removed by peeling operation. Water sprayers used in first step assist peeling besides loosening the dirt. Peeling may be effected by steaming, radiant heat, or by heating over gas flames & tumbling in washer flame. The last technique is used for peeling of onion & garlics. In small scale units, hand operated peeling machine are used for removing the outer layers of garlic. The peeling process is again followed by the washing by spraying water.

SULPHITATION

Prior to dehydration, another operation is sometimes performed with certain limitations. This process is known as sulphitation. A small amount of sodium metabisulfite solution is spread on the sliced garlic prior to steaming. Sulphitation greatly prolongs the storage life of vegetables. garlics & onions, but treatment reduces their pungency. Sulphitation also protects the garlic and other vegetables against scorching damage during dehydration.

DEHYDRATION

The modern process of dehydration consists of the removal of moisture from garlic by the application of heat usually in the presence of controlled flow of air. If the air used in drying garlic is allowed to escape into the atmosphere after it passage through the dehydrator, a great deal of heat is lost. The garlic may become overdried if the spent air is recirculated in larger quantities. This condition is avoided to a large extent of the relative humidity of the air is increased sufficiently, which can be done to a large degree by return of some of the spent air. Because of these facts, it is customary in modern dehydrators to provide for recirculation of a portion of air used in drying.

The air in the dehydrator should be so furnished as to be applied to the product to be dried in evenly distributed manner. By placing baffles on the walls of the dehydrator or on the trolleys it is possible to force the air into the desired channels. Various types of dehydrators are available commercially and used for the dehydration techniques :

1. Kiln Drier.
2. Tower or stack Drier.
3. Oregon Tunnel Drier.
4. Vacuum Dehydrator.
5. Forced draft tunnel dehydrator.
6. Circulating Air Blast type funnel dehydrator.

Various types of dehydrator trays are in use which vary

greatly in size design and materials of the construction. The trays used for garlic dehydration are of 6' x 3' size with wooden slot bottoms. The tray load is about 1 1/4 lb/sq. ft. Garlic is dried to 8% moisture in dehydrators. The drying is completed in bins at 45-50°C to obtain moisture less than 6.5%.

PACKAGING

The packing of garlic flakes is done completely in hermetically soaked container, so that no air from outside will go into the package and no air from inside will come out of the package. The product will remain good for a longer period.

STORAGE

The product after packaging in hermetically sealed container is now stored at low temperature. (0-2^0) to prevent the product from non-enzymatic browning reaction. The product will remain good in low temperature storage conditions.

SAFETY PRECAUTIONS & OTHER CARES IN GARLIC DEHYDRATION

In accordance with the fruit produce order 1965 Government of India the undermentioned requirements in respect of the hygienic conditions for the manufacturing premising have to be fulfilled:

1. The premises shall be cleaned adequately lighted and ventilated and shall be cleaned of required by lime washing or colour washing or painting or disinfecting deodorizing.

2. Windows, doors and other openings suited to screening shall be fly-proof. The doors should have spring so that they may close automatically. The ceiling of the roof shall be of

permanent nature. The floor should be cemented, tiled or laid in stone.

3. The premises shall be located in sanitary place and free from filthy surroundings.

4. All out-houses stores and approaches to the premises shall be kept clean and sanitary.

5. Equipment & machinery when employed shall be of such design which will permit easy cleaning. Adequate arrangements for cleaning of containers tables, working parts of machinery etc. shall be provided.

6. No vessel, container or other equipments, the use of which is likely to cause metallic contamination, injurious to health shall be employed in the preparation, packing or storage of the fruit products (copper & brass vessel shall be always kept tinned, no iron or galvanized iron shall come into contact with fruit provisions).

7. The water used in the manufacture shall be potable.

8. There should be efficient drainage system and adequate provision for disposal of reuse. The drains should be kept covered.

9. Wherever cooking is done by open fire, proper arrangement will be made for outlet of smoke and soot.

10. No workers suffering from infections or contagious diseases shall be allowed to work in the factory. Arrangements shall be made for examining all the workers once a year to check disease. They shall be inoculated and vaccinated against the entries group of disease once a year. In case of epidemic all workers should be inoculated.

11. Workers working in the process and preparation shall

be provided with proper clean apron headwears etc.

PLANT ECONOMICS

Rated Plant Capacity = 200.00 Kgs./Day

LAND & BUILDING

Land Area 600 Sq. Mt. = Rs. 12,04,000.00

PLANT & MACHINERY

1. Fruit & Vegetable washing machine
2. Garlic Peeler
3. Hot air drying oven model 1D-IV electrically or steam heated thermostatically controlled
4. Garlic slicer
5. Steam Generator
6. Steam blancher, tunnel
7. M.G. Impact 20" pulverizer
8. Polyethylene bag sealer floor model, sealing
9. Sieving set
10. Other equipment, pipelines & accessories

FIXED CAPITAL

1.	Land & Building	Rs.	12,04,000.00
2.	Plant & Machinery	Rs.	1,90,500.00
3.	Other Fixed Assets	Rs.	50,000.00
	Total	Rs.	14,44,500.00

RAW MATERIALS

1. Garlic Bulbs

TOTAL WORKING CAPITAL/MONTH

1.	Raw Material	Rs.	1,50,000.00
2.	Salary & Wages	Rs.	1,53,750.00
3.	Utilities & Overheads	Rs.	66,000.00
	Total	Rs.	3,69,750.00

TOTAL CAPITAL INVESTMENT

Total Fixed Capital	Rs.	14,44,500.00
Total Working Capital For 3 Months	Rs.	11,09,250.00
Total	Rs.	25,53,750.00

TURN OVER/ANNUM

Receipt by sale of 200x300=60000 kg. of Garlic powder/Annum Rs. 60,00,000.00

PROFIT SALES RATIO = Profit/Sales x 100 = 14.81%

RATE OF RETURN = Operating profit/T.C.I x 100 = 34.80%

BREAK EVEN POINT (B.E.P) = 66.05%

33

MUSTARD POWDER

Mustard powder is one type of spice used either individually with blend of several spices for preparation of various Indian dishes both vegetable & non-veg food items. It is prepared in two types.

1. Whole mustard seeds powder.
2. Dehulled Mustard powder.

Uses & Application

Mustard powder is one of the ingredient of various mixed spices.

It is also used ass individual spice for various preparations of food items viz. Curries, Dals, Gravy, Chutney, Pickles, Samosa Stuffings, Pakoda Stuffings, Sambar, Coconut, Dahi chutney and lot of other south indian and north india food preparation.

It is used in pizza, Dosa, Vada, Idli preparations.

It is consumed by hotels, restaurants, pickles, snack manufactures and others.

It is also mixed with various spices to prepare various masalas like Baba, Ashok, M.D.H etc.

MANUFACTURING PROCESS

Mustard Powder can be manufactured by following

processing steps described as below.

1. Procurement of mustard seeds of food quality from market.
2. Weighing into desired quantity
3. Cleaning by automatic vibro screen to remove dust, soils chaffs, leaves and unwanted foreign matters from seeds.
4. Quality checking of mustard seeds.
5. Pulverizing or grinding of seeds to desired particle size.
6. Mustard powder packing in nitrogen flush metallised printed plastic pouches by automatic weighing filling, nitrogen gas flushing and pouch sealing machine.
7. Quality checking/Testing to be done for its long shelf life.
8. Then it is packed in corrugated cardboard boxes, sealed and then stored.
9. It is now dispatched for market.

PLANT ECONOMICS

Rated Plant Capacity = 2.00 Ton/Day

LAND & BUILDING

Land Area 1000 Sq.Mt. = Rs. 24,50,000.00

PLANT & MACHINERY

1. Plate Form Weighing Balance
2. Vibroscreen
3. Pulveriser
4. Bucket Elevator
5. Automatic Weighing Filling & Pouch Sealing Machine
6. Testing Equipment
7. Misc. Tools, Jigs, Fixtores Etc.
8. Conveyor belt with Magnetic Separator

FIXED CAPITAL

1.	Land & Building	Rs.	24,50,000.00
2.	Plant & Machinery	Rs.	15,45,000.00
3.	Other Fixed Assets	Rs.	4,25,000.00
	Total	Rs.	44,20,000.00

RAW MATERIALS

1. Mustard Seeds
2. Pouches, Packaging Materials, Corrugated Cardboard boxes, Adhesive Tapes, box straps lables, Nitrogen Gas etc.
3. Laboratory Chemicals

TOTAL WORKING CAPITAL/MONTH

1.	Raw Material	Rs.	8,52,251.00
2.	Salary & Wages	Rs.	1,27,500.00
3.	Utilities & Overheads	Rs.	1,20,500.00
	Total	Rs.	11,00,251.00

TOTAL CAPITAL INVESTMENT

Total Fixed Capital	Rs.	44,20,000.00
Total Working Capital For 3 Months	Rs.	33,00,753.00
Total	Rs.	77,20,753.00

TURN OVER/ANNUM

By Sale of 600000/- Kgs. Mustard Powder in Nitrogen Gas Flush Pouch Rs. 1,92,00,000.00

PROFIT SALES RATIO = Profit/Sales x 100 = 19.66%
RATE OF RETURN = Operating profit/T.C.I x 100 = 48.90%
BREAK EVEN POINT (B.E.P) = 47.47%

34

OLEOREis FROM CHILLY & GINGER (EXTRACTION)

Uses & Application

As Food Flavourant

Dry chilly is extensively used as a spice in all types a curried dishes in India are abroad. Curry powder is made by grinding roasted dry chilli with other ingredient such as coriander, cumin, turmeric and farinaceous matter, etc. It is also used for seasoning of egg, fish and meat preparation,s sauces, chutneys, pickles, frankfurters, sausages, etc.

Bird chilli is used in making hot sauces such as pepper sauce. 'Mandram' is a West Indies stomatic preparation made by adding cucumber, shallot, lime juice and Madaria wine to meshed fruits of bird chilli.

ROLE IN HUMAN PHYSIOLOGY :

Chillies, when taken with food, stimulate our taste buds there by increase the flow of saliva which contains the enzyme 'amylase' which, in turn, helps in the digestion of starchy or cereal foods, etc. into the easily assimilable sugar namely glucose.

When eaten fresh with salads, they, being rich in vitamins C and A, Serve as a good vitamin supplement in addition to their being an appetizer. Thus green chillies are more nutritious than ripe. Dried chillies or chilli powder, as most of the vitamins are lost during drying.

PAPRIKA AS COLOURANT AND FLAVOURANT

Paprika, Red Pepper, Kashmiri Mirch or Degchi Mirch which are mild in pungency, are used to colour flavour and garnish dishes, and shimla Mirch, which is not pungent and issued as curried vegetable, is specially rich in vitamin C. One simla Mirch a day fulfils our daily requirements of vitamin C. It is necessary that its used must be encouraged and popularised. Use of attractive red paprika in tomato ketch-up and sauces should also be encouraged for improving their colour since addition of synthetic colour is no longer allowed in tomato ketchup under the latest food laws of the country.

PRODUCTION OF SPICE OLEORESIN (CAPSICUM)

1. SELECTION OF PROPER VARIETY OF SPICE

The difference in quality and yield of both essential oils and oleoresins have been noticed in varieties of important spices such as cardamom, chillies, ginger, pepper, and turmeric grown in India. The oleoresin content of chillies varies from 12 to 10%, while in pepper varies from 10 to 12%, ginger 5 to 7%, and turmeric 4 to 7%

2. CONDITIONING OR DRYING

The spice selected must be dried thoroughly to bring down the moisture to a critical level, which is different from the moisture content for the prevention of mold growth. This level also depends on the nature of the solvent to be used. For water soluble solvents such as alcohol and acetone, the moisture level should be very low, otherwise it dilutes the solvent, and this, in turn, lowers the solubility of certain flavoring compounds. Besides if spices are not dried, they require larger quantities of solvent and larger equipments, with the added difficulty of extraction mentioned above.

3. Preparation of Material for Pulverizing, in chillies, the calyx should be removed so that it does not impart a greenish tinge to the oleoresin. Properly dried spices should be cleaned to get rid of all extraous matter. Chilli powder is ground to 0.5 and 0.35 mm mean mesh which gives about 12% and 16% oleoresin respectively.

4. CHOICE OF SOLVENT

The selection of solvent has received due attention from several workers. Sabel and warren reported that, out of a number of solvents studied, acetone, ethanol, and isopropanol could be used very satisfactorily for the recovery of oleoresin from ginger. This was little to chose among these three solvent. Mathew studied the comparative efficiency of hexane, ethanol and ethylene dichloride and concluded that hexane was a poor solvent for extraction of capsaicin from capsicums or chillies. On the other hand, alcohol did not extract the color efficiently. Furthermore, alcohol, especially hot alcohol, gives a product that is semi solid instead of usual free flowing products. Thus ethylene dichloride is a good solvent for the extraction of chilli oleoresin, getting yields up to 13 to 14%.

CONDITIONS OF EXTRACTION

Several conditions of extraction, such as the time taken for the solvent to wet the bed of material and the rate of flow of the extract, are commonly influenced by the size of the particles, the density of packing, the bed height, the area, the rate of percolation etc. Optimum conditions for quick and efficient extraction have thus to be worked out for each spice, since time is a very important factor in commercial operation of the process. The method of extraction is yet another important factor to consider. Systematic work done at CFTRI, Mysore, shows that three-stage batch counter current extraction is satisfactory for all the major splices (pepper, ginger chillies, turmeric etc.). In addition, ethylene dichloride has been found to be the most suitable solvent because (1) the final product is clear and (2) open distillation can be used for desolventization.

SOLVENT STRIPPING FROM MISCELLA

Great care should be exercised to minimize the heat damage to the product during the disolventization of the miscella. Cannel has observed that excessive heating during removal of solvent from ginger extract can cause the formation of shogao, zingerone, and aliphatic aldehydes. This can result in a decrease in pungency as well as the development of off-flavours. Thus, it is very necessary to control the temperature of the material carefully during distillation by use of vacuum. Constant stirring prevents overheating near the walls of the still. Volatile oil losses can be minimized by controlling the rate of distillation and by using tall columns. High essential oil content in oleoresin is necessary to get a good quality oleoresin of the desired pleasent aroma. Chilli oleoresin is, of course, an exception, since it does not contain any essential oil.

Unlike pepper, there is no necessity for "contact time" in the case of chillies for maximum extraction of solids. The diffusion of solubles into the solvent is fairly quick. Handling of both chilli powder and extract requires special precautions, since they are highly pungent and irritate the skin and mucous membrane.

The last traces of solvent are removed from oleoresin by vacuum distillation, followed by an azeotropic distillation technique.

Location of Oleoresin Plant:

The location of the extraction plant, whether at the source or near the market, affects the marketing and economic aspects of oleoresin. Following are the major considerations to be taken into account at the time of location of a plant.

1. Availability of contemplated raw material
2. Reasonable cost of good quality of raw material
3. Scope for marketing of the product
4. Efficient plant design with minimum losses in recovery.
5. Availability of technical expertise and management
6. Reasonable facilities for labour, transport and utilities.
7. Assurance of reasonable profits.
8. Government regulations regarding labour and transport.
9. Availability of sufficient financing.
10. Facility for economic disposal of spice waste etc.

However the ultimate success of plant or project lies in the entrepreneur's ability to interpret the facts correctly, to translate his ideas into action and to achieve the goals he has set for himself and the enterprise. System and check lists help in organising routines, but in the final analysis the key to success lies in the people who are behind the undertaking. This is true for all human endeavor and so also for spice extraction whether at the source or at the market.

PROCESS OF MANUFACTURE

Oleoresin from chillies consists of fixed oil, capsaicin, pigment, sugar and resins. The oleoresin yield from chilli varies from 8.7-16 % with 2-3 % capsion and about 0.114 % colour in B-caroten ethylene chloride is good solvent for oleoresin extraction.

The process of solvent extraction of chillies oil from chillies involves the following steps which are otherwise simple and do not require high technology.

1. Drying :

The green chilli from crop and dried in air and sun as to evaporate all moisture. If the received raw materiel is red chilli these are also placed in sun for some hours to ensure the evaporation of all moisture contents.

2. Grinding :

The red dried chillies are ground in ordinary grinding mills. These chillies are ground to a proper size.

3. Solventization :

The ground chilli so formed is then powered into a specially designed apparatus containing the required solvent is ethylene dichloride. After some time of reaction the oil of chilly is carried away by solvent leaving behind chilli with very low oil contents to accomplish complete yield, this process is again replaced with fresh batch of solvent until all the oil of chilly is extracted from the chilli cake. The left over its known as cake. This process is continue with new batch of grind chilly and fresh batch of solvent to extract the oil of chilli.

Recovery of solvent :-

The solvent from oil of chilly is separated by fractional distillation process.

Cake grinding :-

The cake is dried and ground and sold at a comparatively lower price as chilli powder in market.

PROCESS FLOW CHART

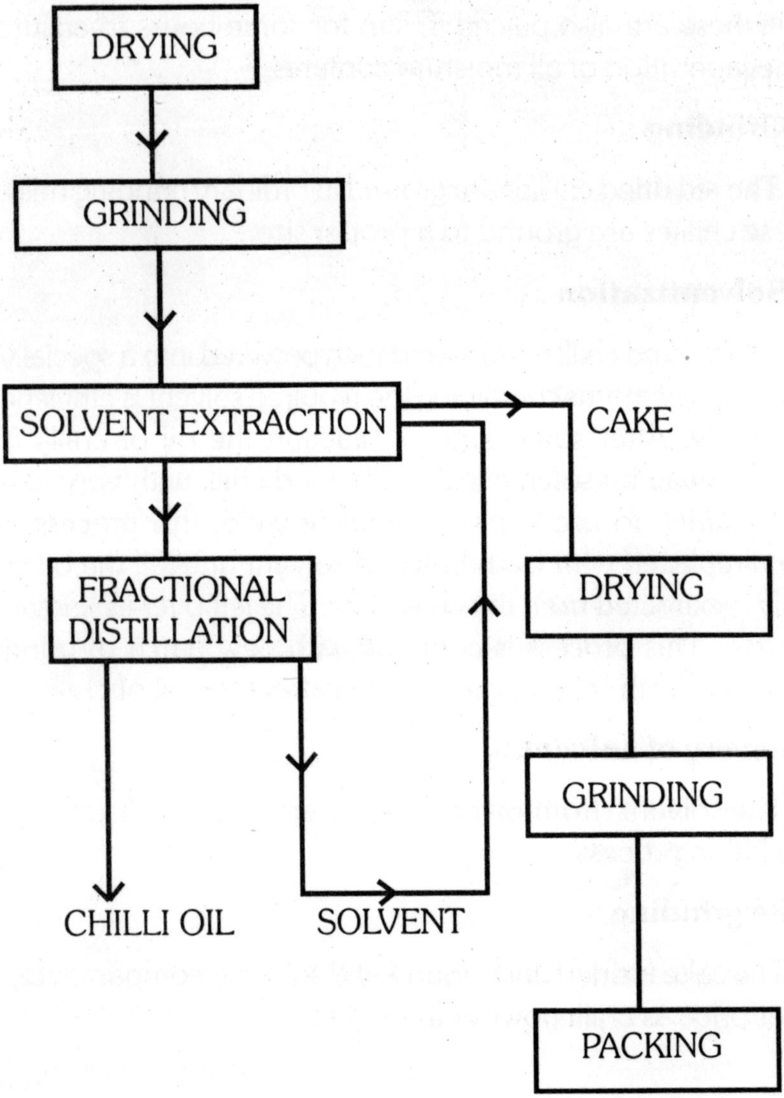

GINGER OIL & OLEORESIN MANUFACTURING PROCESS

Preparation of raw Material

Distillation of ginger oil on an industrial scale does differ some what from distillation of essential oils in general.

Cleaning

Prior to any combination, the spice must be freed from extraneous matters, such as dust, dirt, pebbles and metallic objects. For this purpose salting machine with a magnetic screen and screens of different diameters are used.

Milling

For the grinding of ginger, mills of different type are used, some are equipped with rotating tooth disk, some are hammer mills and for some special purposes, triple- roller mills are used. Both the rotating tooth disk mills and the hammer mills have a considerable airflow, which causes a certain loss of volatile oil from the ground ginger.

The rotating disk mill may be adjusted to the desired grain size of the milled product, but frictioned heat develops during grinding and therefore they are with a cooling device. Hammer mills are not practicable when the material is small and contains a relatively high percentage of fats. For such case crushing in triple roller mills, which rotates at different velocties and have ribbed rollers is the appropriate method of comminution.

Soaking

Ames and Mathews mention the desirability of (1968) soaking of some plant material for instance, cinnamon bank & also of grinding the spice prior to distillation.

Loading or Charging

Ground ginger must be loaded into the still and distilled without any delays otherwise, losses of Essential oil and deteriotion through Oxidation are inevitable. The oil distiller must realize that this valuable product will some day be used in food without nay further preliminary purification. Contamination of essential oil with rust, dirt, salt of copper or water can not be tolerated. Therefore, the distillation apparatus should preferably be made of stainless steel. As a minimum requirement the lid of the still, the gooseneck, the condenser and the flerentine flask or oil receiver should be made of this material.

Bleaching of Ginger

The peeled ginger hands are washed in water and kept steeped in plain water for 2 to 3 hours. Thereafter, they are takenout and steeped in about 1.5 to 200% lime (Cao) Solution for about 6 hours. They are then drained and sun dried on mats, barbecues, or a clean cement floor. This liming or bleaching of ginger not only improves its colours but also helps to preserve it better. Case should be taken to use the best quality slaked lime in order to get better whiteners.

Application of these chemicals requires proper control especially in the bleaching of ginger.

Manufacturing Process

Ginger Oil is Obtained by the steam distillation of the dried Ginger. The best raw material is African ginger. It is not only lower priced than other qualities but also gives a higher yield of oil. In general the yield varies from 1.5 to 3 percent of volatile oil. averaging 2%. Prior to distillation the dry material should be comminuted, then charged into the stills immediately. Care must be taken to distribute the mass evenly on several trays. Within the still Distillation is Carried out with direct steam depending upon the charge in the still and the steam depending upon the charge in the still and the steam pressure Applied, distillation of one charge may require up to 20 hour. The distillation water may require cohobation.

Peeling and shaving of the rhizomes constitute an excellent material for distillation, giving a good yield of oil, provided distillation is carried out immediately after peeling.

PLANT ECONOMICS

Rated Plant Capacity = 10000 Kgs./Day

LAND & BUILDING

Land Area 1000 Sq.Mt. = Rs. 16,25,000.00

PLANT & MACHINERY

1. Boiler
2. Disintegrator Beater type with motor,
3. Solvent Extractor
4. Vacuum Distillation Still
5. Desolventiser
6. Vibrating Screen
7. Platform balance,
8. Laboratory Equipment, pipe & fitting etc.
9. Condenser (S.S tubes)

FIXED CAPITAL

1.	Land & Building	Rs.	16,25,000.00
2.	Plant & Machinery	Rs.	24,35,000.00
3.	Other Fixed Assets	Rs.	6,70,000.00
	Total	Rs.	47,30,000.00

RAW MATERIALS

1. Chillies
2. Ginger dry,
3. Solvent n-Hexane, acetone
4. Packing container glass bottles
5. Lab testing chemicals
6. Cartons, labels adhesive tapes

TOTAL WORKING CAPITAL/MONTH

1.	Raw Material	Rs.	44,32,600.00
2.	Salary & Wages	Rs.	1,30,375.00
3.	Utilities & Overheads	Rs.	2,67,000.00
	Total	Rs.	48,29,975.00

TOTAL CAPITAL INVESTMENT

Total Fixed Capital	Rs.	47,30,000.00
Total Working Capital for 3 Months	Rs.	1,44,89,925.00
Total	Rs.	1,92,19,925.00

TURN OVER/ANNUM

By sale of chilly oleoresin 108000 Kgs.
By sale of ginger oleoresin Rs. 7,38,00,000.00

PROFIT SALES RATIO = Profit/Sales x 100 = 15.56%
RATE OF RETURN = Operating profit/T.C.I x 100 = 59.75 %
BREAK EVEN POINT (B.E.P) = 35.30 %

35

TURMERIC POWDER

Turmeric is botanical known C.longa. It is the rhizomes which are short and thick, constitute the turmeric of commerce. Turmeric is used both as a colouring material and as a condiment. The characteristic yellow matter, distributed throughout the plant, is especially concentrated in the rhizomes.

Uses & Application

Turmeric powder is an auspicious article in all religious observances in Hindu holds. It is a normal constituents of condiments, curry powders and prepared mustards.

It is also used for dyeing wool, silk and unmordanted Cotton to which it imports a yellow shade in an acid bath. Inspite of its poor light fastness it is still used for dyeing cotton, sometimes in combination with other natural dyes like indigo and safflower to import different shades.

In Indian systems of medicines turmeric is used to some extent as a stomachic, tonic and blood purifier. It is also preseribed as an antoperiodic alterative. Mixed with warm milk it is said to be beneficial in common Cold. The juice of fresh rhizomes is used as an antiparasitic for many skin affections. Externally it is applied to indolent ulcers, and a paste made from the powdered rhizomes along with lime forms a remedy for inflamed joints. A decoction of the rhizome is said to relieve the pain of purulent ophtalmia.

PROCESS OF MANUFACTURE

The clean, pre washed and dried, rhizomes of turmeric are taken in a hammer mill and crushed to smaller particle size.

The smaller particle of turmeric is now pulverized to very fine particle size. The particles of turmeric should very fine and should conform the B.I.S. Specificataion. The product is now Sieved through an automatic closed sieving machine. Then the product is packed in polyethene bags by automatic powder weighting, filling and sealing Machine.

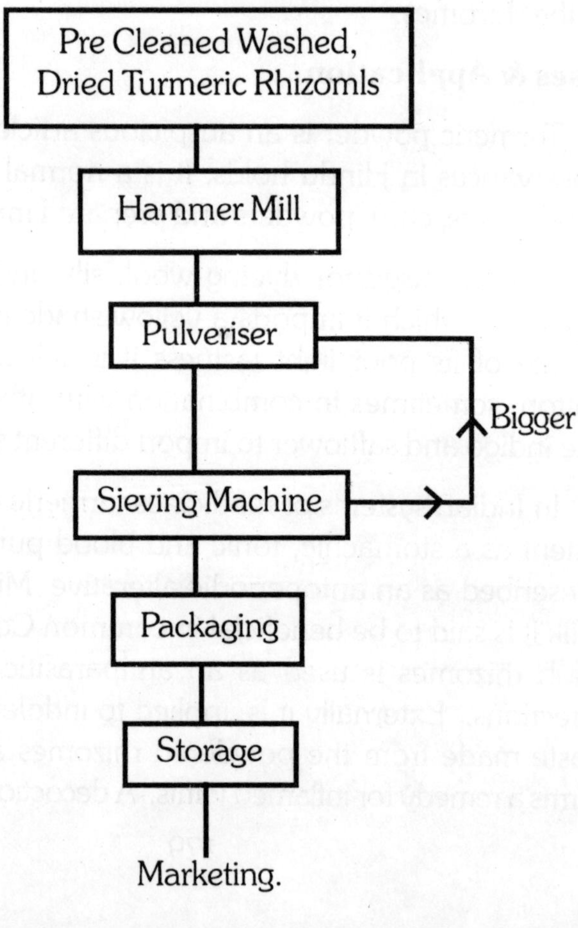

PLANT ECONOMICS

Rated Plant Capacity = 1.00 Mt./Day

LAND & BUILDING

Land Area 250 Sq. Mt. = Rs. 7,07,500.00

PLANT & MACHINERY

1. Hammer mill
2. Pulveriser
3. Automatic sieving machine
4. Powder weighing, filling, sealing machine
5. Conveyer belt, bucket elevator etc.
6. Miscellaneous plant and machinery

FIXED CAPITAL

1.	Land & Building	Rs.	7,07,500.00
2.	Plant & Machinery	Rs.	6,60,000.00
3.	Other Fixed Assets	Rs.	2,55,000.00
	Total	Rs.	16,22,500.00

RAW MATERIALS

1. Turmeric Rhizomes
2. Packaging materials

TOTAL WORKING CAPITAL/MONTH

1.	Raw Material	Rs.	6,23,000.00
2.	Salary & Wages	Rs.	21,250.00
3.	Utilities & Overheads	Rs.	38,600.00
	Total	Rs.	6,82,850.00

TOTAL CAPITAL INVESTMENT

Total Fixed Capital		Rs.	16,22,500.00
Total Working Capital For 3 Months		Rs.	20,48,550.00
	Total	Rs.	36,71,050.00

TURN OVER/ANNUM

By sale of 300 Mt. Turmeric Powder Rs. 1,05,00,000.00

PROFIT SALES RATIO = Profit/Sales x 100 = 12.28%

RATE OF RETURN = Operating profit/T.C.I x 100 = 35.11%

BREAK EVEN POINT (B.E.P) = 50.29%

36

TAMARIND SEED POWDER

Uses & Application

The tamarind is used in making chutney and also pickles. It's products are very tasty. Apart from these, the tamarind powder has use in tamarind gum. The gums are used in food as stabilizers and thickness. They from viscous solutions which prevent aggregation of the small particles of the disposed phase. In this way they aid in keeping solid dispersed in chocolate milk, air in whipping creams and in Confectioneries flier, thickening and stabilizing properties make them useful in water base paints, printing inks and drilling muds. Because of these properties they also are used in cosmetics and pharmaceuticals as emulsifiers or bases for ointments, greaseless creams, toothpaste, lotions, demulcents, and emollients. Gums are used to modify texture and increase moisture holding capacity for example as gelling agents in canned meats or fish, mash-mallows, jellied caudies, and fruit jellies. Their adhesive properties make them useful in the production of card-board, postage stamps, gummed envelopes, and as pill binders other application include the production of dental impression mold, fibres, soluble surgery films and gauge, blood anti coagulants plasma extenders, beverage clarifying agents, bacteriological culture media, half cell bridge and tungsten wire-drawing lubricants.

MANUFACTURING PROCESS

Tamarind seed powder is prepared by decorticating the tamarind seeds powder and pulverizing tamarind seeds are thoroughly washed with water to free them from any adhering pulp, the bad and hollow seeds floating on the surface of water during washing are discovered. The kernels are separated from the washed seeds by soaking in water or roasting. The submerged seeds are taken out and fumigated with sulphur dioxide gas or soaked in 25 % brine solution for an hour.

The seeds are then dried, sorted out and stored in dry pipa.

Variation of these processes are followed for the preparation of tamarind powder on both large and cottage industry scale.

The production of tamarind powder from the seeds is done by any of the three methods.

First Method :-

In the first method; which is economical method suggested for the production of good quality tamarind seed powder is as follows :

The outline steps of the process enumerated as :

1. Washing of the tamarind seeds
2. Fumigation
3. Roasting
4. Cooling for 7 to 8 days
5. Decortication (hull removal of kernel collection)
6. Grading of kernels
7. Washing of properly parched kernels in cold water
8. Soaking in 0.5 % sulphur dioxide solution for 3-4 hours.
9. Washing in water

10. Drying in hot air chamber
11. Grinding (pulverizing) and collection of powder through air cyclones
12. Packing.

1. Washing of the Tamarind Seeds :-

Washing is necessary to free the tamarind seeds from any adhering pulp. The seeds which float on the surface of water are discovered. Washing is carried out in a washing tank (MS) where high jets of water are provided and an agitator is also provided for agitating while washing, if required.

2. Fumigation :-

After washing of tamarind seeds with water & separating from bad & hollow ones, they are fed into fumigation tank. In same processes So_2 is used for fumigation, but here in this process, an alternative method is employed.

The seeds are soaked in a soaking tank (MS) in 25% brine solution for about 12 hours.

After fumigation, the seeds are dried in a tray dryer.

The dried seeds are then sorted out and stored in a dry place.

Cleaning :-

The dried tamarind seeds are cleaned for removal of the spoiled seeds and other foreign materials present. This is carried out manually.

3. Roasting :-

Roasting is carried out in mechanically open pans with sand. The dried tamarind seeds are parched for 30 minutes on hot sand or in a hot air chamber or roaster at 145°-150°C to remove the testa. The seeds are parched.

While roasting is carried out, care must be taken to see that the kernel inside the seeds is not damaged or over-roasted. Over-roasting destroys the starch quality and a cream colored starch results in case of over-roasted stuff.

4. Cooling :-

After roasting, the tamarind seeds are cooled. Then they are kept as such for 7-8 days. This process is done because by giving a lobger gap period after roasting helps in easy hull removal in the decorticators after cooling. During roasting the oil content and moisture content of the kernel is reduced and during cooling period for 7-8 days, the kernel shrinks a little which helps easy removal of hull in the decorticators and the percentage of the decorticated seeds will be less. It may be noted that roasting and cooling of seed imparts resistance against attack by insect to the seeds and well roasted seeds can be done for a longer period of this time without due spoilage.

5. Decortication (Hull Removal & Kernel Collection)

The roasted (parched) and cooled tamarind seeds are then fed into a grain cleaner provided with beaters and an exhaust fan to remove testa and dirt.

Or the roasted and cooled tamarind seeds are then charged into the decorticators where the hull is removed and separated from kernels. For every 10 Kgs. of roasted and cooled seeds feed only 60% of kernels are obtained.

6. Grading of Kernels :-

Grading is done to prepare feed for pulverizing. Grading section is the section where more kernels are separated by grading decorticated seeds. The kernels as obtained from the decorticator have about 5% of under corticated seeds.

This process of grading is carried out mechanically. Grading will thus increase the efficiency of the pulverizing step. To maintain the overall efficiency and performance of the process of manufacture of decorticated seeds from grading section are again feed to the decortication tank.

7. Washing of Properly Parched Kernels in Cold Water :-

The properly parched kernels are washed in cold water.

8. Soaking in 0.5 % Sulphur Dioxide Solution for 3-4 Hours :-

After washing in cold water, the kernels are soaked for 3 or 4 hours in 0.5 % sulphur dioxide solution.

9. Washing in Water :-

Then the kernels are washed again in water.

10. Drying in Hot Air :-

Then they are dried on sand bath or in a hot air chamber at 110°C to a moisture content of 5%.

11. Grinding (Pulverizing) :-

The kernels are charged to the pulverizer for pulverizing. For pulverizing the tamarind seed kernels machine or 2 tons/ day or 250 Kgs/hour capacity with a fineness of 100-250 mesh size is used.

The kernels are powdered in the pulverizer and the powder is collected through air blower cyclones. In the pulverizer, the kernels are broken by the hammers. Wastage is about 1.55 %.

12. Packing :-

The product is then packed.

PLANT ECONOMICS

Rated Plant Capacity = 1.00 Mt./Day

LAND & BUILDING

Land area 400 Sq. Mt. = Rs. 7,85,000.00

PLANT & MACHINERY

1. Soaking tank M.S. for soaking of tamarind seeds
2. Washing tank (M.S.),
3. Crusher/Impact grinder
4. Disintegrator/pulverizer
5. Decorticator
6. Air blower
7. Roaster
8. Dryer (tray) for drying of seeds
9. Packing machine
10. Hot air chamber
11. Testing equipments
12. Instrumentation & process control
13. Miscellaneous

FIXED CAPITAL

1.	Land & Building	Rs.	7,85,000.00
2.	Plant & Machinery	Rs.	6,46,000.00
3.	Other Fixed Assets	Rs.	1,82,000.00
	Total	Rs.	16,13,000.00

RAW MATERIALS

1. Tamarind seeds,
2. NaCl
3. Packing materials

TOTAL WORKING CAPITAL/MONTH

1.	Raw Material	Rs.	1,18,000.00
2.	Salary & Wages	Rs.	47,625.00
3.	Utilities & Overheads	Rs.	28,800.00
	Total	Rs.	1,94,425.00

TOTAL CAPITAL INVESTMENT

Total Fixed Capital	Rs.	16,13,000.00
Total Working Capital For 3 Months	Rs.	5,83,275.00
Total	Rs.	21,96,275.00

TURN OVER/ANNUM

By sale of 300 Tons of Tamarind seed powder	Rs.	34,50,000.00

PROFIT SALES RATIO = Profit/Sales x 100 = 15.81%

RATE OF RETURN = Operating profit/T.C.I x 100 = 24.83%

BREAK EVEN POINT (B.E.P) = 63.24 %

37

PROCESS OF MANUFACTURE & FORMULAES

Processing of fine spice and **Curry Powder** involve the operations as under:

S.No	Item	Qty (Parts/Wt.)
1.	Dhania	70
2.	Salt	5
3.	Yellow Saranso	5
4.	Red Chilli	5
5.	Haldi	5
6.	Black Pepper	2
7.	Tej Pat	2
8.	Jai Phal	1
9.	Shalati	1
10.	Saunt	1
11.	Jeera	1

KACHHI BIRYANI

S.No	Item	Qty (Parts/Wt.)
1.	Lahsoon	30
2.	Adarak	30
3.	Salt	50
4.	Chilli	15
5.	Haldi	30

SOUTH INDIAN CURRY

S.No	Item	Qty (Parts/Wt.)
1.	Besan	500
2.	Hing	250
3.	Chilli	1
4.	Jeera	6
5.	Rai	12
6.	Dhania	2

FISH MASALA

S.No	Item	Qty (Parts/Wt.)
1.	Jeera	50
2.	Long	3
3.	Ilaichi	3
4.	Jafran	1
5.	Chilli	6
6.	Black Pepper	6
7.	Lahsoon	50
8.	Dal chini	3
9.	Salt	20
10.	Dhania	20

FISH KABAB MASALA

S.No	Item	Qty (Parts/Wt.)
1.	Dalchini	2
2.	Salt	15
3.	Long	2
4.	Ilaichi	2
5.	Chilli	6
6.	Black Pepper	6

FISH PULAO MASALA

S.No	Item	Qty (Parts/Wt.)
1.	Sugar	250
2.	Badam	100
3.	Kishmish	90

POTATO MEAT PURI MASALA

S.No	Item	Qty (Parts/Wt.)
1.	Garam Masala	6
2.	Chilli	6

MASALA FOR RICE OF FISH

S.No	Item	Qty (Parts/Wt.)
1.	Salt	100
2.	Jeera	50

for 300 grms of fish & 100 grm of Rice.

PICKLE MASALA (MANGO)

(Quantity %)

1	Saunf	12
2.	Maithi	15
3.	Salt White	50
4.	Chilli	10
5.	Kalaunji	8
6.	Haldi	5
		100

THANDAI - POWDER

1.	Saunf	10
2.	Rose - Flower	10
3.	Kali Mirch (Black Pepper)	10
4.	Badam Giri (Almonds Kernel)	20
5.	Poppy - Seeds (Khas Khas)	20
6.	Melon - Giri (Magaz)	30
		100

CHAT MASALA

(Quantity %)

1.	Salt White	25
2.	Salt Black	8
3.	Amchur	15
4.	Jeera 6 Jeera (Roasted) 6	12
5.	Chilli (Yellow)	8
6.	Kali Mirch (Black Pepper)	8
7.	Pudina Leaf	3
8.	Anardana (Pomegranate Seeds)	5
9.	Hing (Asafoetida)	0. 100grn.
10.	Long Pepper (Bari-Pipal)	2
11.	Musk Melon	6

12.	Dhania (Coriander Seed)	5
13.	Bishop's Weed (Ajwain)	3
		100

FISH - MASALA

1.	Dhania	20
2.	Chilli (Kashmiri)	10
3.	Jeera (Cumin-Seed)	15
4.	Garlic (Lehsun)	30
5.	Black Pepper (Kali Mirch)	4
6.	Salt White	15
7.	Cinnamon (Dal Chini)	2
8.	Cardamom	2
9.	Clove (Laung)	2
10.	Zafran (Saffron)	q.s
		100

JAL - JEERA

1.	Salt White	25
2.	Salt Black	20
	Salt Rock (Sendha)	2
3.	Amchur	25
4.	Pudina Leaf	6
5.	Saunth (Dry-Ginger)	4
6.	Jeera Siah (Caraway) 6	12
	Jeera (Roasted) 6	
7.	Chilli Yellow	3
8.	Pippla (Long Pepper)	1
9.	Hing (Roasted) (Asafoetida)	0 - 150 gm.
10.	Citric Acid (Tatri)	2
11.	Laung (Clove)	0 - 150 gm.
		100

CURRY - POWDER

S.No	Item	Qty (Parts/Wt.)
1.	Cumin	25--25
2.	Ginger	10
3.	Cardamom-Seed	5
4.	Black Pepper	15
5.	Clove	2
6.	Nutmeg	2
7.	Pulse Arhan	8
8.	Salt	4
9.	Mustard	5
10.	Fenugreek	3
11.	Mace	0.25--0.25
12.	Poppy-Seed	1
13.	Garlic	2
14.	Asafoetida	0.10
15.	Coriander	5
16.	Turmeric	5
17.	Chilli	5
18.	Cassia	2

TANDOORI CHICKEN POWDER

S.No	Item	Qty (Parts/Wt.)
1.	Coriander	15
2.	Cumin	10
3.	Red Chilli	8
4.	Black Pepper	5

5.	Ginger	4
6.	Garlic	10
7.	Turmeric	6
8.	Cassia	4
9.	Nutmeg	1
10.	Cloves	5
11.	Mace	1
12.	Salt White	10
13.	Arhar/Chana Dal	10
14.	Poppy Seed	5--3
15.	Mustard	4
16.	Fenugreek	5

SAMBHAR POWDER

S.No	Item	Qty (Parts/Wt.)
1.	Coriander	30
2.	Chilli	20
3.	Arhar Dal	8
4.	Turmeric	6
5.	Fenugreek	6
6.	Salt White	5
7.	Cumin	2
8.	Black Pepper	6
9.	Poppy Seed	6
10.	Rai	4
11.	Mustard	5
12.	Asafoetida	0.05
13.	Cloves	0.25
14.	Nutmeg	0.25
15.	Mace	0.25
16.	Caraway	0.25

GARAM MASALA

S.No	Item	Qty (Parts/Wt.)
1.	Cumin	30
2.	Black Pepper	20
3.	Coriander	20
4.	Ginger (Dry)	15
5.	Clove	5
6.	Cassia	8
7.	Caraway	0.4
8.	Cinnamon	0.5
9.	Cardamom Seed (Big)	2
10.	Cardamom (Small)	0.20

MUTTON BIRYANI MASALA

S.No	Item	Qty (Parts/Wt.)
1.	Garlic	20
2.	Turmeric	20
3.	Chilli Red	10
4.	Ginger	15
5.	Salt White	20
6.	Coriander Seed	10
7.	Cumin Seed	5

PICKLE MASALA (MANGO)

S.No	Item	Qty (Parts/Wt.)
1.	Saunf	.15
2.	Maithi	.15
3.	Salt white	1
4.	Chilli	.2
5.	Kalaunji	.1

CURRY POWDER No.1

S.No	Item	Qty (Parts/Wt.)
1.	Dhaniya	5
2.	Haldi	5

3.	Ilaichi	40
4.	Black Pepper	10
5.	Maithi	40

No.2

1.	Dhaniya	18
2.	Black Pepper	1.5
3.	Haldi	1.5
4.	Adarak	1.5
5.	Jai Phal	0.5
6.	Long	0.5
7.	Saunt	0.5
8.	Shalati	0.5
9.	Ilaichi	0.5

FORMULAE FOR SPICES

KITCHEN KING: for every 1kg of spice. By Weight.

1. Coriander
2. Chillies
3. Turmeric
4. Cumin
5. Pulses
6. Black Pepper
7. Fenugreek
8. Cardamom Seeds
9. Dry Ginger
10. Poppy Seeds
11. Mustard
12. Cassia
13. White Slat
14. Nutmeg
15. Cloves
16. Mace
17. Cinnamon
18. White Pepper
19. Garlic Powder
20. Caraway &
21. Asafoetida.

All these individual items are mixed in the proportion in order to come up to the ISI specification.

RAITA MASALA

1. Salt White
2. Dry Mango
3. Salt Black
4. Cumin
5. Black Pepper
6. Chillies
7. Pomegranate
8. Coriander
9. Dry Ginger
10. Longer Pepper
11. Bishopsweed
12. Nutmeg
13. Cloves
14. Salt Amoniac Asafoetida

N.B: This Same combination is used for dahi curry masala too. This formula in the market is termed as *Chat Masala.*

JALJIRA

S.No	Item	Qty (Parts/Wt.)
1.	Salt White	1
2.	Salt Black	1
3.	Dry Mango	1
4.	Citric	1½
5.	Chillies	1

6.	Dry Ginger	1
7.	Salt Amoniac	
	Asafoetida	1½
8.	Long Pepper	1
9.	Caraway	1
10.	Cloves	½

Similarly other Masalas & Powders too have their specific combinations of raw material like additives.

FORMULATIONS OF CURRY POWDERS

MADRAS CURRY POWDER

No. 1

Item	Qty (Parts/Wt.)
Chillies	24.5
Coriander	32.0
Turmeric	15.0
Garlic	10.0
Cumin	1.0
Black Pepper	1.0
Cinnamon	1.0
Clovers	0.5
Dal	12.0
Salt	3.0

SAMBAR POWDER

Formula No.2	Parts/Wt.
Coriander	40
Chillies	40
Fenugreek	2
Urad Dal	4
Thoor Dal	4
Asafoetida	3
Curry Leaf	2
Turmeric	5

GARAM MASALA

Formula No.3	Parts/Wt.
Chillies	32
Coriander	35
Garlic	10
Black Pepper	5
Cumin	1
Cloves	1
Cardamom	1
Nutmeg	11
Star Aniseed	2
Khus Khus	1
Cinnamon	2
Fenugreek	6
Salt	3

SOME FORMULATIONS OF MASALA (SPICES)

CHAAT MASALA

S.No	Item	Qty (Parts/Wt.)
1.	Salt White	3
2.	Dry Mango	2
3.	Salt Black	1
4.	Cumin	2
5.	Black Pepper	1
6.	Chillies	1
7.	Pomegranate Seeds	1
8.	Musk melon	1
9.	Coriander	1
10.	Mini Leaves	1

11.	Long Pepper	1
12.	Bishop's Seeds	1/2
13.	Asafoetida	1/2

JAL JIRA

S.No	Item	Qty (Parts/Wt.)
1.	Salt White	1
2.	Salt Black	1
3.	Dry Mango	1
4.	Citric	1/2
5.	Chillies	1
6.	Dry Ginger	1
7.	Salt amoniac	1
8.	Long Pepper	1
9.	Asafoetida	1/2
10.	Caraway	1
11.	Clove	1/2

SAMBHAR

S.No	Item	Qty (Parts/Wt.)
1.	Coriander	1
2.	Pulse Arhar	7.5
3.	Cumin	1.1
4.	Turmeric	1/2
5.	Fenugreek Seeds	1
6.	Chillies	1
7.	Rai	1/ 2
8.	Black Pepper	1/2
9.	Poppy Seeds	1/2
10.	Mustard	1/2
11.	Cloves	1/4
12.	Nutmeg	1/ 4
13.	Mace	1/4
14.	Caraway	1/4
15.	Asafoetida	1/4
16.	Salt	1

MEAT MASALA

S.No	Item	Qty (Parts/Wt.)
1.	Coriander	.40
2.	Chillies	.84
3.	Turmeric	1.02
4.	Cumin	1.25
5.	Pulse	4.1
6.	Black Pepper	1.2
7.	Fenugreek	0.4
8.	Cardamom Seeds	0.6
9.	Dry Ginger	0.7
10.	Poppy Seeds	0.2
11.	Mustard	0.8
12.	Cassia	0.6
13.	Nutmeg	1.1
14.	Garlic Powder	1.7
15.	Asafoetida	.6
16.	Salt White	2

TANDOORI CHICKEN POWDER

S.No	Item	Qty (Parts/Wt.)
1.	Coriander	1.2
2.	Pulse	3.8
3.	Turmeric	1
4.	Chillies	1
5.	Cassia	0.4
6.	Cumin	1.0
7.	Poppy Seeds	0.8
8.	Fenugreek	0.7
9.	Black Pepper	1.2
10.	Garlic	0.6
11.	Mustard	0.5
12.	Dry Ginger	0.5
13.	Cloves	0.6

14.	Nutmeg	0.72
15.	Mace	0.2
16.	Salt White	2

PUNJABI CHOLA KA MASALA

S.No	Item	Qty (Parts/Wt.)
1.	Coriander	1.2
2.	Dry Mango	1
3.	Pomegranate Seeds	0.4
4.	Salt White	2
5.	Chillies	1
6	Cumin	0.8
7.	Fenugreek	0.6
8.	Cassia	0.4
9.	Black Pepper	0.8
10.	Dry Ginger	0.8
11.	Cardamom Seed	0.6
12.	Mini Leaves	1
13.	Mustard	0.8
14.	Nutmeg	0.6
15.	Mace	0.4
16.	Cloves	0.6
17.	Chinnamon	0.5
18.	Caraway	0.5

CURRY POWDER

S.No	Item	Qty (Parts/Wt.)
1.	Coriander	1.4
2.	Pulse	2.6
3.	Turmeric	1
4.	Chillies	1.2
5.	Cassia	0.6
6.	Cumin	1.0
7.	Poppy Seeds	0.6
8.	Fenugreek	0.6
9.	Cardamom	0.8
10.	Black Pepper	1
11.	Garlic	0.8
12.	Mustard	0.6
13.	Dry Ginger	0.6
14.	Cloves	0.8
15.	Nutmeg	0.8
16.	Mace	0.3
17.	Salt White	2.2
18.	Asafoetida	0.5
19.	Caraway	0.5

GARAM MASALA

S.No	Item	Qty (Parts/Wt.)
1.	Cariander	1
2.	Cumin	1
3.	Dry Ginger	1
4.	Laung	1
5.	Black Pepper	1
6.	Mini Leaves	1/2
7.	Caraway	0.4
8.	Ilaichi (Small)	0.25
9.	Ilaichi (Big)	0.5

THANDAI MASALA

S.No	Item	Qty (Parts/Wt.)
1.	Kharboji ke seeds	2
2.	Badam	2
3.	Khas	0.4
4.	Gulab Patti	0.4
5.	Black Pepper	0.4

PICKLE MASALA (MANGO)

S.No	Item	Qty (Parts/Wt.)
1.	Saunf	.15
2.	Maithi	.15
3.	Salt White	1
4.	Chilli	.2
5.	Kalaunji	.1

CURRY POWDER

No.1.

S.No	Item	Qty (Parts/Wt.)
1.	Dhaniya	5
2.	Haldi	5
3.	Ilaichi	40
4.	Black pepper	10
5.	Maithi	40

No.2.

S.No	Item	Qty (Parts/Wt.)
1.	Dhaniya	18
2.	Black Pepper	1.5
3.	Haldi	1.5
4.	Adarak	1.5
5.	Jai Phal	0.5
6.	Laung	0.5
7.	Saunth	0.5
8.	Shalati	0.5
9.	Ilaichi	0.5

No.3.

S.No	Item	Qty (Parts/Wt.)
1.	Dhania	70
2.	Salt	5
3.	Yellow Sarason	5
4.	Red Chilli	5
5.	Haldi	5
6.	Black Pepper	2
7.	Tej Pat	2
8.	Jai Phal	1
9.	Shalati	1
10.	Saunt	1
11.	Jeera	1

KACHHI BIRYANI

S.No	Item	Qty (Parts/Wt.)
1.	Lahsoon	30
2.	Adarak	30
3.	Salt	50
4.	Chilli	15
5.	Haldi	30

SOUTH INDIAN CURRY

S.No	Item	Qty (Parts/Wt.)
1.	Besan	500
2.	Hing	250
3.	Chilli	1
4.	Jeera	6
5.	Rai	12
6.	Dhania	2

FISH MASALA

S.No	Item	Qty (Parts/Wt.)
1.	Jeera	50
2.	Laung	3
3.	Ilaichi	3
4.	Jafran	1
5.	Chilli	6
6.	Black Pepper	6
7.	Lahsoon	50
8.	Dal Chini	3

9.	Salt	20
10	Dhania	20

S.No	Item	Qty (Parts/Wt.)
1.	Dalchini	2
2.	Salt	15
3.	Laung	2
4.	Ilaichi	2
5.	Chilli	6
6.	Black Pepper	6

FISH PULAO MASALA

S.No	Item	Qty (Parts/Wt.)
1.	Sugar	250
2.	Badam	100
3.	Kishmish	90

POTATO MEAT PURI MASALA

S.No	Item	Qty (Parts/Wt.)
1.	Garam Masala	6
2.	Chilli	6

MASALA FOR RICE OF FISH

S.No	Item	Qty (Parts/Wt.)
1.	Salt	100
2.	Jeera	50

for 300 grms of fish & 100 grm of Rice.

DISINTEGRATING AND POWDERING

This process is carried out in a disintegrator which is designed to break up the bates seeds to smaller pieces. The disintegrators are made with two or three hairs of horizontal rollers which are either plain or grounded according to the class of the seed to be treated.

In the above operation, the spice are ground. We must have a cooling arrangement for grinder. It is because of sufficient amount of heat is produced during grinding operation. The grinding is done to protect pulverizer

After crushing with the disintegrator, the mixture is brought to the micropulveriser which turns the composition into powder of very fine grade.

PRINCIPLES OF OPERATIONS

DRYING

All the spices are dried in sun in consideration with the cost factor. This operation should be carried out at a place from which dust & dirt is away.

GRINDING

The spices are ground. We must have a cooling arrangement for grinder. It is because sufficient amount of heat is produced during grinding operation. The grinding is done on Impact Pulverizer.

PRINCIPLES OF OPERATIONS

The standard pulverizer consists of an encased main rotor carrying swing hammers, fineness regulator and exhaust fan. Raw materials from the feed hopper enters the roll feeder and, as the feeder pockets rotates, spilis into the grinding chamber to be reduced by Impact with rotating hammers and sides of the chamber. The air steam flowing through the

Pulveriser carries the ground material towards the outlet, the oversize particles being rejected by the fineness regulators and returned for further grinding. Classified material is then conveyed through the fan and into the cyclone for separation from the air system. Clean air is returned to the inlet of the pulverizer for recirculation. The small quantity of air entering the feeder with the raw material is usually exhausted directly to a dust collector with an almost negligible quantity of dust.

The Impact Pulverizer has a cast iron beater chamber, fan chamber and regulator chamber fitted with adjustable whizzers for varying the fineness of the ground products, the whole being mounted on a cast iron bedplate.

Renewable pulverizing hammers are mounted on the main shaft of shock resisting steel which is supported in two dusttight housing fitted with heavy duty rolled bearing. The beater chamber is fitted with renewable liners.

The roll feader is super imposed on the pulverizer and is operated by means of a rocket and pawl mechanism driven through a reduction gear from the main beater shaft.

In the beater chamber, a pocket is arranged for the purpose of removing foreign material such as tramp iron which might be unintentionally introduced with the feed into the pulverizer.

MIXING

After the process of grinding of different spices is done, the different separate hardened spice are mixed together in the requisite quantities as per the formulation of the spice to form the required product in a slow speed mixer for the manufacture of different spices or masalas, the spices are then mixed with diffferent quantities as given in this book.

PACKING

Finally, the powdered spices are packed in polythene bags of requisite quantity and sealed in packs of 1 kg.

The packed and sealed spices in polythene bags are then further packed in a suitable size of cardboard boxes of suitable sizes. This cardboard box is further wrapped with polythene covering or thin HDPE film and secured from all stores by pasting, and then sent to the market.

Thus, the spices will remain unaffected by atmospheric moisture, heat and dust, etc. Such a fine sophisticated and attractive packing is all the more a desirability for export purposes. However, it is further recommended to keep in dry, cool and dust free place only.

38

PACKAGING OF SPICES

Major spices/masalas exported are pepper, cardamom, turmeric, ginger, chillies, cumin and coriander. Boosting of export is engaging the attention of the spice industry. One of the measures in this regard is the export of quality products in attractive and functional consumer packs. The advent of flexible consumer packs for retail distribution has heralded a concept of packaging catering to both functional and economic needs. Use of flexible packages will help in establishing image of Indian brands and yield higher return. In internal markets also use of flexible consumer packs for ground spices and spice products have gained wider consumer preference in view of assured unadulterated quality products. Further, they have logistic advantages such as low cost, tailor made functionality, light weight and saving in freight charges. As such they are becoming more popular. In view of the vast scope and great need, studies have been made at CFTRI, Mysore to develop appropriate functional consumer packages for ground spices.

PACKAGING OF GROUND SPICES

Ground spices in general are highly sensitive to vagaries of climate and are prone to various types of deteriorative changes such as loss of volatile oil, free flow properties (caking of the product), microbial spoilage and insect infestation during storage and transportation. Colour pigments in green pepper and red chillies get discoloured considerably when exposed to light and oxygen. Further, losses of essential oils result from considerable seepage and oozing out of volatile oils through packs. A functional package for ground spices should possess attributes like.

1) ability to protect the contents from spoilage and spillage.

2) should offer protection against physico-chemical and microbiological spoilage due to environmental conditions like humidity, temperature, light and oxygen. This means good barrier materials for packaging.

3) prevent loss of volatile oils and also prevent pickup of foreign odour.

4) good oil and fat resistance characteristics.

5) Prevent insect infestation and protect from insect damage.

6) assist in selling by suitable attractive outer graphics and also should conform to the food laws of the importing and exporting countries.

7) should be economical and easily available.

The selection and design of a suitable packaging media is dictated by factors like product characteristics, the type of environmental and distributional hazards encountered, the expected storage life and economic consideration.

With a view to arrive at appropriate functional packs for powdered spices, detailed packaging and storage studies in consumer unit packs of 100 g of size 11 x 14 cm. made out of different flexibles having varied functional properties have been carried out under different conditions of storage. Spice powders like pepper, turmeric, cumin, coriander and chilli powders were used. Considering their wider availability and moisture barrier properties, the following packaging materials with water vapour transmission rate (WVTR) indicated in brackets were used in the studies.

1. 250 gauge printed low density polyethylene (LDPE)(6.0)
2. 350 gauge LDPE (5.0)
3. 200 gauge high density polyethylene (HDPE) (3.0)
4. 200 gauge polyropylene (PP) (4.6)
5. 350 gauge PP (3.0)
6. 300 MXXT Cellophane (8.0)
7. Double pouch of glassine gusset pouch inside and 250 gauge printed LDPE outside (6.0)
8. Double pouch of 300 MSAT cellophane (15.7) inside and 250 gauge printed LDPE (6.0) outside.
9. Glassine/150 gauge poly laminate (9.6)
10. Saran coated cellophane /150 gauge poly laminate (7.0).
11. Metallised polyester 12micron/150 gauge poly laminate (0.8)
12. Paper/0.009 mm aluminium foil/150 gauge poly laminate (nil)

* Figures in brackets are values of WVTR in g/sq.cm/day under 90% RH gradient at 38^0 C.

Approximate shelf-life of the different spice powders under two conditions of storage namely i) 92% RH and 38°C (accelerated) and ii) 65% RH and 27°C (BIS standard condition) are presented in Tables 1&2. The shelf-life in days reported is based on ingress of moisture leading to predominantly unacceptable change of lumping or caking. Also presented in Table 1&2 is the percentage volatile oil loss in the packs at the end of shelf-life period or at a particular storage period.

The important findings of the study are as follows :

a) The polyethylene, (both low density and high density) and polypropylene film pouches of various thickness retard only the ingress of water vapour and are inadequate in offering protection against volatile oil loss as considerable amount of volatile oils in turmeric, pepper and cumin packs are lost (within 60 days) of storage under both conditions. Further, printing on the printed polyethylene pouches (especially in turmeric and pepper packs) gradually get disfigured and smudged to great extent due to solubility and diffusion of

TABLE 1

PROBABLE SHELF LIFE OF GROUND SPICES IN DIFFERENT FLEXIBLE POUCHES IN 100g . CONSUMER PACKS AT 92 % RH &38%C (ACCELERATED STORAGE CONDITION)

Sl. No.	Pouch packaging Material	Pepper S.L.*	Pepper %loss**	Turmeric S.L.*	Turmeric %loss**	Cumin S.L.*	Cumin %loss**	Coriander S.L.*	Chilli S.L.*
	Initial Moisture Content (% by wt.)	9.5		9.5		6.0		6.0	6.0
	Critical moisture content (%by wt.)w.r.t. caking & lumping	11-12		11-12		9-10		10-11	10-11
1.	200 g. (LDPE) low density polyethylene	30	80	25	35	70	75	80	-
2.	350g. LDPE	50	75	45	30	-	-	-	60
3.	200g. (HDPE) high density polyethlyene	60	75	-	-	-	-	-	70
4.	200g. Polypropylene (PP)	40	50	35	30	70	50	-	-
5.	350 g. PP	60	60	50	20	-	-		-
6.	300 MXXT Cellophane	25	10	30	5	-	-	70	-
7.	Double pouch of glassine gusset inside+ 250g. LDPE	35	50	45	20	-	-	80	-
8.	Double pouch of 300 MSAT cellophane inside+ 250g. LDPE	40	10	45	15	80	10	80	-
9.	Glassine / 150g. Polyamide	-	-	20	5	-	-	-	-
10.	Saran coated cello/ploy laminate	-	-	40	5	-	-	-	50
11.	Metallised polyester 12 micron 150g. LDPE laminate	120	20	120	10	120-150	30	150-180	150-180
12.	Paper/0.009mm Al/foil/150g. poly	expected 1 yr.	21% 180 days	expected 1 yr.	5% 180 days	expected 1 yr.	-	expected 1 yr.	expected 1 yr.

* Shelf-life respect to caking and lumping.

** % loss of volatile oil at the end of shelf-life.

TABLE 2
PROBABLE SHELF LIFE OF GROUND SPICES IN DIFFERENT FLEXIBLE POUCHES IN 100g. CONSUMER PACKS AT 65% RH & 27°C (INDIAN STANDARD CONDITION)

Sl. No.	Pouch packaging Material	Pepper		Turmeric		Cumin		Coriander	Chilli	Remarks on Packging materials
		S.L.*	%loss** of V.O. at 120 days	S.L.*	% loss** of V.O. at 180 days	S.L.	% loss** of V.O. at 120 days	S.L*	S.L.*	
	Maximum moisture content content (% by wt. of the product in an atmoshphere of 65% RH & 27°C	10.0		11.0		9.0		10.0	11.0	
1.	200 g guage IDPE	60	80	30	50	60	75	80	90	1,2,3,4 & 5 are good moisture
2.	350g. LDPE	60	75	30	50	60	-	60	90	barriers but poor volatile barriers
3.	200g guage HDPE	90	75	60	-	90	-	90	120	
4.	200g. Polypropylene (PP)	90	65	60-90	40	90	45	120	150	
5.	350 g. PP	120	60	60-90	20	120	-	150	200	
6.	300 MXXT Cellophane	200	10	200	10	200	-	200	200	6, fairly moisture proof, good v.o. barrier
7.	Double pouch of glassine gusset inside + 250g. LDPE	120	50	120	15	120	-	150	150	7, moisture proof, fair barrier to v.o.
8.	Double pouch of 300 MSAT cellophane inside + 250g. LDPE	200	10	200	10	200	20	200	200	8, good barrier to both moisture & v.o.
9.	Glassine / 150g. Poly	120	-	120	15	120	-	120	150	9, 10 fairly moisture proof, good barrier
10.	Saran coated cello/ploy	200	-	200	10	200	-	200	200	to v.o.
11.	Metallised polyester 12 micron/150g. LDPE	1 yr.	10-20	1 yr.	20-30	1 yr.	10	1 yr.	1 yr.	11, good moisture & v.o. barriers
12.	Paper/0.009mm Alfoil/150g. Poly.	1 yr.	5	1 yr.	10	1 yr.	-	1 yr.	1 yr.	12, very good moisture & v.o. barrier.

* Shelf life w.r.t. overall quality refers to probable quality changes due to consaderable loss in volatile oil, colour & flavour leading to overall loss in freshness of ground spices.

** As the product attains maximum moisture content which is slightly below the critical level of moisture, the shelf life with respect to lumping or caking is not a problem at and below 65% R.H. & 27 °C.

organic volatile oils through these polymeric packaging materials. However, these hydrophobic films offer good moisture protection during storage and are suited for short-term storage. 200 gauge polypropylene and 200 gauge HDPE are better suited than LDPE and these two offer about 90 days of storage life at Indian Standard condition of, storage at the sacrifice of 20-50% volatile oil loss in turmeric and pepper powder and 120-150 days for cumin, coriander and chill powder.

b) The pouches made of cellophane or polyester have less permeability for organic volatile oils and offer better protection against loss of volatile oils. However, these materials with high affinity to water vapour, are inadequate in offering protection against moisture ingress especially under high humid conditions. A double pouch of cellophane inside and 250 gauge printed LDPE pouch outside is found to offer desired protection against loss of volatiles and ingress of moisture. The disfiguring and smudging of printing on the outer printed LDPE pouch is also considerably minimised. A shelf-life (based on overall quality) of about 200 days under Indian Standard condition can be obtained for all spice powders in this pouch.

c) Pouches made from laminates of cellophane/poly, glassine/poly and 300 MXXT cellophane retain volatile oil and provide adequate moisture protection for about 200 days under Indian Standard condition of storage (65% RH and 27^{0}C). However, they are inadequate in providing protection against ingress of moisture particularly at high temperature and humid conditions.

d) Metallised polyester/poly and paper/foil/poly laminate pouches, which are very good barriers to moisture and volatile oils can offer adequate protection for about one year for different ground spices under Indian Standard condition. The

.oss of volatile oils and moisture ingress in these pouches are not considerable even after long term storage under both the conditions of storage. However, in case of metallised polyester/poly laminate pouches containing turmeric and pepper powder which are rich in volatile oils, slight delamination of the laminate was observed during long term storage and the shelf-life was 120 days at 92% RH and 38° C as there was higher moisture pickup due to delamination. In such cases, a hree ply laminate such as PET/Met PET/Poly is better suited.

e) At 65% RH and 27°C, as all the spice powders attain naximum moisture content which is slightly lower than the critical moisture content, they do not pose caking or lumping problems. However, as pointed out earlier, polyolefins, the volatile oil loss was considerable and as such their use is imited. Laminate pouches of cello/poly, metallised polyester/poly and paper/foil/poly are well suited for long term storage of 200 days, one year and over one year respectively under ndian Standard storage condition of 65% RH and 27°C. For hort term storage of about 90 days, 200 gauge polypropylene or high density polyethylene pouches can be preferred in view of their low cost. It may be also emphasised that as low moisture content as possible in the product at the time of acking will minimise the problem of caking and lumping luring long term storage especially in high humid conditions.

BULK PACKAGING AND STORAGE OF WHOLE SPICES

The traditional method of storage of whole spices is in ıte bags. A twill, B twill or and DW gunny bags are used epending upon the value of the spices. The weave clearance f A twill, B twill and DW gunny bags are 1-2%, 3-5% and -6% respectively which prevents spillage and also restricts ısect movement into bags. Sometimes double bags are used get better physical barrier. Polyethylene lined gunny bags nd HDPE woven sacks are being used to restrict moisture ingress during storage. For cardamom capsules, polyethylene lined plywood boxes are being used. Multiwall paper bags or cotton bags are also sometimes used.

In whole spices, the flavour is protected by outer natural coating and losses during storage are negligible. However, in ground spices due to opening of cells during grinding, the flavours are released and the losses in flavours are considerable during storage. Thus in whole spices the packaging problems are reduced to prevention of moisture ingress and insect attack. But in ground bulk spices the loss of volatile oils is a major problem. For ground spices, multiwall paper bags, textile bags, metal containers and HDPE woven sacks are commonly employed.

In whole pepper packed in-double burlap bags with polyethylene liners of 75 micron, moisture increase was hardly 0.4% even in monsoon conditions. In the case of dry whole chillies, due to low bulk density, package becomes voluminous and suitable method has been developed to compress the chillies to reduce bulk density. Moisture content of 10% and pressure of 2.5 kg/sq.cm was found optimum and it reduced the volume by 78% of its original value. Compressed packages of 10 and 25 kgs are packed in 300 gauge polyethylene.

39

METHOD OF TEST FOR SPICES & CONDIMENTS

SCOPE

This standard precribes physical and chemical methods of test for spices and condiments.

EXTRANEOUS MATTER

Thoroughly mix the sample, take in accordance with Indian Standard Methods of samplings of spices and condiments (under preparation) and weight 100 to 2000 g of it depending on the nature of the material; separate the extraneous matter from the material and transfer it to a dry tared watch-glass. Weight the watch-glass with the extraneous matter in an analytical balance. The difference between the two weighings gives the extraneous matter in the test portion. Calculates from this the percentage by mass of extraneous matter

GRINDING OF SAMPLE FOR CHEMICAL ANALYSIS

This method is applicable to the majority of spices and condiments. However, in view of their large number and their diversity, it may be necessary in certain special cases (such as considerable hardness, high content of water and essential oil of fat to carry out some modifications or even to choose a more suitable method. These modifications or other methods would be indicated in the corresponding Indian Standard specifications.

PRINCIPLE

Spices should be ground so as to pass through 1-mm IS Sieve [see IS : 460 (part I) - 2985*]

TOTAL ASH

Apparatus

Dish : Flat-bottomed, having a surface area of at least 15 cm^2, made of platinum or of other material unaffected by the conditions of the test.

Muffle Furnace - regulated at 550 ± 25°C

Determination

Pour about 2 ml of ethanol on the material in the tared dish and ignite it. When the ethanol is burnt off, heat the dish carefully over a small flame to char the material. Then ignite in the muffle furnace at 550°C ± 25°C for 2 hours. Cool and wet the ash with several drops of water, evaporate carefully to dryness and heat in the muffle furnace for further 1 hour at 550 ± 25°C. If the wetting shows the ash to be carbon-free, remove the dish to a desiccator containing fresh and efficient desiccant; allow to cool to room temperature and weight without delay. If the wetting shows the presence of carbon, repeat the wetting and heating and heating until no specks of carbon are visible and ignite in the muffle furnace for 1 hour after the disappearance of carbon. If carbon is still visible, leach the ash with hot water, filter through has ashless filter paper, wash the filter paper thoroughly, transfer the filter paper and contents to the ashing dish, dry and ignite in the muffle furnace at 550 ± 25°C until the ash is white. Cool the dish, add the filterate and evaporate it to dryness on a water-bath. Heat in the muffle furnace again at 550 ± 25°C, cool in the desiccator and weight as previously. Heat again in the muffle furnace at 550 ± 25°C 1 hour, cool and weigh. Repeat these operations until the difference in mass between tow successive weighings is less than 0.001 g. Record the lowest mass. Reserve the total ash for determining the water-soluble ash and the acid-insoluble ash

WATER-INSOLUBLE ASH

To the reserved ash in the dish, add distilled water, heat nearly to boiling, and filter through an ashless filter paper. Wash the filter paper with hot water until the combined filterate and washings measure about 60 ml. Return the filter paper and the contents to the dish, evaporate the water carefully on a water -bath and igniting at 550±25°C for 1 hour. Cool in the desiccator and weigh. Ignite again, cool and weigh. Repeat the process of igniting, cooling and weighting till the difference in mass between two successive weighings is less than 0.001g. Note the lowest mass.

ACID INSOLUBLE ASH

Hydrochloric Acid Solution - Concentrated hydrochloric acid (r.d.1.19 at 20°C) diluted in water 2:5 (v/v)

Silver Nitrate Solution - 10 Percent (m/v)

PROCEDURE

Test Portion - Use the total ash obtained in 6.2.3.

Determination - Add to the test portion 15 to 25 ml of the hydrochloric acid and boil for 10 minutes, covering the dish with a watch-glass through the ashless filter paper (medium-fine). Wash the filter paper with hot water until the washings are free from hydrochloric acid, at tested by silver nitrate solution and return it to the dish. Evaporate carefully on the water-bath and ignite in the muffle furnace at 550 ± 25°C for 1 hour. Cool the dish in the desiccator and weight. Repeat the operations of igniting for 1 hour, cooling and weighting till the different in mass between two successive weighings is less than 0.001 g. Note the lowest mass.

MOISTURE CONTENT

Principle-The amount of water is determined by first disti the material with an organic liquid not miscible with water and then collecting the distillate in a graduated tube.

TERMINOLOGY FOR SPICES AND CONDIMENTS

SCOPE

This standard prescribes list of botanical names of the plants classified under spices and condiments. This standard also gives the part of the plant used ad the common English and Hindi names of spices and condiments and grown in the country.

TERMINOLOGY

The list of spices and condiments together with the botanical names, their common English and Hindi names, of the part used as the spice or condiment is given in Table 1.

TABLE 1 LIST OF SPICES AND CONDIMENTS

Sl. No.	BOTANICAL NAME	PART USED	ENGLISH COMMON NAME
1.	Acrous calamus Linnacus	Rhizome	Sweet-flag
2.	Allium cepa Linnaeus	Bulb	Onion
3.	Allium sativum Linnacus	Bulb	Garlic
4.	Alpinia galanga (Linnaeus) Wildenow	Rhizome	Garlanga
5.	Amomum subulatum Roxburg	Fruit and seed	Greater indian cardamom Nepal

			cardamoms Cardamom ammomum
6.	Anethum graveolens Linnaeus	Fruit	Dill seed
7.	Apium graveolens Linnaeus	Fruit	Celery seed
8.	Brassica juncea (Linnaeus) Czernajev & Cosson	Seed	Indian mustard
9.	Brassica nigra (Linnaeus) W.D.H.Koch	Seed	Black mustard
10.	Capparis spinosa Linnaeus	Unopened flower bud	Caper
11.	Capsicum frutescens Linnaeus/Capsicum annum Linnaeus	Fruit	Chillies or Capsicum
12.	Carum carvi Linnaeus	Fruit	Caraway seed
13.	Cinnamomum aromaticum	Bark	Cassia China or Cassia
14.	Cinnamomum burmanii C.G.Nees ex Blume	Bark	Batavia cassia or Java cassia or Cassia Vera or Padang cinnamon Cassia, Indian
15.	Cinnamomum tamala (Buch Ham) Nees & Ebermaier	Leaf	Cassia, India
16.	Cinnamomum Zeylanicum Blume	Bark	Cinnamon
17.	Coriandrum Sativum Linnaeus	Leaf and seed	Coriander
18.	Crocus Sativus Linnaeus	Stigma	Saffron
19.	Cuminum cyminum Linnaeus	Fruit	Cumin seed
20.	Curcuma longa Linnaeus	Rhizome	Turmeric
21.	Elettaria Cardamomum (Linnaeus)Maton	Fruit and seed	Cardamom
22.	Eugenia caryopyllus	Unopened	Cloves

	(C.Sprengel) Bullock et Harrison [Synonym Syzygium aromaticum (L) Merril et Perry]	flower bud	
23.	Ferula alliacea Boiss [Synonym Ferula rubricaulis Boiss]	Olegum resin from rhizome and thickened root	Asafoetida (HING)
24.	Ferula foetida Regal	Oleogum resin from thickened root	Hingra
25.	Foeniculum vulgare P.Miller	Fruit	Fennel
26.	Garcinia inica Choisy	Peel of	Kokum fruit(cured)
27.	Hyssopus Officinalis Linnaeus	Leaves	Hyssop
28.	Juniperus communis Linnaeus	Berry	Juniper
29.	Levistcum officinatlis W.D.J.Koch	Fruit and root	Lovage
30.	Mangifera Indica Linnaeus	Unripe fruit	Mango silces or powder Mint
32.	Murraya koenigii (Linnaeus) C.Sprengel	Leaf	Curry leaves
33.	Myristica fragrans Hottuyn	Arillus	Mace
34.	Myristica fragrans Hottuyn	Kernel	Nutmeg
35.	Bigella sativa Linnaeus	Fruit	Cumin,black
36.	Ocimum basilicum Linnaeus	Leaf	Sweet basil
37.	Papaver somniferum Linnaeus	Seed	Poppy seed
38.	Petroselium erispum (P.Miller) Nyman ex A.W.Hill	Leaf and Seed	Parsely
39.	Pimpinella anisum Linnaeus	Fruit	Aniseed

40.	Piper longum Linnaeus	Seed and Leaves	Long pepper (Pipli or Pipal)
41.	Piper nigrum Linnaeus	Berry	Black pepper, White pepper
42.	Piper granatum Linnaeus	Seed(drined with flesh)	Pomegranate
43.	Satureia hotensis Linnaeus	Leaf and flowering top	Savory
44.	Sinapis alba (Linnaeus) Boisser	Seed	White mustard Yellow mustard
45.	Tamarindus indica Linnaeus	Fruit	Tamarind
46.	Thymus serphyllum Linnaeus	Leaf and flowering top	Wild thyme
47.	Thymus vulgaris Linnaeus	Leaf and flowering top	Thyme
48.	Trachyspermum ammi(Linnaeus) Sprague ex Turrill	Fruit	Bishops weed or Ajowan
49.	Trigonella foenumgraecum Linnaeus	Seed	Fenugreek
50.	Vanilla fragrans (Salisbury) Ames [Synonym vanilla Planifolia Andrews]	Pod (fruit)	Vanilla
51.	Vanilla pompona Schneiden	Pod (fruit)	Vanilla
52.	Vanilla tahitensis Moore	Pod(cured fruit)	Vanilla
53.	Zingiber officinate Roscoe	Rhizome	Dried Ginger

40

AGMARK

SYMBOL OF QUALITY & PURITY

What is Agmark ?

Agmark is a symbol of quality & purity which is affixed on agricultural & allied products like rice, wheat atta, maida, suzi, pulses, spices, ghee, butter, edible oils, honey, asafoetida, tamarind, fruits, eggs, etc. This symbol by way of a label or a replica is affixed only after testing the quality & purity of the product.

Why Agmark ?

Due to the increase in prices of food items of daily consumption, there is a tendency to sell adulterated and sub-standard items which are slightly less costly. These items may cost less in terms of money, but they cost the consumer much more in items of health because the adulterated food items can cause fatal diseases. As Agmark symbol is affixed only after testing the purity and quality of each item, the products bearing Agmark label or replica are without any doubt, pure and unadulterated.

How Agmark Certification is done ?

Persons, firms or organizations having certificate of Authorisation (Licence) issued by the Agricultural Marketing Adviser to the Government of India alone are authorised to affix the Agmark label or replica on the products. For this, the authorised packer who holds the Certificate of Authorisation should have access to laboratory testing facilities premises for processing and packing the product, trained technical personnel for testing etc.

Affixing the Agmark label involves four stages :-

1. The commodity or the product reaching the authorised grading or certification premises is subjected to preliminary testing.

2. From the product, inspecting officers take representative samples.

3. Technically qualified and experienced officers test the samples and assign Agmark quality grades.

4. Afterwards, the commodity is packed using Agmark label or Agmark replica on pouches/containers.

During all stages of these operations, there is direct supervision of the inspecting officers. Even after sending to the markets, Agmark products are subjected to continous checks. Samples are collected from various outlets in the market and tested in the various Regional Agmark Laboratories of the Government of India. In case the products are found to be substandard, are authorised packer is directed to withdraw the entire batch from the market and afterwards his/their activities of grading the commodity under the Agmark are subjected to observation. Still, if it is found that the quality standard of the Authoried Packer is going down, his C.A. (Licence) is suspended or cancelled.

While buying Agmark products please ensure that :-

1. Agmark label printed on water mark paper bears the words "this label is the property of Government of India".

2. Agmark words are printed in a map of India on the centre

of the label vertically and horizontally. Commodity and grade are written in English and Hindi.

3. The Agmark seal is not mutilated or spoiled and is legible.

4. The packet has not been tampered with.

5. The container is new.

6. Lable number or replica number, lot number, date of packing and address of the authorised packer are mentioned on the package.

CONSUMER SATISFACTION

Buy Agmark products automatically ensures quality and purity, still, if a consumer is not satisfied, he can get the product replaced free of cost or money refunded as per rules. Still if he has any complaint against the quality of Agmark products, he may file a written complaint giving particulars of the package, i.e. commodity grade, Agmark label number, date of packing, name and full address of the authorised packer and the full address of the shop from where the purchase has been made enclosing the original cash memo to any one of the following address :-

1. Agricultural Marketing adviser to the Government of India
Directorate of Marketing & Inspection
Ministry of Rural Area & Employment

C.G.O. Complex, N.H. IV
Faridabad-120001 (Haryana)
Tel. : 216568, 215710, 212519

2. Dy. Agricultural Marketing Adviser

Directorate of Marketing & Inspection

Northern Region
4/20, Asaf Ali Road
New Delhi - 110 002
Ph:. 3264635, 3277295

41

PRESENT MANUFACTURERS/ SUPPLIERS OF PLANT & EQUIPMENTS FOR SPICES

PULVERISER/GRINDER

M/s. Advance Quality Controls
Ph:. 0129-5263017, 5291556
E Mail : aqc1@rediffmail.com

M/s. Ambika Vijay Works
1H, Laxmi East Link Road
West, Mumbai - 53
Ph:. 6366894

M/s. Babbar Engineering
688/335, Munshi Ram Bagh
Near Ranjit Nagar
New Delhi - 110 008
Ph:. 5705367, 5705363
Also at: 8007/11
Multani Dhanda,
Paharganj
New Delhi - 110 055
Ph:. 3522232, 3677804
Fax: 3512178

M/s. Chandra Orgo-Chem Combines
306, Belscot Tower, Link Road
Lokhand Wala Complex
Andheri, Mumbai - 53
Ph:. 3430789

M/s. Dhiman Udyog
6026, Kapurthala Road
Nakodar - 144040
(Dist.: Jalandhar) Punjab
Ph: 01821-20891, 22891, 22991
Fax: 0091-1821-20891
Website:www.dhimanudyog.com

M/s. Dolphin Engineering Works
6, Baburam Ghosh Lane
P.O. Hatkhola
Kolkatta - 5 (West Bengal)
Ph:. 2399378

M/s. D.P. Pulveriser Works
76, Nagindas Master Road
Fort, Mumbai - 23
Ph:. 2675724, 2670976
Fax: 022-2676435

M/s. Flour Tech Engineers (P) Ltd.
16/5, Mathura Road
Faridabad - 121002
(Haryana)
Ph:.0129-5291556, 5263017
E-Mail :
flourtech@rediffmail.com

M/s. Frigmaires Engineers
Post Box:16353
Janta Industrial Estate No.8L
Parel, Mumbai - 13
Ph:. 4941694

M/s. Hind Pulverizer Works
B-3/2, Ambica East
Near Sukhram Nagar
Ahemdabad - 23 (Guj.)
Ph:. 2747451, 2744018
Fax : 079-2747451

M/s. JDP Enterprises
13, Kharwa Lane,
Samad Building
Mumbai - 400004
Ph:. 3810054

M/s. Jikosha Engineering Corp.
2, Ratna Jyoti Ind. Estate,
Vile Parle West, Mumbai - 56
Ph:. 6711312

M/s. K.B. Engineering
B-58, Kiran Industrial Estate
M.G Road,
Goregaon (West)
Mumbai - 62
Ph:. 8720616

M/s. Kaps Engineers
831, GIDC, Makarpura
Baroda - 10 (Gujarat)
Ph:. 5781933, 011-5756760
Website : www.vmkaps.com
E-Mail :
kapsvm@ad1.vsnl.net.in

M/s. Kabir Engineers Works
Niramay,
B/H Suvidha Centre
Paldi,
Ahemdabad - 7
Gujarat
Ph:. 6620270
Fax: 6576497

M/s. Kaps Engineers
Samrat Silk Mills Compound
L.B.S. Marg,
Vikhroli (West),
Mumbai - 400079 (M.S)
Ph:. 91-22-5781933
Fax: 5785741
E-Mail :
vmsrehls@bom4.vsnl.net.in

M/s. Litho Tech Engineers
Sector-10/B25/Sh-13
Shanti Nagar
Mira Road - East
Mumbai - 7
Ph:. 8110182

M/s. Micro Pulverizer Manufacturing Work
Universal Compound,
Old Nagar Das Road,
Andheri (East),
Mumbai - 69
Ph:. 8209725

M/s. Modern Fabricators
25/4, Industrial Area
Anand Parbat,
New Delhi - 110005
Ph:. 5722888

M/s. Precious Fab-Cast Pvt. Ltd.
4809, Ph-4, GIDC, Vatva
Ahmedabad - 445
Gujarat
Ph:. 5832237
Fax : 5830026

M/s. Premier Engineering Works
7/23, Gali No. 7
Anand Parbat
Industrial Area
New Delhi - 110005
Ph:.5730730

M/s. Ruby Engineering Work
Memnee Building
1750, Imtimkar Road,
Nagpada, Mumbai - 8
Ph:. 3088552

M/s. Sreema Engineering Works Pvt. Ltd.
148/1A, Ultadanga
Main Road
Kolkata - 67
Ph:. 3561639

M/s. S.S. Industries
Netaji Palkar Road
Asalpe Ghatkopar
West, Mumbai - 84
Ph:.5110336

M/s. Saxena Indusrtries
W-300, TTC, MIDC Rabale
New Bombay - 400701
Ph:.7692445

M/s. Techmac Engineering Works
310, Usha Kiran Building,
Commercial Complex
Azadpur, Delhi - 110 033
Ph:. 7137027

M/s. Trover Pharmamach
6214, Kapurthala Road
Opp. Suraj Palace
Nakodar - 144040
(Distt. Jalandhar)
Ph:. 1821-20318

Fax : 91-1821-23599
E-Mail :
sanjeev@troverindia.com

M/s. Vimal Enterprises
40, Than Ranchhod
Chawl Rabari Colony
Amwadi, Ahemdabad - 26
Ph:. 2168420

M/s. Vohra & Co.
523, Rishi Nagar
Rani Bagh
New Delhi - 34
Ph:. 7104651

MIXER

M/s. A-One Packaging Machine
D-312, Sector-10
Noida
Distt. Ghaziabad (U.P.)
Ph:. 914 - 443437
Fax:. 01180-4526188

M/s. Ambika Vijay Works
1H, Laxmi East Link Road
West, Mumbai - 53
Ph:. 6366894

M/s. Babbar Engineering
688/335, Munshi Ram Bagh
Near Ranjit Nagar
New Delhi - 110 008
Ph:. 5705367, 5705363

Also at: 8007/11,
Multani Dhanda,
Paharganj
New Delhi - 110 055
Ph:.3522232, 3677804
Fax: 3512178

M/s. B.R. Pouch Packing Pvt. Ltd.
C-22/15, Sector-57
Noida - 201301(U.P.)
Ph:. 914582871
Fax:. 011-84584930
E-Mail :
info@bropouchkngmchs.com
Website :
www.brpouchpkngmchs.com

M/s. Citra Engineers
23, Narmada Estate,
Odhav, Ahemdabad - 415
Ph: 2876516
Fax: 079-2891666

M/s. Dolphin Engg. Works
6, Baburam Ghosh Lane
P.O. Hatkhola
Kolkata - 5
Ph:. 2399378

M/s. Mix Well Industries
Plot No. 2, Lane-6
Gopal Pur Village
Delhi - 110009
Ph:. 7653086

M/s. M-Tech Engineers
Plot No. 33, Gali No.1
Sewa Sadan Block, Fazalpur
Mandawali, Delhi - 110 092
Ph:. 2232356

M/s. Pharmatech Engineering Works
L-96, Shiv Vatika
N. Mandir Road
Shastri Nagar
New Delhi - 110 052
Ph:. 3640095

M/s. Premier Engineering Works
B-136, Okhla Industrial Area
Phase-1,
New Delhi - 110 020
Ph: 6818210

M/s. Precious Fab-Cast Pvt. Ltd.
4809, Phase-4, GIDC,
Vatva, Ahmedabad - 445
Gujarat
Ph:. 5832237
Fax : 5830026

M/s. Sreema Engineering Works Pvt. Ltd.
148/1A, Ultadanga
Main Road
Kolkatta - 67
Ph:. 3561639

M/s. S.K.L Mineral Processing Equipment
B-205, O.P Commerce
Centre Jesal
Park Bhayander (East)
Distt. Thane - 105 (M.S)
Ph:. 8160889
Fax: 8160889

M/s. Vimal Enterprises
40, Than Ranchhod
Chawl Rabari Colony,
Amwadi,
Ahemdabad - 26
Gujarat
Ph:. 2168420

DISINTEGRATER

M/s. Dolphin Engineering Works
6, Baburam Ghosh Lane
P.O. Hatkhola
Kolkata - 5
Ph:. 2399378

PACKAGING MACHINES (MANUAL/SEMI-AUTOMATIC/ AUTOMATIC)

M/s. Authentic Designer's
C-112, Sector-10
Noida - 201301 (U.P)
Ph:. 91-4540451, 4550649

Fax:0118-91-4540451
E-Mail :
authdesi@nda.vsnl.net.in
Website :
www.authenticdesigners.com

M/s. A.D. Industries
29, Dhan Laxmi
Industrial Estate,
Shahibaug,
Ahmedabad -380004
Gujarat
Ph:. 079-5624978

M/s. A-One Packaging Machine
D-312, Sector-10
Noida,
Distt. Ghaziabad (U.P.)
Ph:. 914443437
Fax:. 01180-4526188

M/s. Aarem Engineering
M-4, Kasturi Industrial Estate
Panchal Road
Bhayander East,
Mumbai - 401105
Thane
Ph:.022-8188560
Fax: 8183927

M/s. Advance Packaging
17, Jaimataji Society
Asalpha,
Mumbai - 84
Ph:. 5101665

M/s. Aprotech Engineers Pvt. Ltd.
1573, Sector-7
Faridabad - 121006
Haryana
Ph:. 0129-5242140

M/s. B.R. Pouch Packing Pvt. Ltd.
C-22/15, Sector-57
Noida - 201301
Distt. Ghaziabad (U.P.)
Ph:. 914582871
Fax:. 011-84584930
E-Mail :
info@bropouchkngmchs.com
Website :
www.brpouchpkngmchs.com

M/s. Baba Packaging
14, Krishna Palace,
Neelam Flyover,
Faridabad - 07 (Haryana)
Ph:0191-129-5291107,
5239168, 5235284
E-Mail:baba@ndb.vsnl.net.in
Website:www.babapackaging.com

M/s. Excelsior Engineers
131, Parvesh Marg
Railway Road
Faridabad - 121002
Haryana
Ph:. 011-91-5265199
E-Mail :
excel_pack@satyam.net.in

M/s. Eclat Auto Packs Pvt. Ltd.
301, Misha Gardens
Tarbund - 9
Ph:. 7818896
E-Mail:eclatap@satyam.net.in

M/s. E.C. Packaging Pvt. Ltd.
14/7, Mile Stone
Mathura Road
Faridabad - 121003
Ph:. (0129)-5277-796, 5277-698, 5277-407
Fax:(0129)-5255-602

M/s. Ganga Packaging
279-C, Sector-59
HSIDC, Faridabad - 4
Haryana
Ph:. 5232670, 0129-5441224
E-Mail : gangapac@mantraonline.com

M/s. M-Tech Engineers
Plot No. 33, Gali No.1
Sewa Sadan Block,
Fazalpur,
Mandawali, Delhi - 110 092
Ph:. 2232356

M/s. Modern Packaging System
2, Garstin Place,
2nd Floor,
Kolkata - 700001
Ph:.248-9369,3894
Fax:033-248-3894

M/s. N.S. Packaging Pvt. Ltd.
C-69, Sector-2
Noida
Distt. Ghaziabad (U.P.)
Ph:. 914535119
Fax:91-4514973
E-Mail : nsindia@mantraonline.com

M/s. Packmech Engineers
23/4, Kailash Industrial Estate
B/h CMC Odhav
Ahemdabad - 382415
Ph:. 079-2876893

M/s. Polygraph Printing Technologies Ltd.
88, Mistry Industrial Complex
MIDC Cross Road-A
Andheri East
Mumbai - 400093
Ph:. 022-8223963

M/s. Qasco Engineers
Badkhal Village, N.I.T
Faridabad - 121001
Ph:. 0129-5419252, 5414963
Fax: 5414963

M/s. R.D. Singal & Co.
A-81/2, Wazirpur Indl. Area,
Delhi - 110052
Ph:. 7242692, 7241958, 7125654
Fax:91-11-7187224

M/s. Rado Packaging Machine (P) Ltd.
A-41, Sector-10
Noida - 201301 (U.P)
Ph:. 011-91-4555190
E-Mail:rado41@hotmail.com

M/s. Star Packaging
D-87, Sector-10
Noida - 201301
Ph:.0118-4521120

M/s. Shivam Sealers
66, Ezra Street, 1st Floor
Kolkata - 700001
Ph:. 2254367

M/s. Saurabh Engineers
132, Ft. Ring Road
Ahmedabad-380051
Ph:. 6425115, 6448292
Fax:91-79-6425115, 2740288
E-Mail : indvac@ad1.vsnl.net.in

M/s. Shree Chamunda Micro Industries
9, Ravi Estate
Ahmedabad - 23
Ph:. 2741094

M/s. Shreeji Engineers & Fabricators
Plot No. 1112
Phase-3, GIDC Vatva
Ahmedabad - 445
Ph:. 5890029
Fax:. 079-5890029

M/s. SPR Marketing Pvt. Ltd.
C-2/8, Mayapuri
Industrial Area, Phase-2,
New Delhi - 64
Ph:.5400105, 5404131
Fax:5404799
E-Mail:ssind@vsnl.com

M/s. Tool Tech
Plot No. 21,
CIE Gandhi Nagar
Bala Nagar
Hyderabad - 500037
Ph:. 040-3091849

M/s. Unique Associates
5C/18, B.P, NIT
Faridabad - 121 001
Ph:. 915411450
Fax : 5413458
E-Mail :
info@uniwueassociates.com

42

PLANT & MACHINERY USED

Pulveriser/Grinder

The machinery required to produce spices/masala (ground) is Pulveriser/grinding plant. The machinery used is Impack Pulverizer machine which is used for grinding spices. It is a versities grinding unit of heavy and rugged construction; and built for continuous operation day after day. The unit is designed especially for the medium fine and fine grinding.

Size:- 32" Impact Pulverizer

Power capacity : 50 H.P. motor used.

Outstanding Features

(i) Combines ruggedness, dependability high efficiency and automatic operation.

(ii) Dust free, completely integrated system for grinding and classifying.

(iii) Assures low cost production with consistent uniform product.

(iv) Operates at peak effiency and highest tonnage per H.P.

(v) Flexible control over product fineness

(vi) Requires minimum attention other than ordinary maintenance.

Standard Equipment

One Cyclone Collector of M.S. (Mild Steel) construction with manhole frame, supporting cleats, and fitted with flap valve discharge. One Tabulam dust Collector with its lower receiving hopper fitted with a butterfly-type cut-off value.

One set of Interconnecting piping to locate the Cyclone and dust collector. This piping is of M.S. plate construction and is supplied complete with necessary bolts, nuts, washers and joining material. All interconnecting piping is supplied with loose flanges to facilitate site erection. The loose flanges are lightly tack welded on to the pipes is supplied with loose flanges to facilitate site erection. The loose flanges are lightly tack welded on to the pipes for security in transit.

Space Requirement

For Impact pulverizer space required is 15 feet X 17 feet height.

PACKING MACHINES

Developments in Vertical from-fill- Seal Machines

Packaging in flexible pouches offers many products the best value for money compared to other kinds of packaging. It is also the first kind of packaging that is used if packaging form-, fill-, seal machinery. A trend to replace plastics by other packaging material is not visible for reason that plastics have big advantages in terms of efficiency, transparency, weight and volume, hygiene and safety.

Replacement of plastics by offer packaging materials would mean that the weight of the materials multiplies by four, the waste will increase by 25%, the energy consumption by 500% and the cost of packaging material will increase by 210%. Now-a-days in Western Europe and other industrial countries, still many packages are found that consist of a bag in a carton, the so-called bag-in-box package. For environmental reasons, there is a trend towards single packaging instead of double packaging. This means that the block-bottom-bag is of increasing interest. Growth is especially expected in packaging of product such as cereals, dry baby food, fast noodles and rice.

In the past, intermittent operating machines were produced, but in the last few years the continuous-motion machines are a fast-growing segment. Where intermittent machines reach speeds up to 120 bags per minute, the continuous-mition machines achieve speeds up to 180 bags per minute (depending on product, film and bag shape).

Intermittent machines have stationary sealing bars. They close, seal the bottom of the bag, catch the falling product, and open again. Subsequently, the film transport accelerates from zero to one to 1.5 m/sec and stops to enable the sealing of the top of the bag. On stopping of the film run, extra forces are applied by the product on the bottomseal. Therefore, an optimum film-thickness, is required.

In continuous-motion-machines, the film speed is lower but is not interrupted. Therefore, the seal-load is lower which allows the use of thinner films. Instead of 40 microns, one may use 20 to 30 microns. As the sealing bars are not stationary but move along with the film during a certain time, the percentage of sealing time as part of the total cycle can be extended. This is what is needed to enable the achievement of higher speeds. With high and controllable sealing pressures, it is possible to realize strong and goodlooking seals at lower sealing temperature.

Another trend is the application of automation and servo technolgy. Through these, it is possible to very sealing temperature and sealing pressure step-wise within certain areas, and the same aplies to the movements in the sealing-mechanism. By this technology, the flexibility of the packaging machine can be considerably improved. In the old jaw draw off system, a big disadvantage was that the function that needed the longest time determined the speed of the machine, while of functions were dependant on one main sheft.

In the belt-draw off machines, this disadvantage is no longer there and film-transport and sealing time could be controlled independently. Through automation and servo technology, it will be possible to make machine designs that consist of interrelated functions that are translated into modules. Each module is a control circuit with its own controls. An overall control system connects and integrates the controls of each module. Here the possibilities of the information-technology enable us to make the system flexible (Table). Moreover, the overall control-system is no longer a dedicated design, but just an industrial personal computer. The software is becoming the most important part of the control system. This is not only for the vertical form-fill-and seal machine, but also for the complete system including dosing and downstream equipment. It will also be possible to control more than one packaging line by only one control system and to connect the control system to computer networks to enable real-time remote control. The total efficiency can also be increased by these technolotgies and especially by diagnostic systems that give information on downtime, causes for downline, and so on.

Another possibility of the information technology is remade diagnosis by the producer of machines at the customer through moderns. This can reduce the need of assistance by service engineers and reduce downtime.

In conclusion it can be said that the packaging/packaging

machine must fulfil customer needs and keep things as uncomplicated as possible, which can be achieved by the present-day modern technologies.

TABLE -2

FFS MACHINES FOR PACKAGING OF FOOD PRODUCTS	
Innovation	
Until 1981	Central main sheft
From 1981	Cyclefree Machine
From 1991	Continuous Motion Operation
Future	Cyclefree Functions

Tables 3 and 4 give the main requirements of a packaging machinery, which could be used as a checklist to design the machinery and fullfil customer requirements.

TABLE 3

REQUIREMENTS OF PACKAGING MACHINERY
* **High Perfomance**
* Short cycle time; if possible no intermittent operation
* Knowledge of physical restrictions in advance
* High efficiency
* **High Availability**
* Good design
* Quick service
* Easy operation
* Easy set up; versatility
* Low maintenance
* Low breakdown
* Easy repair

TABLE - 4

REQUIREMENTS OF PACKAGING MACHINERY
*** Low personnel need**
* Multiple machine operation
* High level of automation
* Twin models
*** Preparedness to design on order**
* Flexible machine concepts; modular design
* Flexible organisation
* Creative, experienced designers
* Close co-operation between customer and manufacturer
* Turn key responsibility for complex installations
* Easy synchronisation single machines
* Well trained project engineers
* Good value for money

PEDAL OPERATED POUCH SEALER

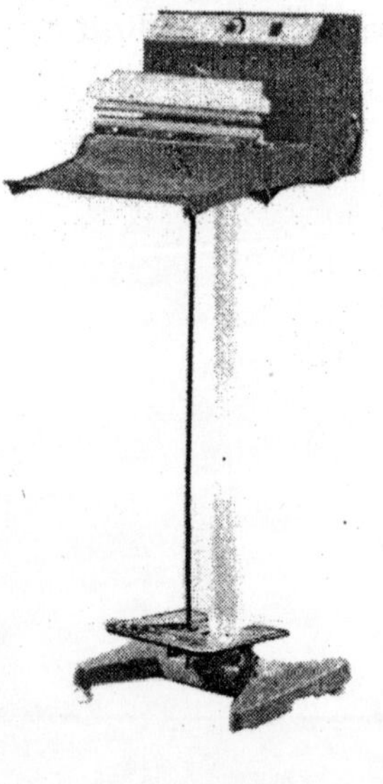

AUTO POUCH SEALER EMF OPERATED

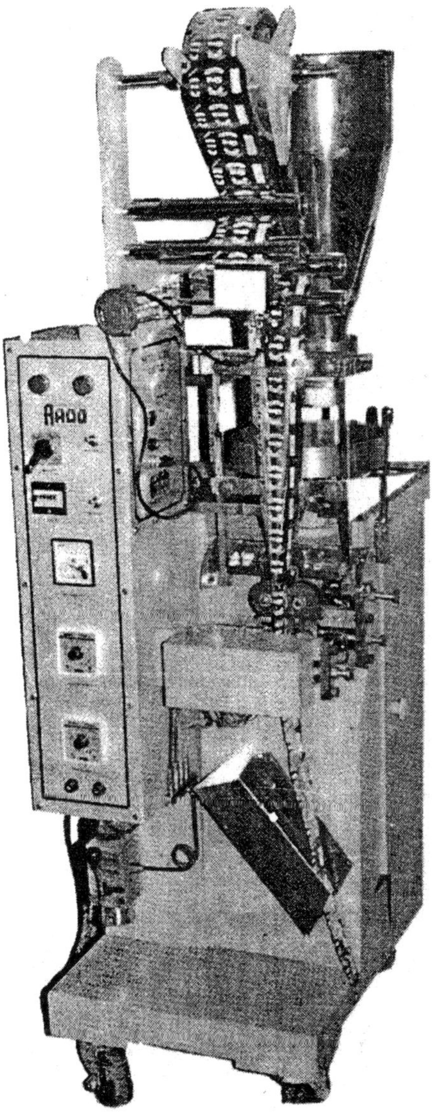

Use :

For Automatic Packing of Spices/Powders, Pan Masala, Granules, Tablets, Tobacco, Tea Dust & Ground Coffee etc.

Packing Range :

2 gm.-250 gm. (Depending on gravity of the product to be packed)

Bag Size :

L - 40 - 240 mm.
W - 20 - 125 mm.

Speed :

40 - 90 Pouches per minute (Depending on the flow & volume of the product to be packed)

43

NATIONAL STANDARDS ON PACKAGING CODE FOR SPICES AND CONDIMENTS

SPICES & CONDIMENTS

Whole Spices

The code has laid down guidelines on packaging of spices and condiments. The spices should be packed in new, clean and sound jute cloth, paper or polyethylene bags or LDPE coated jute bags, LDPE coated raffia bags. If the purchaser specifies packing in double gunny bags, the outer bag may be old and the inner bag should be new. The bags should be free from any fungal or insect infestation and any undesirable smell.

Black Pepper, Whole

Black pepper should be packed in clean and sound jute bags with or without moisture-proof lining or LDPE coated raffia bags which do not impart any foreign smell to black pepper. The mouth of each bag should be either machine-stitched or rolled over and hand stitched.

Miscellaneous

Ginger, Whole

Whole ginger should be packed in sound double or single

jute bags with water-proof lining. The bags may be lined inside with cloth or polyethylene. The material may also be packed in LDPE coated raffia bags.

Ginger, Ground

Ground ginger should be packed in sealed, clean and sound tinplate or glass containers or paper cartons properly lined with water-proof or in moisture proof bags or pouches made from PET/EVA or BOPP/EVA which do not impart any smell to the ginger. The quantities packed in each container may be 0.5, 1.0 and 2.0 kg or as required. A suitable number of such containers should be packed in wooden or cardboard cases.

Curry Powder

Curry powder should be packed in sealed, clean and sound tin-plate or glass containers, or paper cartons properly lined with water-proof paper or in moisture-proof bags or pouches made from PET/EVA or BOPP/EVA which does not impart any smell to the curry powder. The quantities packed in each container may be 0.5, 1.0 and 2.0 kg or as required.

Chillies

Chilies should be packed in clean and should jute bags or in pouches made from PET/EVA or BOPP/EVA or in suitably lined wooden cases. The material may also be packed in LDPE coated raffia bags.

Saffron

Saffron should be supplied in water-tight, should and clean packing made of PET/LDPE or BOPP/LDPE laminates.

Tamarind Concentrate

Tamarind concentrate should be packed in tinplate or

glass containers which should be appropriately sealed. The containers may be either plain or lacquered, if lacquered, the lacquer should be of the acid resistant type. The contcentrate may also be packed in pouches made from metallized polyester laminate or metallized BOPP/ionomer laminate.

Cloves

Whole and ground cloves should be packed in clean and sound air-tight containers, made of a material which does not affect the cloves. Packing in PET/LDPE bags may be considered.

44

IMPORTERS OF SPICES

Mandy S.A.
Frage 71
1427 Buenos Aires
Argentina
C.P : Dithurbide Juru Carlos
President
Tel. : 541-854-5141
Fax. : 541-854-0074
(Black Pepper. White Pepper Cloves, Turmeric Cardamom (Small), Celery Seed, Garlic, Parsely and other spices)

Corona Manufacturing Pvt. Ltd.
595 Burwood Highway,
Knoxfield Vic 3180,
Victoria, Australia
C.P. : John Batkin, CEO
Tel.: 0061-3-9801-9800
Fax.: 0061-3-9800-1265
(Chillies dry, Black pepper, Nutmeg, Paprika)

Max Spices Pty. Limited
A.C.N. 067 115 879
11/28 Vore Street
Silve water Nsw 2141
Australia
C.P. : Pratap Thakker
Director
Tel. : 0061-2-7379094
Fax. : 0061-2-9648606
(Cumin Seed, Coriander Seed, Chillies Powder, Turmeric Powder, Fenugreek Seed, Ajwanseed (Bishop Wood), Pepper Powder, Black Pepper, Mustard Seed)

Spencers General Food Pte. Ltd.
4 Adams Street, o'conner 6163,
Western Australia
Australia
C.P.: Wayne Honore
Business Manager
Tel.: 0061-9-314-1133
Fax.: 0061-9-314-1304
(Curry masala, Tamarind pastes/ Concentrate, ajwanseed (bishop weed), Basil cardamom (large), Cardamom (small)&(large), Powder, Chilli dry dehydrated, Green pepper, Pomegrante seed, all type of spices)

Unifoods Pvt. Ltd.
20-22 Cambridge Street
Epping, Nsw 2121, Australia
C.P. : Ken Towers
Senior Buying Manager
Tel. : 0061-2-9869-6382
Fax. : 0061-2-9869-6320
(Curry Powder)

Waters Trading Pty. Ltd.
P.O.Box 190
ryde N.S.W.-2112
Australia
C.P. : Brian Butler
Purchasing Manager
Tel. : 0061-29-80-74-544
Fax. : 0061-29-80-96-898
(Black pepper, White pepper, Chillies dry, Chillies powder, Chillies crushed, Ginger dry, Ginger powder, Turmeric, Turpowder, Celery seed, All type of spices)

Chunilal Purushottam & Co.
P.O. Box No. 4, Manama
Baharain
C.P.: C.V. Chemand Patel
Chairman
Tel. : 00973-210738, 210739
Fax. : 00973-210750
(Coriander Seed, Chillies Dry, Black Pepper, Cardamom (small), Cloves, All types of Spices, Coriander Powder, Chillies Powder, Pepper Powder)

Kazerooni Brothers
P.O.Box No. 5844
Manama Baharain
C.P. : K.T.Babu
Asst. Purchasing Manager
Tel. : 00973-246369
Fax. : 00973-276758
(Black pepper, Chillies dry, Turmeric, fennel seed, Fenugreek seed, Coriander seed greater galanga, Ginger dry)

M.M.Joofri & Sons
P.O.Box No.52
Manama, Baharain
C.P. : Abdul Gaffer,
Ismail Mohtisham
Tel. : 00973-223354
Fax. : 00973-223356
(All type of spices)

P.Haridassons Co. WII.
P.O.Box No. 434
Manama, Baharain
C.P. Bhagwan L. Asarpota
Director
Tel. : 00973-223689
Fax. : 00973-223648
(Pepper powder, Chillies powder, Cumin powder, Curry powder, Curry masala, Coriander powder, dehy, Garlic powder, Ginger powder, Turmeric powder, All type of spices)

Salehalsaleh Co.Wll.
P.O. Box No. 176
Manama, Baharain

C.P.: Pradeep K. Bhatia
Marketing Manager
Tel. : 00973-270362, 253411
Fax. : 00973-231671
(Black pepper, Cardamom (small), Cassia, Fenugreek seed, Cloves, Chillies powder, Coriander powder, Turmeric powder, Curry masala)

G.D.I.N.V.
Wolventofstraat,
8870 12 Egem, Belgium
C.P.: Guido Deprez, M.D.
Tel. : 0032-51313628
Fax. : 0032-51314881
(Herbal spices)

Taiga International N.V.
Hoek 76, Unit 48, 2840 Boom
Belgium
C.P. : M. Paul Voute, M.D.
Tel.: 0032-3-8440176
Fax. : 0032-3-8445406
(Spice oleoresins)

Classic Foods & Produce Ltd.
5050-76th Alberta T2C 2x2
Canada
Tel. : 403-270-6267
Fax. : 403-279-6515
E-mail :
clasicfd@cadvision.Com
(Black pepper, Pepper/Turmeric/ Curry powder, Chillies crushed, Chillies dry)

Farahimpex Limited
110, Barbados BLVD
Scarborough, Ont mij 1 k 9
Canada
C.P.Siraj China M.D.
Tel. 001-416-267-4227
Fax. 001-416-439-1174
(Chillies dry, Chillies powder, Cumin seed, Cumin powder, Coriander seed, Coriander powder, Black pepper, Powder, Turmeric powder, Ginger powder, All type of spices)

G.S.Teja Limited
160-2620, Simpson Road
Richmond, B.C. V6X 2p9
Canada
C.P.: David Teja, President
Tel. : 604-273-7862 Fax: 7534
(Black pepper, White pepper, Turmeric, Chillies powder, Cumin seed, Coriander seed, Chillies dry, Chillies crushed, Cloves, Curry powder)

Golden Boy Foods Inc.
8820 Northbrook Court
Burnaby, BC, V5J Canada
C.P. Nizar Virani
Executive vice President
Tel. 001-604-433-2200
Fax. 001-604-433-0051
E-mail: goldenboy foods@bc sympatico.com
(All spice, Aniseed, Bay leaf, Basil, Cardamom (small), Seed cardamom, Cardamom powder,

Caraway seed, Celery seed, Cumin seed)

K.I.Lister Ltd.
251, Bartley Drive Toronto,
Ontario M4A 2N7, Canada
C.P. Mark Crawford
Tel. 001-416-752-7913
Fax. 001-416-752-4197
(Black pepper, Pepper powder, Chillies dry, Chillies powder, Chillies crushed, Turmeric, Ginger dry, Celery seed, Cumin seed, Dill seed & All type of spices)

Les Aliments Rose Hill
Foods Inc.
5778, Rue Cypihot St.
Laurent,
Quebec H4S 1Y5, Canada
C.P. George Sarbains
Tel. 514-745-1153
Fax. 514-745-5795
(Black pepper, Pepper powder, Chillies crushed, Chillies powder, Cinnamon)

Shah Trading Company Ltd.
3451 McNicoll Ave,
Scarborough,
Ontario M1V 2V3, Canada
C.P.Shashi Shah, Director
Tel. 1-416-292 6927 Fax. 7932
(Turmeric, Cumin seed, Chillies crushed, Chillies dry, Chillies powder, Fenugreek seed, Fennel seed, Dill seed, Celery seed & all type of spices)

Albrecht & Dill. GMBH
Brand Stucken 23,22549
Hamburg, Germany
C.P. Jurgen Sahling, Director
Tel. 0049-40-8009101
Fax. 0049-40-8002659
(Dehy, Green pepper, Black pepper, Curry powder, Mace)

Dragoco Gerberding & Co.
Aktiengesellschft, Dragocostr.1
D-37601 Holzminden,
Germany
C.P. Rolf Merkentrup
Tel. 0049-5531/97-1588
Fax. 0049-5531/97-1588
(Black pepper, Nutmeg, Mace, Chillies dry, Turmeric, Celery seed)

Eramex
Burggrafenstrabe 2,
40545 Dusseldorf
Post Box.110328, 40503
Germany
C.P. Marcus Sinell
Tel. 0049-211-557390
Fax. 0049-211-555568
(Spice oils, Spice oleoresins)

HONGKONG

Bentech International Ltd.
2/F Shui on Court
I-#, Tai Yuen Street Wanchai
Hongkong
C.P. : Mabel K Wok

Export/Export Cordinator
Tel.: 852-2803-4348
Fax.: 852-2508-6959
E-mail:
bentech@asianonline.net
(Chillies Dry, Black Pepper, Pepper Powder, White Pepper)

New Delhi Store
T.S.T., P.O.Box : 98109
Kowloon, Hongkong
C.P.: Khosa/Mr. Kulbir Singh
Director
Tel.: 00852- 23693038
Fax.: 00852- 23669488
(Chillies Powder, Turmeric Powder, Coriander Powder, Coriander Seed, Cumin Powder, Cumin Seed)

HUNGARY

Compack Douwe Egberts Ltd.
Istv Ansu 23-25, H-1078
Budapest, Hungary
C.P.: Piroska Nagy
Erzsebet balardine
Tel.: 0036-1- 342-0786
Fax.: 0036-1- 342-6449
(Black Pepper, White Pepper Turmeric Powder)

Silvestris & Szilas Ltd.
H-2143, Kerepes, Vasut Str.42
Hungary
C.P. : Attila Olah
Purchase Manager
Tel. : 0036-28-480-675
: 0036-28-370-389
Fax.: 0036-28-370-099
(Caraway Seed, Dill Seed Fennel Seed, Garlic Juniper Seed, Marjoram Parsely, Sage Thyme, Aniseed and all type of Spices)

INDONESIA

P. T. Island Sun Indonesia
Komplex Ketpang Indan
Block - A2
No. 10-11, J1. K. H. Zainul, Arifin, Jakarta Barat-11140
Indonesia
C.P. Poni Madijukie, Direstor
Tel.: 62-21-6596713
Fax.: 62-21-6596715
(Chillies Dry, Turmeric, Paprika, Ginger Dry, Carway Seed, Garlic Nutmeg, Cloves, Greater Galanga, Black Pepper)

P.T.Sinduro Kencana Sari Coy.
Jalan Kertopaten 33
Surabaya 60145, Indonesia
C.P.: Hensen Susanto, Director
Tel.: 62-31-312879
Fax.: 62-31-319252
(Cumin Seed, Coriander Seed)

Pt. Saricitra Indomandiri
JL. Notaris No. 76
Kreo Cileduk 15156
Tangerang, Indonesia
C.P. Bambang Marsulan S.
Director
Tel.: 021-733-4557

Fax.: 021-585-2305
(Capsicum Oleoresin, Turmeric Ginger Dry, Garlic, Black Pepper, White Pepper, Chillies Powder, Tamarind Fresh)

IRAM

Full-Time Co.Ltd.
P.O.Box - 13145 - 493
Tehran, Iran
C.P.: M.Haghighai-Khou, M.D.
Tel. : 0098-21-677380
Fax. : 0098-21-675926
(All type of Spices)

Mirhadi International Trading
151, Lalezarno Street
P.O. Box : 11365-4954
Tehran, Iran
C.P. : Seyyed Abbas Mirhandi President
Tel. : 0098410-6496966
Fax. : 008410-6457286
(Chillies Dry, Black Pepper, Cumin Seed, Black Cumin, Turmeric, Saffron, Coriander Seed)

Sapah Consumer Co-Operative
Kargar Shomali Ave.
Corner of Dr. Fatemi Ave
Teheran -14144, Iran
C.P. Hosien Modarresi Far
Managing Director
Tel.: 0098-658685
Fax.: 0098-659799
(Turmeric, Black Pepper)

ISRAEL

Indian Sweets Ltd.
Shavezion Street 128
Ashdod, Israel
C.P.: Ashtivkar David, Owner
Tel.: 08 - 8522064
Fax.: 08 - 8563423
(All type of Spices)

Moshe-Mussafi
Mahalat-Bengamin 82 St.
Telaviv - 66525, Israel
C.P. : Joseph, Manager
Tel. : 00-972-3-6827424
Fax. : 00-972-3-6832065
(Cumin Seed, Poppy Seed)

Ta'am Vareach Spices Ltd.
P.O. Box - 3090
Kiryat Arye, Petah Tikva 49130
Israel
C.P. : Jerome Shattenstein
Technical Director
(Black Pepper, White Pepper Turmeric, Cinnamon, Ginger Dry, Cumin Seed, Nutmeg, Coriander Seed, All-spice)

ITALY

SPL Imperial 2 SPA
VIA Tiburtina, Valeria, 475
65131 Pescare, Italy
C.P.: Nicolaas F. Mehagnoul
Import Manager
Tel.: 0039-085-4304220
Fax.: 0039-85-4304232
(Black Pepper, Chillies Dry, Paprika, Cinnamon, all type of

Spices)

Drogheria & Alimentari
VIA Founda Di Mezaana
15-50047 Prato (Firenge)
Italy
C.P. Fagnoni Giovanni
President
Tel. : 0574-575727
Fax. : 0574-571071
(Black Pepper, Chillies Powder, Chillies Crushed, White Pepper Nutmeg, Cinnamon)

Enrico Webb-Jams S.N.C.
57121 Livorno, 26-28, Via Nicolodi Italy
C.P.: Stefano Trumpy, Buyer
Tel.: 586-424725
Fax.: 586-425523
(Chillies Seed & Powder, Black Pepper & Powder, White Pepper, Nutmeg, Cinnamon, Cloves)

I.D.A.V. SRL
Contradale Vecchie 2
80040 Striano (Naples), Italy
C.P.G. Ambrosio General Manager
Tel.: 0039-81-8276963
Fax.: 0039-81-8277670
(Black Pepper)

Macor Di Truccazzano S.R.I.
Viale Monte Grappa 10
20060 Truccazzano (Milano)
Italy
C.P.: P. Melloni
Purchasing Officer
Tel. 0039-2-9583136
Fax. 0039-2-9583707
(Pepper Powder, Chillies Powder, Chillies Crushed, Turmeric Powder, Curry Powder, Cumin Seed, Fennel Seed, Celery Seed, Coriander Seed)

Sundries Food S.A.S.
15/30 Plazza Delha
Vittoria, 16121 Genova, Italy
C.P.: Augusto vianson
Purchasing Manager
Tel. 39-10-589351
Fax. 39-10-565467
(Black Pepper, Chillies Dry, Chillies Seed, Chillies Powders, Turmeric, Turmeric Powder, Turmeric, Turmeric Powder Fr. Dry Green Pepper, Garlic)

JAPAN

Cultor Food Science K.K.
2-3-22, Tordnomon
Minatoku, Tokyo 105, Japan
C.P.: Kuniel Toyoda
Director, Cal Division
Tel.: 81-3-3503-0441
Fax.: 81-3-3503-0447
(Pepper Oleoresin, Ginger Oleoresin, Nutmeg Oleoresin, Pepper Oil, Ginger Oil, Chillies Oleoresin)

M & H Corporation
Sankyo Bekkan Bldg.
1-7-10, IIDabashi
Chiyoda - Ku - Tokyo, Japan
C.P. : Kazuyuki Yoshino
Import Manager
Tel. 0081- 03- 3288 - 5185
Fax. 0081- 03 - 3288 - 5187
(Turmeric, Cumin Seed Cardamom (Small), Fennel Seed, Celery Seed, Poppy Seed Black Pepper)

Mae Chu Co. Ltd.
No.2426 Shimoichi
Shimoichi - Cho
Yoshino- Gum, Nara Pref, Japan
C.P.: Hirotomo Mae, Manager
Tel.: 0081-7475-2-2262
Fax.: 0081-7475-2-9188
(Chillies Dry, Turmeric)

S & B Foods Inc.
38-8, Miyamotocho, Itabashi-Ku
Tokyo-174 Japan
C.P.: Akira Takahashi, G.M.
Tel.: 03-3558-1075
Fax.: 03-3558-6948
(Black Pepper, White Pepper, Chillies Dry, Cumin Seed, Cloves, Nutmeg, Ginger Dry, Paprika, Garlic, Turmeric & All type of Spices)

Saiwai Trading Co. Ltd.
17-25, 1 Chome, Sinkawa
C uou Ku. Tokyo, Japan
C.P.N. Yamamoto, G.M.
Tel. 0081-03-5543-2451
Fex. 0081-03-5543-2458
(Mustrad Seed)

Shonan Trading Co. Ltd.
3-4-5 Kugenuma, Matsugaoka
Fujisawa Konagawa, Japan
C.P.: F. Toyoda, President
Tel.: 0081-466-27-2314
Fax.: 0081-466-27-2491
(Pepper Oil, Ginger Oleoresin, Capsicum Oleoresin, Nutmeg Oil)

Takasagospice Co., Ltd.
1-4-1, Hatchobori Chuo-Ku
Tokyo 104, Japan
C.P.: Yasuto Koyama
Executive Director
Tel.: 81-463-81-6245
Fax.: 81-463-81-7609
(Turmeric, Cumin Seed Coriander Seed, Fenugreek Seed Cardamom (Small), Celery Seed, Ginger Dry, Dill Seed, Celery Seed etc.)

Tokyo Koshin Co.Ltd.
23/1-4-Chome,
Kamiuma Setagaya Ku
Tokyo 154, Japan
C.P.: Shizuka Kato
Tel.: 0081-03-3414-3180, 3156
Fax.: 0081-03-3414-3180
(Black Pepper, Turmeric Cardamom (Small), Cumin Seed)

Yasuma Co. Ltd.
5-23-2 Nishigotanda
Shinagawa, Tokyo, Japan
C.P.: Shizuka Kato
Tel.: 0081-03-3490-5215
Fax.: 0081-03-3490-5265
(Black Pepper, Turmeric Cardamom (Small)

Yuassa Trading Co.Ltd.
13-10, Nihonhashiodenmacho
Chuo-Ku, Tokyo, Japan
C.P.: Takehisa Hashimoto
Manager
Tel.: 81-3-3665-6223
Fax.: 81-3-3665-6267
(Poppy Seed, Chillies Dry, Garlic, Ginger Dry, Turmeric, Basil & Spice Oils)

JORDAN

Arzzaq & Partners Trading Co. Ltd.
P.O. Box.: 16104
Alwahdat - Ammansovdan
Street Address: Middle East Circle, Opp. Islamic Bank
Jordan
C.P.: S.A.Razzaq
Director General
Tel.: 009626-778929,750597
Fax.: 009626-778929
(Black Pepper)

Jordan Commodity Trading & Agencies Co. Ltd.
Amman Commercial Centre
Ist Floor, Abdalli Street
P.O. Box : 910206
Amman -11191, Jordan
C.P.: Maurice C. Akkawi
Managing Director
Tel.: 00962-6-698452
Fax.: 00962-6-698453
(Ajwanseed [Bishop weed], Black Pepper, Coriander seed, Cumin Seed, Curry Powder, Dill Seed, Ginger Dry, Fennel Seed, Fenugreek Seed, Chillies powder & All types of spices).

Samih Khauli Trading Co.
P.O.Box-6940, Amman -11118
Jordan
C.P.: Samih Khauli
General Manager
Tel.: 00962-6-623460
Fax.: 00962-6-627011
(Black Pepper, Turmeric Chillies Dry)

KENYA

Karman Wholesalers
P.O. Box - 45327, Nairobi
Kenya
C.P.: Arun D. Shah
Manager
Tel.: 254-2-222842, 224742
Fax.: 254-2-222842
(Black Pepper, Cardamom (Small), Cardamom (Large), Cinnamon, Turmeric, Cassia)

Vipee's
P.O.Box 81342
Mombasa, Kenya
C.P.: R. P. Shah, Partner
Tel. 00254-224078
Fax. 00254-313335
(Cumin Seed, Fennel Seed, Ajwanseed (Bishop Weed), Dill Seed, Fenugreek Seed, Coriander Seed, Ginger Dry, Turmerics)

MALAYSIA

Bhatgwansingh Melasing Sdn Bhd
32, Jalan Tuanku Ablul Rahman
P.O.Box-10386
50712, Kuala Lumpur Malaysia
C.P.: Sam S.S. Sambhi
Managing Director
Tel.: 03-2927282, 2982661
Fax.: 03-2982661
(Coriander Seed, Cumin Seed Fennel Seed, Chillies Dry, Black Cumin, Coriander Powder, Cumin Powder, Chillies Powder)

Enrico Sdn Bhd
16, Puncak Perusahaan Satu
136000 Perai, Malaysia
C.P.: S.K. Sundaraam
Managing Director
Tel.:0060-4-3973363, 3996745
Fax.: 0060-4-3905724
(Chillies Dry, Turmeric Cumin Seed, Fennel Seed)

Gaban Spice Manufacturing (M) Sdn. Bhd.
No.2042, MK.I,
Solok Perusahaan Satu,
Kompleks Perindustrian Prai.
136000 PRAI, Malaysia
C. P.: Edward A.K. Teoh
Asst. General Manager
Tel.: 0060-3908236
Fax.: 0060-4-3993166
(Black Pepper, Turmeric, Cumin Seed, Fennel Seed),

Hua Loung Heng Trading Co.
46-Lorong Riang Tamin Riang
Butter Worth Malaysia
C.P.: Koay Wee Long
Manager
(Chillies Dry, Coriander Seed, Fennel Seed, Black Pepper Poppy Seed)

45

EXPORTERS OF SPICES

Al-Gayathri Trading Co. Pvt. Ltd.
Darragh Smail Centre
2nd Floor, 5th Croess Road,
Willingdon Island, Cochin
Kerala - 682003
C.P.: P. Nanda Kumar M.D
Tel.: 91-0484-668556, 668754
Fax.: 91-0484-668547
E-mail:
algaytri@nd2.vsnl.net.in
(Black Pepper)

Elecom Exports Pvt. Ltd.
25-A, Camac Street
"Vardaan" Suite # 403
Kolkatta, West Bengal-700016
C.P.: Rajiv Bahety, Director
Tel.: 91-033-2474932,
2402358
Fax.: 91-033-2476872
E-mail : elecom@cal.vsnl.net.in
(Black Pepper)

Gandhi Sons
C-20/21, Mezz, Floor,
Satyam Shopping Centre,
M.G.Road, Ghatkopar (E)
Mumbai, Maharashtra - 400 077
C.P.: Harshed D Gandhi
Managing Partner
Tel.:91-022-5142121,5142122
Fax.: 91-022-5111144
E-mail:
gandhi@bom3.vsnl.net.in
(Black Pepper)

I.T.C. Ltd.
IB Division - ATBG, 1st Floor,
"Rajhans" No. 36, VII Cross,
Vasantha Nagar, Bangalore
Karnataka-560 052
C.P.: Ninad Bhosle
Tel. 91-080-2205288, 2205172
Fax.: 91-080-2205170
(Black Pepper)

Indain Products Ltd.
No. 39, Cunningham Rd. Cross
Bangalore, Karnataka - 560 052
C. P.: Ashwin J. Shah
Tel. 91-080-2268687
Fax. 91-080-2255271
E-mail: ashwin@jayanti.com
(Black Pepper)

Priyanka Overseas Ltd.
D-18, Connaught Place,
New Delhi-110001
C.P.: R. K. Jain, Chairman
Tel.:91-011-3327150, 3324210
Fax.: 91-011-3324642
(Black Pepper)

Accelerated Freeze Drying Co. Ltd.
Amalgam House, Bristow Road
Willingdon Island
Cochin, Kerala - 682 003
C.P.: Sashi Menon
Sr. General Manager
Tel.: 91-0484-668680
Fax.: 91-0484-668130, 668133
E-mail:
amalgam@giasmldo1.vsnl.net.in
(Frozen/green pepper)

AVT Mccormick Ingredients Ltd.
Spice Enclave, Panampilly Nagar, Cochin, Kerala - 682036
C.P.: Msa Kumar, Exe. Director
Tel.: 91-0484-317903, 317905
Fax.: 91-0484-317916
E-mail : Kumar avtmcc@satyam
(Cardamom small)

Groversons
Dharam Jyot, 96 Kazi Sayed St.
Mumbai, Maharashtra 400 003
C.P.: Manoj M.Grover
Tel.: 91-022-3420638,3401706
Fax.: 91-022-3420638
E-mail :
bhavan@bom3.vsnl.net.in
(Cardamom-small)

Goyal Marketing Pvt. Ltd.
2, Asia House, K.G. Marg
New Delhi - 110001
C.P: Anil Goyal, Director
Tel. 91-11-3389217, 3326756
Fax.: 91-011-3382343
(Cardamom small)

U.Karunakaran
15, T.C. Godown Street
Virudhunagar, Tamilnadu 1
C.P.: U.Karunakaran
Sole Proprietor
Tel. 91-04562-44240
Fax. 91-04562-47093
E-mail: aanukudy@psynet.net
(Cardamom small)

Laxmichand Dayabhai (Export) Co.
512/16, Rewa Chambers
31, New Marine Lines
Mumbai - 400 020
C.P.: Nisheeth M.Vasa
Tel. 91-022-2014173, 2014266
Fax.: 91-022-2062901
E-Mail : abjopati@vsnl.com
(Cardamom small)

S.P.G. Ramasamy Nadar & Sons
77, South Car Street
Virudhunagar, Tamilnadu 1
C.P.: S.P.G.R. Nithyanandan
Sr. Partner & Chief Exe.
Tel. 91-04562-43364, 44164
Fax. 91-04562-44964,45339

(Cardamom small)

Atlantic Corporation
Unit No. 111.
A/2 Shah & Nahar Ind. Estate
Dhanraj Mill Compound,
Lower Parel (W)
Mumbai, Maharashtra - 400 013
C.P.: Hitesh C. Gutka, Partner
Tel.: 91-022-4932087,4932092
Fax.: 91-022-4930478
E-mail : gutka@vsnl.com
(Chilli Powder)

Avt Mccormick Ingredients Ltd.
Spice Encleve, Panampilly Ng.
Cochin, Kerala - 682036
C.P.: Msa Kumar
Exe. Director
Tel. 91-0484-317903, 317905
Fax. 91-0484-317916
(Chilli Powder)

Chillies Export House Ltd.
35, M.C. Chidambara Nadar
Street, Virudhunagar
Kamaraj Dist. Tamilnadu - 1
C.P.: A. P. Murugan
Tel. 91-04562-43315, 45017
Fax. 91-04562-45089
E-mail:
paprika@giasmd01.vsnl.net.in
(Chilli Powder)

Indian Exporters
C-1-7, G.I.D.C.
Nadiad, Gujarat 387 001
C.P.: Vasudev Meghraj Taheliani
Tel.: 91-0268-64102, 64103
Fax.: 91-0268-64101
(Chilli Powder)

Kanu Krishna Corporation
502/503, Goradia House
5th Flr. 100/104 Kazi Sayed St.
Mumbai - 400 003
C.P.: Dipak K. Parikh Partner
Tel.91-022-3427676, 3412565
Fax.: 91-022-3401676
E-mail:
kkcdipak@bom3.vsnl.net.in
(Chilli Powder)

K.P.Industries
28,GIDC Estate
Dhrangadhra, Gujarat - 363310
C.P.: Kishore Panjwani
Tel.: 91-02754-22075,22275
Fax.: 91-02754-22686
(Chilli Powder)

ABS Food Ingredients
Near Raj Chambers
Khodiyar Colony
Jamnagar, Gujarat 361006
C.P.: Avadhnaresh B.Sharma
Proprietor
Tel.: 91-0288-555665,502864
Fax.: 91-0288-555195
(Ginger Powder)

Krishna & Co.
Krishna Kunj, Pallaiarakavu Rd.
Cochin, Kerala - 682 002
C.P.: Krishnakumar
Managing Partner
Tel. 91-0484-221989

Fax.: 91-0484-224001

E-mail:

krishna@giamd01.vsnl.net.in

(Chilli Powder)

P. Mittulaul Lalah & Sons

54, Nelson Manickam Road

Aminjikarai, Chennai

Tamilnadu - 600 029

C.P.: N.S.R. Mandraadiar

Tel.91-044-4839124, 4839607

Fax.: 91-044-4837772

E-Mail :

lalahs@md@.vsnl.net.in

(Ginger Powder)

Nanji topanbhai & Co.

Bazar Road. Mattancherry

Cochin, Kerala 682 002

C.P.H.N.Dattani

Partner

Tel.: 91-0484-222180,224180

Fax.: 91-0484-223180

E-Mail :

nanjee@md2.vsnl.net.in

(Ginger Powder)

Sipco Masalas (P) Ltd.

VI/207, Jew Town, Cochin

Kerala - 682002

C.P.: T.Vidyasagar

Tel.: 91-0484-224628, 224832

Fax.: 91-0484-225939

E-Mail: sipce@md2.vsnl.net.in

(Ginger Powder)

Unigue Exports

G - 8, Namrata Apartments,

L.B.S.Road,Mulund (West),

Mumbai - 400080

C.P.: Paresh B.Bhatt

Tel.: 91-22-5642488, 5686135

(Ginger Powder)

46

PRESENT MANUFACTURERS OF SPICES

Shree Ranganatha Seed Corp.
Opp. Municipal Office
Congress Bhavan
Anantapur-515001 (A.P.)
Ph. 23852,32448
Chilli Dry, Mustard Seed Coriander Seed, Turmeric Dry, Garlic

S.R.Food Products
Kalakada Mandal
Chittoor 517001 (A.P.)
Ph. 25102
Curry Powder, Chilli Powder
Coriander Powder, Coriander Seed

Jain Turmerics
Dt-Guntur
Duggirala 522330 (A.P.)
Ph. 77372, 77160
Turmeric Dry

Durga Devi Dall Mill
Main Bazar
Eluru-534001 (A.P.)
Ph. 23455, 20882
Chilli Dry Coriander Seed

Sri Lakshmi Vankatashwara Traders
Agraharam
Opp. Kanakadyrgamma Temple
Eluru-534001 (A.P.)
Ph. 20994,23455
Chilli Dry

Neppalli Venkala Nenkala Narayana
Pedavadlapuri
Manglagiri Manglam
Guntur-522302 (A.P.)
Ph. 82392551
Curry Leal Powder

Ravi Raj Spces Exporters (P) Ltd.
Sadhu Complex
Eluru Bazar
Guntur 522003 (A.P.)
Ph. 222168,222178
Chilli Dry, Turmeric Dry
Coriender Seed, Curry Masala, Curry Powder

S.S. Enterprises
5-87-34/7, 2nd Line Main Road
Lakshmi Puram
Guntur -522007 (A.P.)
Ph. 350943

Mirch Grawars Association
C/O Si Lakshmio Traders
Near Post Office
Main Road
Gurazala - 522415 (A.P.)
Ph. 58520 PP
Chilli Dry

Maruthi Overseas Enterprises
B-8.Padma Building
Main Bazar
Hindupur -515201(A.P)
Ph. 30307
Cardamom (S), Chilli Dry
Turmeric Dry, Ajwan Seed.
Tamarind

Omkar Enterprises
D No-16-1-34
M.F.Road
Hindupur -515201 (A.P)
Ph. 22414
Chilli Dry. Tamarind

Eco Safe Systems Pvt. Ltd.
DNS -3-6-168/7
1st Floor
Hyderabad-29 (A.P)
Ph. 597537,243689
Coriander Seed, Chilli Dry
Ginger Dry, Turmeric Dry. Garlic

Muthyala Narendra
Plot No-8-3-976/96
Salivatena Nagar
Srinagar Colony Post
Hyderabad -500073 (A.P)
Ph.3748733
Turmeric Dry

R. Vishwanath
Charterod Accounted
H.No-5-9-224/A
Chirag Ali Lane, ABIDS
Hyderabad-500001 (A.P)
Ph. 203780
Chilli Dry. Turmeric Dry

Raaghavachendara Exports Pvt. Ltd.
Flat No-102
Chandra Apartment Complex
New Bakaram, Gandhinagar
Hyderabad-500080 (A.P)
Ph. 7613112
Chilli Dry. Chilli Powder
Turmeric Dry, Turmeric Powder,
Coriander Seed

Sneha Exports Ltd.
446 Road No.19 Jublee Hills
Hyderabad -500034 (A.P)
Ph. 238720

Tongmin Perme
Jia Village
Via Roing
Dt.-Dibang Valley
Jia-792110 (A.P)
Ph. 520
Ginger Fresh, Chilli Dry

K.Doraswamy Raju
Padmasarassu
Dt-Chittoor
Karveti Nagar-517582 (A.P)
Tamarind, Chilli Dry

Sri Suguna Cold Storage
H. No. 2-2-211
Gandhi Chowk
Khamgam-507003 (AP)
Ph. 24028, 25206

Chilli Dry. Tamarind

Sri Krishna Oil Traders
Opp. Tobacco Company
Banaganapalli Road
Kollkuntle
Dt-Kumool
Kollkuntla-518134 (A.P)
Ph. 65139,65049
Coriander Seed, Chilli Dry
Turmeric Dry

M. Sulaman & Sons
511, Laxmlvarpeteluru-534005 (A.P)
Ph. 20480, 20885
Chilli Dry, Tamarind, Turmeric Dry

G. C. Chowdhary
H.No-5-11-63
Shanthinagar
Nalgonda -508001 (A.P)
Ph. 32543
Chilli Dry. Coriender Seed

Pothula Buehapa Naidu
Ramnagar, 4th Line
Ongole
Prakasam-523001 (A.P)
Ph. 23522,23625
Chilli Dry

G. Srinivasulu
22/102, Vasanthapet
Proddatur -516360 (A.P)
Ph. 51888
Qurry Leaf Powder, Turmeric
Powder Chilli Dry

K. Venkata Mohan
S/O K.V. Mohan Rao
Near Old Police Lines
Dt. East Godhavari
Rasanagaram-533294 (A.P)
Chilli Dry, Tumeric Dry,
Coriander Seed, Garlic, Tamarind

Deshmukh Range Rao
H.No. 11-3-357/8/1/A
Parsl Gutta
Secunderabad -500061 (A.P)
Ajwan Seed

G. Prabhakar
Navbharat House
Dt-Kartin Nagar
Sircilla -505301 (A.P)
Ph. 2164
Chilli Dry

Shalini International
14-3-38, Badurlapeta
Sri Kakulam-532001 (A.P)
Ph. 22961
Curry Powder,Chilli Powder
Turmeric Powder, Coriander
Powder, Cumin Powder.

Joythi Enterprises
D No-2-20-11
S.S.complex, Nehru Road
Gandhi Chowk
Tenali-522201 (A.P)
Turmeric Dry Powder, Chilli Dry
Coriander Seed, Coriander Powder
Guntur Sannam

P.N.V. Ramana
No-24, Ist Floor
Municipal Employess Colony
Reservoir Road
Tirupathi-517501 (A.P)
Ph. 27707, 23297
Curry Leaf Powder Chilli Dry

K.V.K.Mohan
Falt No-1-A
Indrakeeladri Apartments
Lalitha Nagar, Bhavanipuram
Vijayawada-520012 (A.P)
Turmeric Dry

Modern Cattle Food Co.
Patamala
Vijayawada-500010 (AP)
Ph. 476237, 476598
Chilli Dry, Turmeric Dry

Modern Food Products
Behind Krishna Bottling Co.
100, Feet Road End, Autonagar
Vijayawada-520007 (AP)
Ph. 540632,542020
Chilli Dry. Tumeric Dry
Tamarind, Coriender Seed. Curry
Leaf

Panangudi Exports
C-7-3,Bhanu Apartments
Moghalarajapuram
Vijayawada -520010 (A.P)
Ph. 471972
Chilli Dry, Turmeric Dry, Turmeric
Powder, Tamarind

AL-Ameon Traders
Room No-1, Jamanasjid
Vikasabad-501101 (A.P)
Chilli Dry, Tamarind
Ginger Dry, Turmeric Dry, Turmeric
Powder

Eaith Food Products
Flat No. D, High Place Apartments
Balaji Hills
Vishakhapatnam -530013 (A.P)
Ph. 550697,5582247
Black Pepper, Chilli Dry, Ginger
Dry & Fresh, Turmeric, Dry. Garlic

Bobbula Vendateshwarlu
Grain Market Area
Warangal -506007 (A.P)
Ph. 26346, 60622
Dry Red Chilli, 54, Tomato chilli
Turmeric, Chilli Flake, 54 Jwala

Domakuntla Kasinadham
H.No-13-2-211, Mattewada
Warangal-506002, (A.P)
Ph. 60035, 25092
Chilli Dry, Tamarind, Coriander
Seed

Karani Spices
7/61, Janpak Shabeed
Pragathi Industrial Estate
Narsampet Road
Warangal -506013 (A.P)
Ph. 60351, 23901
Chilli Powder, Turmeric Powder
Turmeric Dry

Alam Food Products
Akbar Patty Road
Near Masjid C/O Ambar Ali
Paskar, Dibragarh (Assam)
Ph. 30082
Ginger Fresh, Ginger Dry

Ishani Sharma
Woodlands
Digbol-786171 (Assam)
Ph. 2401
Bay Leaf

Dipak Kumar Chotia
D.A. Goan, Tetalital
Golaghat-785621 (Assam)
Ph. 20876
Ginger Fresh, Turmeric Dry

C.M.Traders
Fancy Bazar (T.R.P. Road)
Guwahati-781001 (Assam)
Ph. 34412,34413
Chilli Dry

Mishra & Co.
Nabagraha Road, Silpukhuri
Guwahati 781003 (Assam)
Ph. 521026
Ginger Fresh, Chilli Dry

Keshri Chand Bhuru & Co.
East Market, Karimganj Bazar
Karimganj -788711 (Assam)
Ph. 2279,2049
Chilli Dry, Ginger Fresh

Bhakalis Spices
C/O R.C. Bhakali Principal,
Dimorla Collage
Dt-Khetri (Kamoup)
Khetri-782403 (Assam)
Ph. 87237
Cinnamon, Bay Leaf, Ginger Fresh

Debashish Ghosh
Subhashpally Dt-B.A.C.
Kokrajhar-783370 (Assam)
Ph. 70491
Cardamom (L), Chilli Dry
Black Pepper, Ginger Fresh,
Turmeric Dry

Abhuday
P.O.Maugalpur

Bagaha-2
Dt-West Dhamparan
Bagaha-845105 (Bihar)
Chilli Dry, Turmeric Dry ,Coriander Seed, Fenugreck Seed, Mustard Seed

Assam Traders
Station Road, Balla
Begusarai - 851211 (Bihar)
Ph. 66731,66734
Chilli Dry

Dr. Veresh Kumar
Birpur, Begusarai - 851127 (Bihar)
Chilli Dry, Ginger Dry/Fresh Turmeric Dry, Coriender Seed, Fenugreek Seed

Rajesh Trading Co.
Bakhasi Bazar
Begusarai - 851101 (Bihar)
Chilli Dry. Tumeric Dry

Swastik Agro Agency
Kachahari Road
Begusarai-851101 (Bihar)
Ph. 22151, 22142
Dehy. Grum Chilli, Chilli dry Turmeric Dry. Coriender Seed, Cumin White

Coral Trend Setter
Near Motanl Petrol Pump,
Supriya Cinema, Road Bettish
Bettiah -84538 (Bihar)
Turmeric Powder, Coriender Powder

Satayandra Saran
Kavivar Nagpal Path
Bettiah -845438 (Bihar)
Ph. 32168,31053
Turmeric Dry, Ginger Dry
Mustard Seed. Garlic, Chilli Dry

Vijay Vikaram Mishra
Deaori Road, Barasi
Bhagalpur - 812001 (Bihar)
Chilli Dry, Ginger Dry/Fresh Turmeric Dry, Coriender Seed, Ani Seed

Natural Agro Plantation
Basantpur Road, Birpur
Dt. Supaul, Birpur 854340 (Bihar)
Ph. 2052
Cardamom L & S, Ginger Dry Fresh Turmeric Dry, Coriender Seed, Cumin White

Adarsh Saving & Housing Dev. Co. Ltd.
K-4 Ram Mandir, Sector No.I
Bokaro-827001 (Bihar)
Turmeric Powder, Chilli Powder Curry Powder

Sathyandra Kumar
C/O Sh. T.N. Barua
Executive Engineer I.E.O.
Jamyada Dawaka, Dawka (Bihar)
Turmeric Dry, Corinder Seed Ajween Seed,Chilli Dry, Ani Seed

Saroj General Industries
Karhaniwad, Dt-B.Deoghar
Deoghar-814112 (Bihar)
Ph. 22471
Turmeric Powder, Coriender Powder Chilli Powdor, Pepper Powder, Cumin Powder

Emkay Enterprises
Noor Complex, Dak Bangalow Road
Opp. Civil Lines,Gaya-823001
Ph. 23455
Chilli Dry, Coriender Seed Turmeric

S.S.Chodhary & Co.
Bara Bazar, Mill Road Katihar
Katihar -854105 (Bihar)
Ph. 33201,33206
Black Pepper, Cardamom (S)
Ginger Fresh, Cumin White, Basil

Brajnandan Dwevedi
Shaktishali Bhashm, Aushdhalaya,
Motihari-845401 (Bihar)
Ph. 33158 PP
Ajwan Seed

Mata Deen Mahila Manch
Village & P.O.Ramnagar
Via Bouchalla, Dt-Muzaffarpur
Muzaffarpur-842001 (Bihar)
Chilli Dry, Turmeric Dry, Coriender Seed, Cumin White, Black Pepper

Amrapali Foods Ltd.
2nd Floor, Ujiwal, Ballay Road
Patna -800001 (Bihar)
Ph. 234051,230160
Ginger Dry, Coriender Seed
Turmeric Dry, Chilli Dry

Anuj Kumar
Bhuvanshwar Bag,Pathr Ki Masjeed
Darsah Road, Dt. Mahendra
Patna-800006 (Bihar)
Ph. 658500
Chilli Dry, Turmeric Dry Garlic

Banjara Fast Food
A-25 Ist Floor, Mourya Lok
Patna -800001 (Bihar)
Ph. 236478, 234801
Chilli Dry, Ginger Fresh Turmeric Dry, Coriender Seed. Mustard Seed

C.S. Export & Import Pvt. Ltd.
Gandhi Nagar
Montessori Lane Boring Road
Patna-800001 (Bihar)
Ph. 287454
Chilli Fresh & Dry, Turmeric Dry, Ginger Dry, Coriender Seed, Fonugreek Seed

Himalaya Fruit Products
Dhanki Bhode, Kumhrar
Patna - 800020 (Bihar)
Turmeric, Dry, Coriender Seed Chilli Dry, Cumin White, Chilli Powder

Indcen Medical Trust
Opp. Stadium Mani Gate
Rajender Nagar
Patna - 800016 (Bihar)
Ph 656876
Coriender Seed, Fenugreck Seed
Ajwan Seed

Jai Shree Food Products
Kurjee, Patna - 800010 (Bihar)
Ph. 261574
Chilli Dry, Turmeric Dry Ginger Dry/Fresh, Coriender Seed, Garlic

Krishan Kumar Sharma
Daaur Village,
Anchumanda (Wadha)
Patna -803213 (Bihar)
Ph. 2126
Turmeric Dry, Mustard Seed Coriender Seed, Ani Seed, Ajwan Seed

Mahila Vikas Sangh
Yamuna Ashram,
Sinha Library Road
Patna -800001 (Bihar)
Ph. 222183
Chilli Dry, Fenugreck Seed Turmeric Dry, Coriender Seed, Cumin White

Mruthyanjay Kumar Singh
4 C. Savita Apartment
Boring Patliputra Road
Patna - 800013 (Bihar)
Cardamom(L)&(S), Chilli Dry Ginger Fresh, Turmeric Dry, Corieander Seed

Progressive Enterprises
Station Road, Gulzarbagh
Patna - 800007 (Bihar)
Ph. 645007
Chilli Dry Garlic Dry Fresh Turmeric Dry Coriender Seed Cardamom (L)

S.C.Sarkar
C/O M.M. Industries
New Bys Pass Kankarbagh
Patna-800020 (Bihar)
Ph. 345117, 350326
Chilli Dry Turmeric Dry Coriender Seed Fenugreck Seed Tamarind

Society For Vill. Emp. Rural Awareness
Savera, 12-P-P Colony
Patna - 800013 (Bihar)
Ginger Fresh Garlic

Vindhwasin Enteprises
Station Road, Mokama
Patna - 803302 (Bihar)
Ph . 2490
Chilli Dry, Coriender Seed

Rakendra Bihari
C/o. Sri Bhupendra
Narayan Sinha, Thatia Dt.
Samastipur, Russra -848210 (Bihar)
Chilli Dry. Ginger Dry Turmeric Dry, Coriender Seed. Mustard Seed

Gupta Traders
Sirdilpur P.O.
Shapur Patong District
Samastipur -848161 (Bihar)
Ph. 4632
Chilli Dry, Turmeric Dry

Madhukar Massala Cottage Ind.
Village Alloy, Musari Gharari
Samastipur-848161 (Bihar)
Chilli Powder, Turmeric Powder Coriender Powder Curry Masala

Tirpathi Marketing
Bhola Talkies Chowk
Samastipur-848101 (Bihar)
Ph. 74313
Turmeric Dry Coriender Seed Mustard Seed Chilli Dry

Aarti Enterprises
45, West Avenue Punjabi Bagh
New Delhi - 110026
Ph. 5418146

Aggarwal Trading Co.
30,Gadodia Market, Khari Baoli
Delhi-110006
Ph. 233638

Anant Ram Charan Dass Aggarwal
590 Katra Ishwar Bhawan
Khari Baoli
Delhi - 110006
Ph. 2512704

Anil Traders
2584/1 Mandir Lane, Shadipur
New Delhi - 110008
Ph. 5700323

Apoom Packs
224, Kallash Hills
New Delhi - 110065
Ph. 6830240, 6926819
Saffrom

Apros Trading Pvt. Ltd.
1016, Arunachal
19, Barakhamba Road
New Delhi -110001
Ph. 3312553, 3715981
Drugs, Leather Goods Spices, Pharma Ceuticals

Arbee Overseas
66-C, BW Block
Shalimar Bagh, Delhi
Ph. 7201895, 7201795
Black Pepper, Coriender (L)
Turmeric Dry, Cumin White, Ani Seed

Ashok Masala Co. (Regd).
E-2/177, Shastri Nagar
Sarai Rohilla
New Delhi -110052
Ph. 528238

Avon Agro Industries Pvt. Ltd.
C-35/23, Lawrence Road
Industrial Area
New Delhi - 110035
Ph. 7188661

B.H.Food Products Pvt. Ltd.
2113-14, Khari Baoli
Delhi - 110006
Ph. 091-11-2942429

Bajaj Sons
290 Bank Enclave,Laxmi Nagar
New Delhi - 110092
Ph. 2245882,2455133
Saffron

Bawa Masala Company
G-6 Lawrance Road
Industrial Area
Delhi - 110035
Ph. 7185288
Powdered Splces

Bharat Massala Co. (Regd).
A-736, Shastri Nagar
Delhi - 110052
Ph. 7537812

C.L.Food Industries
Najaf Garh,Delhi - 110043
Ph. 5566596, 5190651

Chander Parkesh & Co.
7150 Beri Wala Bagh
Azad Market, Delhi - 110006
Ph. 2929702
Black Pepper Cardamom (S) Ginger Dry, Turmeric Dry, Coriender Seed

Chilco Enterprises
C-25 Ist Floor, NDSE Part-I
Delhi - 110049
Black Pepper, Cardamom (L)
Chilli Dry, Ginger Dry, Turmeric Dry

Dish Life Industries
370, Chirag Delhi
Delhi - 110017
Ph. 6430720

Docman Laboratories
B-3/50, Ashok Vihar
Phase -II
New Delhi - 110052
Ph. 7240200
Curry Masala, Chilli Dry
Black Pepper

East-West Trading Company
B-153, F.F.C.C., 1 GNOU Road
Neb Sarai
Delhi - 110068
Ph. 6517093, 6517084
Allied Products, Floor Covering
Handicrafts, Spices Handlooms

Enowgule & Co. Ltd.
4th Floor, Allahabad Bank
Building 17, Sansed Marg
New Delhi - 110001
Ph. 310227

Export Lyans
B-23, Ansal Chambers -II
6, Bhikaji Cama Place
New Delhi - 110006
Coffee, Handicrafts, Spices, Tea, Tabacco

Fun Foods Pvt. Ltd.
B-2/17, Shopping Centre
Safderjang Enclave
New Delhi-110029
Ph. 091-11-6106567, 6185940

Goel & Goals Exports
DB-59F, Hari Nagar
New Delhi - 110064
Ph. 5142353
Curry Powder, Curry Masala Pepper Powder Chilli Powder, Cumin Powder,

Gokul Overseas
8/32, Kriti Nagar, Industrial Area
New Delhi - 110015
Ph. 531375

Gopal Enterprises (India) Regd.
P.O. Box No. 8511
New Delhi - 110052
Ph. 7248860, 7411703
Fruits, Pluses

H.B.S. Marketing Services (Regd.)
256, Tegore Park, Model Town
Delhi - 110009
Ph. 7218091

Hamant Kumar
B-7/ Extn. -31,
Ground Floor, Safdarjung Enclave
New Delhi - 110029
Ph. 6885807
Black Pepper, Chilli Dry Ginger Dry, Coriender Seed, Cumin White

Hari Ram & Sons
412, Katra Maidgran
Khari Baoli, Delhi-110006
Ph. 2529878, 2927407
Black Pepper, Ginger Dry,

Coriender Seed, Cumin White Ani Seed

J.C. International
E-503, Narwana Apptt.
I.P. Extension
New Delhi - 110092
Ph. 2220167

Jain Exports
Pocket-A , 15-B Sukhdav Vihar
New Delhi - 110036
Ph. 6832722

Jindal Aromatics
110, Babar Road
Opp. World Trade Center
New Delhi - 110001
Ph. 3719800
Essential Oil, Plastic Goods Spices, Textile, Cosmetics

K.V. Spices (India)
526, Lahori Gate,
Delhi - 110006
Ph. 3956103 (Brand : Sahiba)

Kanchan Masala Co.
E-2/245, Shastri Nagar
Dehli - 110052
Ph. 7775765

Keshri Haldi Company
C-30/4, Lawrence Road
New Delhi - 110035
Ph. 2928304, 2528304

Khaitan Exports
A/3. Asaf All Road, 3rd Floor
Delhi- 110002
Ph. 3278729, 3281482
Cardamom (L) Ginger Fresh Ginger Dry

Mahashian Di-Hatti Pvt. Ltd.,
680, Khari Baoli
New Delhi - 110006
Ph. 3928717
Brand : M.D.H)

Madan Sons
103 Ist Floor
Katra Tobacco, Khari Baoli
Delhi - 110006
Ph. 2526939
Ajwan Seed, Coriander Seed Cumin White, Ajwan Seed Ginger Dry

Janak Chand Aggarwal & Sons
103 Katra Tobacco, Khari Baoli
Delhi - 110006
Ph. 2514377, 2526939
Turmeric Dry Corinder Seed Cumin White, Ajwan Seed Ginger Dry

Janak Chand Sandeep Kumar
44 Katra Tobacco, Khari Baoli
Delhi - 110006
Ph. 2914305, 2526939
Turmeric Dry. Coriender Seed Cumin White, Ajwan Seed, Ginger Dry

National Spice & Detiy Drates
Khasra No. 1110, Gali No-18
Plot No. Fimi Road Village
Rithala, Delhi-110085
Ph. 2935477, 2932594
Lal Mirch , Chana Powder, Kali Mirch, Garam Masala Powder. Meat Masala

Nav Bharat Trading Co
39-A Gadodia Market, Khari Baoli
Delhi - 110006
Ph. 238180, 2942799
Chilli Dry

Nonand Rai Bhola Nath
6691, Khari Baoli,
Delhi - 110006 Ph. 3958525
www.nonandraibholanath.com

New Janta Masala Company
1/6359, Netaji Stadium,
Gandhi Nagar, Delhi-110031
Ph. 2143253

Om Mahashakti Namah
D-175, DDA Flats,Jhilmil Colony
New Delhi - 110095
Ph. 2161351
Cardamom (L) Powder

Om Parkash Ashok Kumar
494, Katra Ishwar Bhawan
Khari Baoli, Delhi - 110006
Ph. 239297

Omega & Omega
2880, Sirki Walan, Hauz Kazi
New Delhi - 110006
Ph. 3283870

Pink City Manufacturing Aganoy
C-24, Shakti Nagar Extension
New Delhi - 110052
Ph. 7212640
Herbal Spices, Saffrm Resomery, Asafoction, Curry Powder

Sanjay Salt Suppliers
A-3, Saral Pipal Thalla Extn.
Azad Pur, Delhi - 110033
Ph. 7119543

Sarvettam Exports
1606, Dr. Mukherjee Nagar
Outram Line
Delhi-110009
Ph. 7422120

Shabha Exports Inc.
2017, Bank Street
Karol Bagh
New Delhi - 110005
Ph. 5767687
Saffron

Shiva Industries
A-72, Group Industrial Area
Delhi - 110052
Ph. 7234261, 7134416
Coriender Seed, Cumin White Fennel Seed, Fonugreck Seed Ani Seed

Shri Lilanand Trading Co.
5180, Lahori Gate
Ist Floor Naya Bazar
Delhi - 110006
Ph. 3018427, 7212640
Hrerbal Spices, Rosemary Saffron Asafoetida, Curry powder

Shubh International
42-B Hanuman Lane First Floor
Connaught Place
New Delhi - 110001
Ph. 3346750. 3346751

Shudh Foods
D-13, Gulmohar Park (Basement)
New Delhi - 110049
Ph. 091-11-6965361
Onion Paste Grary Mix

Star Spices/Masale
3-B,Gopi Nath Market, Khari Baoli
Delhi-110006
Ph. 3952935 Fax : 3934267
Curry Powder

Suri Exports
2/205, Ashish Complex
New Rajdhani Enclave Vikes Marg
New Delhi - 110092
Ph. 2243821, 2243822
Spices

Swadeshi Grain Crushing Mill
105, Keshav Ji Naik Road
Chinch, Bunder
New Delhi - 110009
Ph. 3764693

Traus India International Ltd.
2318, Laxmi Naral N. Street
Pahar Ganj
Delhi - 110055
Ph. 523566

Umesh & Co.
14-B, Gadodia Market, Khari Baoli
Delhi - 110006
Ph. 3926181

Vikas Hybrida & Electornics Ltd.
Exports House B-378
New Friends Colony
New Delhi - 110065
Ph. 6848402, 6835493

Vitasta Exports
85, Kailash Hills
New Delhi - 110065
Ph. 6849788
Saffron Lacha Mongra

Well Brines Chemical Pvt. Ltd
E-95/1, Viender Nagar
Janak Puri Marg
New Delhi - 110058
Ph. 5330304

Westfield Flora Pvt. Ltd.
1521, Devika Tower
6, Nehru Place
New Delhi - 110019
Ph. 6429123
Chilli Dry, Coriander Seed, Cumin White, Fenugreck Seed, Ani Seed

Devarshi Exports
3/33, Adarsh Nagar, Naranpure
Ahmedabad - 380013 (Gujarat)
Ph. 7477758
Cumin White

Grower Intertrade Ltd.
504, Golden Triangle Building
S.P. Stadium Road
Ahmedabed -380014 (Gujarat)
Ph. 465292, 407018
Coriander Seed, Fennel Seed Fenugreck Seed, Mustard, Seed Chilli Dry

Madhur Food Products Ltd.
Madhur Complex, 3rd Floor,
Stadium Cross Road
Ahmedabad-380009 (Gujarat)
Ph. 6563423, 6563422
Chilli Dry, Turmeric Dry Coriender Seed, Cumin White, Black Pepper

Ramdev Exports
Ramdav House, 1097, Madhupura
Opp. Delhi Gate
Ahmedabad-380004 (Gujarat)
Ph. 337022, 337033
Chilli Dry/Powder, Turmeric Dry Coriander Seed, Cumin White/ Powder Garlic.

Shri Jay Enterprises Pvt. Ltd.
Jai Hind Building, Ashram Road
Nr. Gujarat Chember of Commerce
Ahmedabad - 380009 (Gujarat)
Ph. 441734, 6562051
Chilli Dry. Garlic Cumin White, Garlic Dry, Turmeric Dry

Subh Food Improvers Ltd.
Klassic Chambers
Nr. Swastik Cross Road
Navrangpura
Ahmedabad - 380009 (Gujarat)
Ph. 445015, 445091
Cumin White, Fennel Seed Coriender Seed, Ajwan Seed Dill Seed

Vishal Fertilizers
Opp Ankur Travels
Nr. S.T. Stand
Ahmedabad -380002 (Gujarat)
Ph. 2143321, 6635893

Amrut Basic Foods
B-38, Adarsh Nagar
Kamala Nagar Complex, Ajwa Road
Baroda-19 (Gujarat)
Curry Masala

Gujrat Co-Op Onion Growers Fed. Ltd.
1172, Gangotri, Meghani Marg
Ambawadi, Bhavanagar
Bhavnagar-364001 (Gujarat)
Ph. 22289
Garlic Fenugreck Seed Coriander Seed Chilli

Hemant International
Plot No-1/13,Ramdev Nagar
Opp. S.T. Work Shop Chitra
Bhavnagar-364003 (Gujarat)
Chilli Dry. Garlic Cumin White

Gujrat Food Products
Feeder Road
Bilimora -396380 (Gujarat)
Chilli Dry, Garlic Cumin White

Mitesh Trading Company
37/3 Delsar Chakaliya Road
Dahod-389151 (Gujarat)
Agricultural Prod. Pulses Chemical & Allied, Food Grains

Miltop Exports
Milan, 2 Kamdar Colony
Jam Nagar - 361006 (Gujarat)
Ph. 62900, 72900
Carry Powder Canned Vegetable ProcessedFoods, Gutka, Uncoked Snascks

Gujrat Castors Pvt. Ltd.
11-GHB, Commercial Complex
Ranjit Nagar
Jamnagar-361005 (Gujarat)
Ph. 552785
Chilli Dry, Cumin White Mustard Seed Fenugreak Seed, Fennel Seed

Indran Exporters
C-1-17, GIDC
Nadlad-387001 (Gujarat)
Ph. 50917, 50103
Chilli Powder Turmeric Powder Other Spices NES

International Exporters
C/O G.R. Spices
Marida Road, Near Sports Complex
Nadiad -387001 (Gujarat)
Ph. 24191, 51012
Turmeric Powder, Chilli Powder Coriender Powder Curry Massla

B.R & Company
A/52, Marketing Yard
Rajkot-360003 (Gujarat)
Ph. 456182, 456685
Jeera, Souff, Isabgol

Ish Export
4, Vrundevan, Opp. R.K.Ashram
Dr. Yagnik Road
Rajkot -360001 (Gujarat)

Khedut Solvex Pvt. Ltd
Rajkot Jilla Sangh
Gundala Road P.B.No.39
Rajkot -360002 (Gujarat)
Ph. 20204, 20826
Oils Spices Processed Seeds-All Type De-oil Cake

Shubh Exports
2nd Floor, Coins Comer
Dr. Yagink Road
Rajkot -360001 (Gujarat)
Ph. 43069

Vish International
12 Vijay Plot
Rajkot 360002 (Gujarat)
Ph. 64796, 64152
Chilli Dry, Turmeric Dry Coriender Seed. Cumin White Fenugreck Seed

Raj Hiagro Food Intustries Ltd.
Plot No.5529, Road No- 55
Opp. Amar Jyot,GIDC Sachin
Surat - 395003 (Gujarat)
Ph. 870227 , 870180
Curry Masala

G.T.Traders
Gange Ram Tribhovan Dass
140, Golai Met Yard, P.B.No.63
Unjha -630003 (Gujarat)
Ph. 56640, 56642
Seame Seeds Spices Isabgul

Kantilal Pransukhra & Co.
99, Market Yard
Unjha -384170 (Gujarat)
Ph. 53892, 55195
Cumin White Fennel Seed Fenugreck Seed

Patel Parshattambhai Vithalbhai & Co.
16, Ganj Bazar
Unjha 384170 (Gujarat)
Ph. 53892, 55195
Cumin White, Fennel Seed Fenugreck Seed

Shah Kirti Kumar Chhota Lal & Co.
Market Yard
Unjha -384170 (Gujarat)
Ph. 53273, 53721
Cumin Seed, Coriender Seed Fennel Seed Ani Seed Ajwan Seed

Vinod Kumar Pradip Kumar
18 New Ganj Bazar

Unjha - 384170 (Gujarat)
Ph. 52651,54851
Cumin White Fennel Seed
Fungreck Seed

Dhirubhi Dayaljibhai Patal
Ghej Village, Valand Faliya Street
Atgam (VIA) Chikli Taluk
Valsed-396045 (Gujarat)
Mint

Mayur Masala Industrial
Nanheda
Ambala - 133004 (Haryana)
Ph. 643074, 23129
Garam Masala Chana Masala Chat Masala Hing Jaljeera

Bansi Dhar Bajranj Lal
127, Gaushala Market
Bhiwani -125021 (Haryana)
Ph. 43617
Chilli Dry Turmeric Dry Coriender Seed Cumin White Dill Seed

Shivam Masala Udyog
O-5 Industrial Area
Sonepat -131001 (Haryana)
Ph. 41278, 42038
Curry Masala Turmeric Powder Coriender Powder, Chilli Powder Black Powder

Welcome Thinners & Chemical Agency
38, Industrial Estate,Digiana
Jammu- 180010 (JK)
Ph. 20300, 20497
Saffron, Chilli Dry Ginger Dry Pomegranate Seed

Kesar King
The Kings Residence,Kadalbal
Pampore -192121 (JK)
Saffron, Herbal Spices
Lecha Mogra Style, Stamon

Mahavir Saffron Centre
H.O. Pampur
Pampur-192121 (JK)
Ph. 86229, 86559
Saffron

Adimely Spices
Kallarkutty Road, Dt. Idukki
Adimaly -685561 (Kerala)
Black Pepper, Ginger Dry Turmeric Dry

Antony K. Thomas
Kuzhivila Puthanveedu
Pashampalli Chal
Padikapu P.O. Adimati, Dt. Idukki
Adimaly -685561 (Kerala)
Ph. 200 PP
Dehy Green Pepper, Chilli Dry White Pepper, Black Pepper Cardamom (S)

C.V.M. Spices
N.H. Road, Dt- Idukki
Adimaly -685561 (Kerala)
Ph. 22849
Black Pepper Ginger Dry Turmeric Dry

Devicolam Taluk Genreal Mkt. Corp.
No. 1-150, Kallarkutty Road
Dt. Idukki
Adimaly -685561 (Kerala)
Ph. 22404,22115
Black Pepper

Jayabharat Spices
Kallarkutty Road, Dt- Idukki
Adimaly -685561 (Kerala)
Ph. 22635
Black Pepper, Ginger Dry Turmeric

K.M.Kunju Mehammed
Kallarkutty Road, Dt-Idukki
Adimaly- 685561 (Kerala)
Ph. 22307
Ginger Dry Turmeric Dry Black Pepper

Kalapurayu Cardamom Traders
N.H. Road, Dt-Idukki
Adimaly -685561 (Kerala)
Ph 32649
Cardamom (S)

Rocky
Library Road, Dt-Idukki
Adimaly -685561 (Kerala)
Ph. 22989
Cardamom (S)

Southern Spices
Kallarkutty Road, Dt-Idukki
Adimaly -685561 (Kerala)
Ginger Dry, Turmeric Dry Black Pepper

Spices Trading Co.
N.H.Road Dt-Idukki
Adimely-685561 (Kerala)
Ph. 22140
Cardamom (S)

V.G. Eldo
Kallarkutty Road. Dt-Idukki
Adimaly-685561 (Kerala)
Ph. 22465
Turmeric Dry, Ginger Dry, Black Pepper

Verghese Cherian
N.H.Road Dt- Idukki
Adimaly -685561 (Kerala)
Ph. 22141
Cardamom (S)

Kairali Foods
Nadumon P.O., Ezhamkalam
Adoor-691556 (Kerala)
Ph. 442145
Chilli Powder, Coriender Powder Turmeric Powder, Pepper Powder Cardamom (S)

Thayil Agencies
Kalarcode, Allappey-673003 (Kerala)
Ph. 62269
Black Pepper Cardamom (S)
Ginger Fresh Clave

S.K. Traders
12/221, Halwa Bazar
Calicut -673001 (Kerala)
Ph. 60451
Tamarind

Al. Madni Exports
7.645, Fatima Building, Jew Town
Cochin-682002 (Kerala)
Ph. 230817
Black Pepper Ginger Dry
Cardamom (S) Chilli Dry, Turmeric Dry

Alex Mathow
Vazhayil Nestie, B.M.C. Post
Thrikkakkara
Cochin -682021 (Kerala)
Ph. 424892
Cardamom (S) Black Pepper

Impro Exim Co. Ltd.
6/671, Bazar Road
Cochin -682002 (Kerala)
Ph. 227475
Black Peppor Curry Powder Ginger Dry

Jifs. Pvt. Ltd.
40/6839 Nirmal Jyoti Complex
Kanakkatnara Lane
Convent Road Shonoys Junction
Dt-Emakulam
Cochin-682035 (Kerala)
Ph. 373078
Black Pepper Cardamom (S)
Ginger Dry, Turmeric Dry, Trmarind

Khatai Agro Food Pvt. Ltd
Khataimahal VR. Menon Rood
RaiPuram
Cochin-682016 (Kerala)

Kishore Spices Company
P.B.No.262 VI/37 Jew Town
Cochin 682002 (Kerala)
Ph. 225111

Krishna & Company
2/59, Calvetty
Cochin-682002 (Kerala)
Ph. 24175, 24001

Mas Enterprises Ltd.
CC/34/2367 F
First Floor, Mangatt Road
Manangalam
Cochin-682025 (Kerala)
Ph. 345119, 348899

Black Pepper, Cardamom (S) Clave

Mawjee Kanji & Co.
CC/VIII/2152, New Road
Cochin-682002 (Kerala)
Ph. 28734,25805
Chilli Red (Indin), Fennel Seed Coriander Seed

Nirmal Kumar & Co.
6/1296, Kottukulam Road
Cochin -682002 (Kerala)
Ph. 226617, 225953
Ginger Dry Black Pepper White Pepper Turmeric Dry, Nutmeg

South India Produce Company
PB-No.24, Jew Town
Cochin -682002 (Kerala)
Ph. 224628
Spices

Team Paarel
44/2270 Main Road, Kaloor
Cochin 682017 (Kerala)
Ph. 332177
Spices

Vanitha Floor Mills
Bazar Road, Mattancherr
Cochin -682002 (Kerala)
Ph. 223206, 228024
Black Pepper Cardamom (S)
Chilli Dry Ginger Dry Turmeric Dry

Thomas George
Fincon, Brokers Chember
Morninagstar Building
Ist Floor, Dt-Cochin
Kacheripady-682018 (Kerala)
Ph.366493, 366508
Black Pepper Turmeric Dry Ginger Dry Cardamom (S)

A.M. Vasu & Co.
Main Road, Kalady
Dt-Ernakulam
Kalady -683574 (Kerala)
Ph. 2351
Nutmeg Mace

Pottokaran Agencies
M.G.Road, Dt-Kalady (Ernakulam)
Kalady-683574 (Kerala)
Ph. 2541
Nutmeg Mace

Victus Jose
Chittinapilly, Chengal
Dt-Ernakulam
Kalady-683574 (Kerala)
Ph. 468306,468386
Chilli Powder Coriender Powder Turmeric Powder Curry Powder

Hajee P.M.K. Sons
Kattakada, Dt-Trivandrum
Kattakada (Kerala)
Ph. 325
Black Pepper Dhey Grem Pepper Clove Ginger Dry

Hassainar & Bros.
A.M.Road, Dt-Ernakulam
Kayamgulam -686691 (Kerla)
Ginger Dry Turmeric Dry

C.M.Marakkar
Kettapady, Dt-Ernakulam
Kettapady-686695 (Kerala)
Ph. 543347
Ginger Dry Turmeric Dry

M.M. Nagalinga Nadar Sons (P) Ltd.
Post Box No. 329
Chinnakkada AndaMukkom
Kollam -691001 (Kerala)
Ph. 77944, 77994
Curry Powder

Benny & Caria
Kozhipilly, Kothamongalam
Dt-Ernakulam
Kothamangalam-636691 (Kerala)
Ph. 522779
Ginger Dry. Turmeric Dry

Joseph Kunju Kunju
Koloth House, Vettambara
Kulankatukuzh, Dt-Ernakulam
Kothamangalam - 686691 (Kerala)
Ginger Dry

K.P. George
A.M.Road, Dt-Ernakulam
Kothamangalam - 686691 (Kerala)
Ph. 522435
Black Pepper Ginger Dry Turmeric Dry

A. A. Abubacker
Kettapady, Dt-Ernakulam
Kottapady-686695 (Kerala)
Ph. 543347
Ginger Dry, Turmeric Dry

C.M. Verghese
Kottapady, Dt-Ernakulam
Kottapady - 686695 (Kerala)
Ginger Dry, Turmeric Dry

C. N. Gopi
Aroorpadem PO, Dt-Ernakulam
Kottapady-686114 (Kerala)
Ginger Dry, Turmeric Dry

Philip C. Vettiyil.
Vettiyil, Vakathanam P.O.
Kottayam - 686114 (Kerala)
Ph. 462463
Ginger Fresh

Token Masala Works
Puthlya Veedu, Olessa P.O.
Kottayam - 68114 (Kerala)
Turmeric POWDER Curry Masala

Davis Jose & Bros.
Ground Floor
Municipal Office Building
Dt-Ernakulam
Kulady -683574 (Kerala)
Ph. 2660
Nutmeg, Mace

Kurian & Kurian
K.K. Road, Dt-Idukki
Kulady-685509 (Kerala)
Ph. 22264
Cardamom (S)

Kurian Varughese
Palakal, Chackupallom
Dt-Idukki
Kumily-685509 (Kerla)
Black Pepper

Navgothi Traders
K.K. Road
Kumily - 685509 (Kerala)
Ph. 22132,22264
Cardamom (S)

E.G. Bose
Nedungapara,Kurumpampady (VIA)
Dt-Ernakulam
Kurumpampady (Kerala)
Ginger Dry, Turmeric Dry

P.C. Kora
Manathur P.O., Dt-Ernakulam
Kuthattukulam (Kerala)
Ph. 375
Ginger Dry, Turmeric Dry

St. George Rubber & Spices Dealer
Vettimood Junction
Kakkoor P.O., Dt-Ernakulam
Kuthattukulam (Kerala)
Ph. 513
Black Pepper, Ginger Dry Turmeric Dry

T.V. Chacko
Ramapuram Jun, Dt-Ernakulam
Kuthattukulam (Kerala)
Ph. 375
Ginger Dry, Turmeric Dry

Wilson Paul
Thazhakat Puthussery House
Kunnukara P.O.
Kuttipuzha Chengamanad VIA
Dt- Ernakulam
Kuttipuzha (Kerala)
Ph. 478166
Nutmeg

Baby Sabastin
Market Road, Muvatupuzha
Dt-Ernakulam
Muvattupuzha - 686661(Kerala)
Ph. 232438
Black Pepper Ginger Dry Turmeric Dry

Muvattapuzha Traders
Market Road
Muvvattupuzha (Kerala)
Ph. 233206
Black Pepper Ginger Dry Turmeric Dry

Jagdish K.Nair
P.O. Box No. 26,Dt-Ernakulam
N.Parur -683515 (Kerala)
Ph. 443514
Black Pepper Ginger Dry Turmeric Dry

Nedu Manged Taluk Mkt. Coop. Soc.
Dt-Travandrum
Nedumanged -695541 (Kerala)
Ph. 812302
Black Pepper Clave

C.V. Narayanan
Chitralayam, Fort Ward
Neyyattinkara-695121(Kerala)
Ph. 222021
Ginger Fresh

Suresh Kumar S.
Suresh Mandiram, Chunkathara
Oyur P.O., Dt-Quillon
Oyar-691510 (Kerala)
Ph. 466180
Black Popper Ginger Dry Ginger Fresh Tamarind

K. Gopinath
Alakananda
Ayodhanagar Nagar Morey College
Pallipuram P.O.
Pallakkad - 6 (Kerala)
Ph. 538731
Black Pepper Cardamom (S) Clave, Ginger Dry, Turmeric Dry

K.V. Paulose & Sons
A.M. Road,
Dt-Ernakulam Parumbavur (Kerala)
Ph. 22203
Black Pepper Ginger Dry Turmeric Dry

Enjayes Spices & Chemcal Oil (P) Ltd.
Aban Towers Pattanamthita
Pattanamthita - 689645 (Kerala)
Ph. 324095, 324995
Curry Powder Paste, Seed Oil, Foods

Avukadarkutly & Bros.
A.M.Road, Perumbavur
Dt-Emakuram Perumbavur (Kerala)
Black Pepper Ginger Dry Turmeric Dry

P.M. Paulose & Sons
A.M.Road, Dt-Ernakulam
Perumbavur (Kerala)
Black Pepper, Ginger, Dry Turmeic

Pappachan & Bros.
P.P. Road, Dt-Ernakulam
Perumbavur (Kerala)
Black Pepper Ginger Dry Turmeric Dry

Shaji P.P.
A.M. Road, Dt-Ernakulam
Perumbavur (Kerala)
Black Pepper Ginger Dry Turmeric Dry

Koovappady Gen.Mkt. Proc. Coop. Ltd.
Iringolo P.O., Pattal
Dt- Ernakulam
Perumpavur (Kerala)
Black Pepper, Ginger Dry, Turmeric Dry

Cherry Mercontelu Products
K.K. Road, Ponkunnam
Dt-Kottayam
Ponkunnam (Kerala)
Ph. 721332
Black Pepper, Ginger Dry, Turmeric Dry

Excel Trading Co.
K.K. Road, Dt- Kettayam
Ponkunnam (Kerala)
Black Pepper, Ginger Dry, Turmeric Dry

Kerala Trading Co.
K.K. Road, Dt-Kottayam
Ponkunnam (Kerala)
Ph. 721339
Black Pepper Ginger Dry Turmeric Dry

Ponkunnam Marketing Corp. Soc.
K.K. Road, Dt-Kottayam
Ponkurinam (Kerala)
Ph. 721233
Black Pepper

K. K. Ebraham
Plamadi P.O., Kottapady
Dt-Ernakulam
Pottapady (Kerala)
Ph. 543347
Ginger Dry Turmeric Dry

Divya Export Enterprises
Pattathanam, Post Box No. 201
Quilon - 691001 (Kerala)
Ph. 77749, 79007
Cashew Kernels Cashews

Tenrose Exports Ltd.
39/3586 M.G.Road, Dt-Cochin
Ravipuram-682016 (Kerala)
Ph. 362738, 364887
Curry Powder

C.H.& Brotherle Spices
LIC Building, Main Road
Dt-Wynad
Sultan Bathery - 673592 (Kerala)
Ph. 20786
Black Pepper ,Ginger, Fresh Ginger Dry, Turmeric Dry

Quality Food Products
Cheppenool,
Taliparamba - 670141 (Kerala)
Ph. 202805 , 203314
Chilli Powder Turmeric Powder Coriander Powder Pepper Powder, Curry Masala

Santosh Kurian T.
Thekkanath House
Kandassan Kadavu
Thrissur - 680613 (Kerala)
Ph. 631097
Ginger Fresh Ginger Dry Turmaeri Dry Black Pepper Cardamom (S)

Modi Pharma
14/146, Panachery Lane
Koorkenchery
Trichur - 680007 (Kerala)
Ph . 26968, 23742
Black Pepper Cardamom (S) Chilli Dry Turmeric Dry Coriender Seed

Jeevan George
A-11, Jawahar Nagar
Trivandurm (Kerala)
Ph. 61755, 64009,
Cardamom (S) Black Pepper Clave

M. Abdul Majeed
Nadumangad, Trivandrum (Kerala)
Ph. 61755, 64009
Cardamom (S), Black Pepper Clave

M. Nazzar
Nadumangad, Trivandrum (Kerala)
Ph. 812451
Black Pepper

Oasis Exporters
35/1698 Vallkkadayu
Trivandrum - 695008 (Kerala)
Ph. 091-0471451056
Fresh Fruits Rice Fresh Vegetable

Radhakrishanan A.
Krishna Vilasam, Puthumanglam
Mulakkalatukave-P.O.
Dt-Thattathumala
Trivandrum - 695614 (Kerala)
Black Pepper Ginger Dry Turmeric Dry, Cardamom (S) & (L) Clave Mace

Mountain Spices Ltd.
Dt-Idukki
Vandanmedu - 685551 (Kerala)
Ph. 77141
Cardamom (S)

E. M. Gandhi
Chandara Vilasam Mali, Dt-Idukki

Vandanmettu - 685551 (Kerala)
Ph. 77141
Cardamom (S)

Mas Enterprises Ltd.
Mas Junction, Dt-Idukki
Vandanmettu - 585551 (Kerala)
Ph. 77077, 77099
Cardamom (S)

Sunil Joseph
C/O E.V. Joseph
Ernakulam House, Dt - Cochin
Vyttila -682019 (Kerala)
Black Pepper Ginger Fresh

Vijayalakshmi Estate
Dt- Coorg
Balele -571219 (Karnataka)
Ph. 2007
Black Pepper Cardamom (S)

General Commodities Ltd.
39, Cunningham Road Cross
Bangalore -560052 (Karnataka)
Ph.2268687
Jute Goods, Spices

K.C.Somashekara Raddy
C/o. M.M. Jayappa
No.434, 1st Main Domlur Post
Bangalore -560071 (Karnataka)
Tamarind

Maharaja Dry Fruits & Condiments
No. 27 Krishna
Rajendra Road Opp. Asha Kiran
Apartments Basavangudi
Bangalore - 560004 (Karnataka)
Ph. 6614911
Curry Masala

P.R. Cmltiations
18/2, Sarakki Village
P.B. No. 7809
Bangalore - 560078 (Karnataka)
Ph. 6643430
Vanilla Black Pepper Cardamom (S)
Chilli Dry, Ginger Dry

S.Prashanth
H.No. 500/1 Jagdish Nagar
Thippasandhra
Bangalore - 5271776 (Karnataka)
Ph. 5271776
Turmeric Dry Giner Dry Ginger Fresh

Sarasathi Enterprises
No.29-Raja Ram Mohan Ral Raod
Bangalore -27 (Karnataka)
Ph. 2226271
Tamarind

Suraj Exports Pvt. Ltd.
84, IIIrd Cross Ist Main
New Timber Yard Layout Majson Road G.E.F. (P.O)
Bangalore - 560026 (Karnataka)
Ph. 6618055
Coriender Seed, Fenugreek Seed
Mustard Seed

Jayashankar C.T.
23, Basav Colony, Nehru Nagar
Belgaum 590010 (Karnataka)
Garlic Tamerind

Klas Spices
Srilak Industries
B-72 Angol Industrial Estate
Udyambag
Belgaum - 590008 (Karnataka)
Ph. 32232
Curry Powder

J.J.Patel
Byadig - 581106 (Karnataka)
Ph. 58214, 58535
Dry Red Tamarind

R. G. Patic & Co.
Byadgi, Dt-Dharwad
Byadig -581106 (Karnataka)
Ph. 88315, 88515
Chilli Dry Curry Powder

Spices Board India
P.B. No 2277
Palarivattom Po
Cochin -682025 (Karnataka)
Ph. 333610, 333616

Sandesh R. Karj
Sadeshev Nagar,Old Jewargi Road
Near P & T Quarters
Gulbarga-585102 (Karnataka)
Ph. 28564
Chilli Dry

A.J. Patvegar & Co.
Haveri, Haveri -581110 (Karnataka)
Ph. 33054, 32598
Cardamom (S)

Raman Lal Kapur Chand Shah
Dt-Dharwad
Haveri -581110 (Karnataka)
Ph. 32431
Cardamom (S)

S.V. Ankalkoh & Sons
Dt-Dharwad, Haveri - 581110
Ph. 32515, 33012
Cardamom (S), Black Pepper Chilli Dry

Shah Tarachand Jasraj & Co.
Dt- Dharwad, Haveri -581110
Ph. 32425
Cardamom (S)

Sri Lakshmi Narsimaha Masala Powder
Uttaradhi Mutt Street
Fort Holenaraslpur, Dt- Hassan
Holenarasipur - 573211 (Karnataka)
Curry Masala, Turmeric Powder

S. K. S. Raveendra
Attgeri Post, Dt- Dharwad
Hulgur -581126 (Karnataka)
Chilli Dry, Coriender Seed, Garlic, Tamarind

Abirami Spices
Muthoor Tiruvalla,
Kerala - 689107 (Karnataka)
Ph.22288

Green Deal
Kohinoor Road
Madikeri -571201 (Karnataka)
Ph. 29151, 26278
Black Pepper

Mahanad Enterprises
Mahadevpet
Madikeri - 571201 (Karnataka)
Ph. 26877
Black Pepper

Meenakshi Cardamom Agency
Main Road
Madikeri - 571201 (Karnataka)
Ph. 26441, 29401
Cardamom (S), Black Pepper

Vijaya Traders
5-126-2, Mahadevepet
Madikeri - 571201 (Karnataka)
Ph. 26756
Cardamom (S), Coorg Green

Bannimantap Multipurpose Coopsoc.
No. 139, MIG
Bannimantap Extension, HUDCO
Mysore- 570015 (Karnataka)
Tamarind, Chilli Dry

H.R.Home Products Ltd.
No. 343 New Layout, N.M. Mohalla
Mysore (Karnataka)
Chilli Dry Ginger Dry Garlic
Tamarind, Tumeric Dry

Vimaca Trading Co.
K.K. Road Ponkunnam
Dt- Kottayam
Ponkunnam (Karnataka)
Ph. 721322, 721283
Black Pepper Ginger Dry Turmeric Dry

Ambika Cardamom Co.
Saklespur- 573134 (Karnataka)
Ph. 44045
Cardamom Black Pepper

Chandraprabhu Spices
ZB.M.Road, Saklespur-573134 (KR)
Ph. 44543, 44109
Cardamom (S), Black Pepper

Hukmi Chand & Co.
Saklespur - 573134 (Karnataka)
Ph. 44023, 44773
Cardamom (S), Black Pepper

Tulasi Trading Co.
Saklespur (Karnataka)
Ph. 44033, 44773
Cardamom (S), Black Pepper

Vardhman Cardamom Co.
B.M. Road, Dt-Hassan
Saklespur- 573134
(Karnataka)
Ph. 441187 , 44938
Cardamom (S), Black Pepper

Smt. T.N.Mangla
W/O S.Ramachandra Reddy
Maruthi Nilaya
Kundalalgurki Sidlaghartta
Dt-Kolar, Sidlaghata - 562105
Tamarind Chilli Dry Coriander Seed, Ginger Fresh

Narasinh Ganapati Hegde Bhairi
Bastigalli, Dt-North Konara
Sirsi 572103 (Karnataka)
Ph. 75151, 76851
Black Pepper Cardamom (S)

Subhas Danderi
No. 81. Amareshwar
Parmesiticales 1st Floor
IIIrd Main New Tharagpupet
Dt- Bangalore
Tharagupet- 560002 (KR)
Chilli Dry Tamarind

G.A. Sreenivasa Selty
A.P.M.C. Yard, Batawadi
Tumkur -572103 (Karnataka)
Ph. 880064 , 78229
Tamarind

N.G. Sivanna & Sons
A.P.M.C. Yard, Batawadi
Tumkur- 572103 (Karnataka)
Ph. 880990
Chilli Dry Chilli Powder
Tamarind

Atul Kumar Thakarisi
Opp. Newaskar Petrol Pump.
Station Road
Ahmednagar - 414001(M.S)
Ph. 23748
Tamarind

Soil & Water Conservation
Aizawal (M.S)
Ph. 23635
Ginger Fresh & Dry, chilli Dry Turmeric

Jagvijay Enterprises
Ganesh Peth Wasim
Akola- 444505 (M.S)
Ph. 32792
Chilli Dry Ankur Chilli Powder Garlic Swela G-41, Tamarind, Mustard Seed

Khaemchandani Group
New Complex Jaistamph Chowk
Amravati - 444601 (M.S)
Ph. 678788, 672895
Chilli Dry Tamarind

Bright Enterprices
No-2 Sunlta Manisha Colony
Behind Session Court
Aurangabad (M.S)
Ph. 26644, 26741
Chilli Dry, Turmeric Dry Cumin White Garlic, Ginger Dry

Hare Krishan International Export
Raigad, Shivaji Coop HSG
Society Tulsi Ram Nagar
Deopar Dhule - 424002 (M.S)
Agro Products, Spices, General Goods

Manes Food Industries
Commerce Corner, 211763
Dhulia - 424001 (M.S)
Ph. 22907, 22807
Chilli Dry Turmeric Dry Tamerind, Ginger Dry Ginger Fresh

Shri Arihant Paddy Processors
Jai Stambha Square
Gondia -441601 (M.S)
Ph. 22740, 24760
Tamarind

Soni Agro Industries
Hingoli Plot Not-B 5/2
6,7 MIDC Limbala,Parabhanl (Makta)
Hingoli - 431513 (M.S)
Ph. 22057, 22041
Turmeric Powder

Gopal Pulse Processors Pvt. Ltd.
E/48. MIDC P.B. No 31
Jalgaon-425003 (M.S)
Ph. 5708, 6262
Pulses

J.K. Dall Mill
G-89, MIDC Ajanta Road
Jalgaon - 425003 (M.S)
Ph. 210404 , 210405

Sunanda Shelke
Rupali Krishi Faron
Forest Colony, Nandura Road
Dt-Buldona, Khamgam (M.S)
Chilli Dry, Ginger Frech Turmeric Dry, Coriender Seed, Garlic

Anjali Fruit & Vegetable
Post Box No-58, Dt-Ahmednagar
Kopargaon - 423601 (M.S)
Ph.70034
Tamarind Paste

Sukhendu Dutta
Bengalee Girls School Lane
Dt- Shillong
Laban -793004 (M.S)
Ph. 223735

Ginger Fresh Chilli Dry Mizoram

Ram Niwas Darak & Sons
Manasa -458110 (M.S)
Ph. 42061, 42006
Ajwan Seed Fenugreek Seed Dill Seed Coriander Seed

Amrita Export Pvt. Ltd.
118/122, Kazi Syed Street
Main Krip 4th Floor
Mumbai - 400003 (M.S)
Ph. 323777, 323629
Flower Dry Sesame Seed Black Ginger, Cardamom

Anam Overseas
510, Veena Chambers
4th Clive Bunder, Dana Bunder
Mumbai - 400009 (M.S)
Ph. 3769775
Spices

Arbee International
93/93-A, Ratan Manzil
Shop No. Kharatank Road
Mumbai - 400003 (M.S)
Spices

Askok Kumar Gouri Shankar
D-52 APMC Complex Market
Phase 2, Turbhe Vashi
Mumbai - 400705 (M.S)
Ph. 7655368
Turmeric Dry Chilli Dry Fennel Seed Dill Seed Tamarind

Atlantic Exports
Unit No -111, 1st Floor
A-2 Shah & Nahar Indl. Estate
Lower Parel (West)
Mumbai - 400013 (M.S)
Ph. 4932087, 4932092

Bhagwan Das Bherumal & Co.
20/E Sita Ram Building
Crow Ford Market
Mumbai - 400001 (M.S)
Ph. 3438955 , 3438956
Spices, Ginger

Bharat Kumar Jetha Lal & Co.
Gautam Udyog Bhawan
Gali No. 15, Behind L.B.S. Marg,
Bhandup West
Mumbai - 400078 (M.S)
Ph. 5680520

Biz World International
5/C Trisnla Building
122, Sheikh Memon ST.
Mumbai - 400002 (M.S)
PH. 2064494 , 2060662
Spices

Bombay Export House
338 Katha Bazar, 1st Floor
Mumbai - 400009 (M.S)
Ph. 3448697

Bombay Keshar Co.
208 Samuel Street, Ground Floor
Mumbai - 400003 (M.S)
Ph. 3423606, 3445697
Saffron (Lachha), Mogra

Bombay Kiryana Industries
204 Samuel Street, Vadgadi
Mumbai - 400003 (M.S)
Ph. 3427666
Black Pepper Coriender Seed
Cumin White Cardamom (S) & (L),
Fennel Seed

CNJ Packaging Industries
P.O. Box. No. 5043
Mumbai - 400009 (M.S)
Ph. 2612656
Turmeric Powder, Chilli Powder
Cumin Powder, Pepper Powder,
Ginger Powder

Chagan Lal Kalidas Mehta
293, Samll Street, IInd Floor
Mumbai - 400003 (M.S)
Ph. 3422898, 3411248
Turmeric Dry ,Coriander Seed,
Ajwan Seed, Fengreck Seed,
Cumin White

Chanakya Enterprises
157, Sonawala
Bldg No. 2 Tardeo Circle
Mumbai - 400007 (M.S)
Ph. 3086000, 3087356
Coriender Powder, Cumin Powder
Chilli Powder Curry Masala

Chiman Lal Sanlay Kumar
4th Floor, Bhagwan Bhawan
196, Samuel Street
Mumbai - 400009 (M.S)
Ph. 3759850

Commodity Impax
328/330, Samuel Street
Karsan Nath Building
Mumbai - 400003 (M.S)
Ph. 3448876, 3448877
Oilseeds Spices

Coroonation Agro Ind. Ltd.
Yogeshwar Building No. 112,
135/139, Kazi Syed Street
Mumbai - 400003 (M.S)
Ph. 3451181, 3451182
Spices

D.C.W. Home Product Ltd.
Plot No.86, Mehta Estate
S.Mathura Das, Vassanji Road
Andheri (East), Mumbai - 400093
Ph. 8351602

D.L. Tanumal Pvt. Ltd.
280, L.T. Marg, Ram Chardra
Building 2nd Floor,
P.B. 24098, Kalabadevi
Mumbai - 400002 (M.S)
Ph. 2083249 , 2066599
Spice

Dalal Mangal Das Kursandas
103, Swah House
70, Kazi Syed Street
Mumbai - 400003 (M.S)
Ph. 3437593, 3446877
Coriander Seed, Celery Seed,
Cumin White, Chilli Dry,Dill Seed

Davesh International
110, Bora Bazar, 2nd Floor
Mumbai - 400001 (M.S)
Ph. 2613795, 2622971
Spices

Dharni Spices
1/2, Sadanwadi
Lake Road Bhandup (W)
Mumbai - 400078 (M.S)
Ph. 5676463
Black Pepper Nutmeg Curry
Powder Cardamom (S)&(L) Chilli

Dhiraj Lal Mangal Das & Co.
121/127 Kazi Sayed Street
Mandvi Navjivan Building,
Basement - A
Mumbai - 400003 (M.S)
Ph. 3445156, 3438811
Turmeric Powder Chilli Powder
Chilli Dry Curry Powder Cumin
White

Dilip Brothers
D/9 APMC Market-I Phase II
Mumbai - 400705 (M.S)
Ph. 7666077
Chilli Dry 54,56, Bird Eye Coriander
Seed Ajwan Seed

Dolatram Tikam Dass
F-45/46 A P M C Market
Phase-II Vashi Mumbai - 400705
Ph. 3427656

Exim Link
7, Karsha Natha Building
328/30, Samuel Street.
Mumbai - 400003 (M.S)
Ph. 339412
Pulses, Spices Oil-seeds

Gandhi Co.
66/68 Kundan Mans First Floor
Kazi Syed Street
Mumbai - 400003 (M.S)
Ph. 3448657

Gausia Eoports Enterprises
133, Kazi Syed Street.
5th Floor Guru Krupa P.B.No.3168
Mumbai - 400003 (M.S)
Ph. 322749, 344282
Spices

Gautam Export corporation
506 Surat Sadan, Surat Street
Mumbai - 400009 (M.S)
Ph. 3769258, 3738751
Seeds, Spice Powder

Gautam Shah
51/11 Bibijan Street
Mumbai - 400009 (M.S)
Ph. 3412875, 3436509
Chilli Powder Turmeric Powder

Geeitlager (India) Ltd.
Manu Mansion 3rd Floor
16-S, Bharat Singh Road
Mumbai - 400023 (M.S)
Ph. 2662609

Global Exports
Paras Darshan
Ground Floor M.G.Road
Ghatkopar (E) Mumbai - 400077
Ph. 5115590, 5115591
Cardamom (S) Black Pepper Chilli
Powder

Gran Heal Pharma Ltd,
401-402 Vimal Apartments
Opp. Patel Petrol Pump
S.V. Road Goregaon (W)
Mumbai - 400062 (M.S)
Ph. 8756612 , 8756613
Turmeric Dry Cardamom (S)&(L)
Cinnamon Rosemary, Tryme
Oregano

Gum Export Corporation
P.B.No. 3117
202, Nav Jivan Building
125, Kazi Syed Street
Mumbai - 400003 (M.S)
Ph. 346549, 332978
Spices

Hansilia
C-4 Satyam Shopping Center
M.G.Road Ghathopar (East)
Mumbai - 400077 (M.S)
Curry Powder Paste Foods

Haria Export Ltd.
Haria Center,
8 Subhash Road Vile Parle East
Mumbai - 400057 (M.S)
Ph. 8388886, 8688887

Hathi Bhai Bulakhi Dass
86, Masjid Bunder Road
Mumbai- 400003 (M.S)
Ph. 8553327, 8552136
Oils Seeds

Hemani Eximp Corporation
86 Masjid Bunder Road
Mumbai - 400003 (M.S)
Ph. 8553327 85552136
Oils Seeds

J. Harkishan Das & Company
M-I Goradia House
104, Kaji Syed Street

Mumbai - 400001 (M.S)
Ph. 2619182, 2615538
Spices

J.K.H. Exports
B-62, APMC, Complex Market-I
Phase II Sector No. 19, Vashi
Mumbai - 400003 (M.S)
Ph. 672315, 672317

Jairam Dass Khushi Ram
312, Central Facility
BLD, APMC Market Phase -II
Sector-19 Vashi
Mumbai - 400705 (M.S)
Ph. 7665618, 7653178

Jamna Das Preji & Co.
Sugar House
93/95, Kazi Syed Street
Mumbai - 400003 (M.S)
Ph. 3425823 , 3421933
Turmeric Dry

Jatin & Company
10, Ashoka Building, Ground Floor
541-C,H, Adenwala Road Matunga
(CR), Mumbai- 400003 (M.S)
Ph. 4147258, 4111594
Spices, Oil Seeds

Jetha Lal Nemchand
D Black Shop No-16-17-18,
APMC House Phase-II
Market -I Vashi Turbhe
Mumbai - 400705 (M.S)
Ph. 7666737 , 7660547
Chilli Dry

Jitesh Jethalal & Co.
D/9 APMC Market -I
Phase -II Vashi, Mumbai - 400705
Ph. 766077-7666076
Chilli Dry Coriander Seed Chilli Fresh

Kanmore Foods Ltd.
Kannore House
281/87, Narsinatha Street
Mumbai - 400009 (M.S)
Ph. 3758701, 3758702

Kay Cee Exports
106/107 Dalamal Chambors
29, New Marin Lines
Mumbai - 400020 (M.S)
Ph, 2008141, 2008142

Khimasia Traders
28, Kazi Syed Street, Masjid
Mumbai - 400003 (M.S)
Ph. 3449745

Krishna Impex
28, Kazi Syed Hill Road.
Purusarth Building Dongri
Mumbai - 400009 (M.S)
Ph. 3426110, 2763404

Krystal Colloids
119, Navroji Hill Road.
Purusarth Building Dongri
Mumbai - 400009 (M.S)
Ph. 3726110 2763404

Kusum Chandra Damodar
58, Mudi Bazar, Mandvi
Mumbai - 400003 (M.S)
Ph. 3421901 , 3449283
Curry Powder Curry Masala

Kusum Chandra Damodar & Co.
MIDC Plot A-21
PAWNE Khairne Village
Mumbai - 400705 (M.S)
Ph. 7632328, 7632329
Chilli Powder, Turmeric Powder, Coriander Powder, Curry Powder, Pepper Powder

Kusum Masala Pvt Ltd.
T.11 Kumsum House Cama Estate
Goregaon (East)
Mumbai - 400063 (M.S)
Ph. 3759894, 3758347
Curry Masala Curry Powder

Lakhamsi Ghellbhai & Company
505, Church Gate Chambers,
5 New Marine Lines
Mumbai - 400020 (M.S)
Ph. 2625077, 2625078

Laljee Godhoo & Co.
213 Samuel Street
Mumbai - 400003 (M.S)

Laxmi Chand Dayabhai Export Co.
512/16, Rewa Chamber 5th Floor
31, New Marine Lines
Mumbai - 400020 (M.S)
Ph. 201473, 2014266
Food Ingredients, Chemical

Laxmi Enterprises
170/72, Samuel Street
Mumbai - 400009 (M.S)
Ph. 3780151, 3755825

Lovson Commercial Agencies
98 Bajaj Bhawan 9th Floor
Nariman Point, Mumbai - 400021
Ph. 2024071, 3755825

Luxmi Masala Co.
1st Floor Shop. No. 18
105 Keshav Ji Road
Mumbai - 400009 (M.S)
Ph. 3760650

M. Motilal Masalawala
157, Sonawala Building No-2
Tardco Circle, Mumbai - 400007
Ph. 3086000, 3087356
Curry Masala

M.S.International
9/9 ,D. Kastur Mahal Sion
Mumbai - 400022 (M.S)
Ph. 4078320, 4074567
Spices (Whole of Ground)

Mahalaxmi Enterprises
14/15 Dalamal Central
7/18 Worli Surface
Mumbai - 400018 (M.S)
Ph. 4926542

Mahim Masala Mills
140/Sitladeni Indl. Central
Behind Victoria Church
Muhim, Mumbai - 400016 (M.S)
Ph, 4458904 , 6640380
Curry Powder

Mansuk Lal Bros.
Mumbai Mutual
Annox 10/17 , Rustom Sidhwa
Marg Fort, Mumbai - 400001 (MH)
Ph. 2664392

Matra Co. India Ltd.
163-C, Mittal Tower
Nariman Point, Mumbai - 400021
Ph. 2875507, 2875598

Matru Shree Developers Pvt. Ltd
161/B, Mittal Towar
Nariman Point, Mumbai - 400021
Ph. 2852247, 2852248
Chemicals Spices

Modi Associates
101/201, Doli Chamb
Strand Cinema Comp
A Buder Road Colaba
Mumbai - 400002 (M.S)

Mukesh Kumar & Co.
D-5 APMC Market -I
Vashi, Mumbai - 400705 (M.S)
Ph. 7666501
Coriender Seed, PGP,

N.V. Jhadhav
7-8 Central Bank Building
4th Floor, Bruce Street
Mumbai - 400001 (M.S)
Ph. 442343
Chilli Dry, Ginger Dry Fresh Coriander Seed Cumin White, Garlic

Napro Industries
509, Marine Chambers
11, New Marine Lines
Mumbai - 400020 (M.S)
Ph. 2054416 , 2022602
Chilli Dry

Narendra Kumar & Co.
177/179 Nand Ashish
R.B. Mehta Marg
Ghatkoper (East)
Mumbai - 400077 (M.S)
Ph. 5132367, 5113017
Curry Masala Powder, Pepper Powder, Ginger Powder, Cumin

Nehul Export
5 th Avasar Building
70/81, Kazi Syed Street
Post Box Bo. 3054
Mumbai - 400003 (M.S)
Ph. 3493353, 3415707

New Bharat Enterprises
Giyani Court, 263-265, M.A. Road
Off No. 5 Two Tanks
Mumbai - 400008 (M.S)
Ph. 3075875
Chemicals & Allied, Products

Novelties Exports
3/161, Abhyadaya
Nagar Cottongreen
Mumbai - 400033 (M.S)
Ph. 4138651
Chilli Dry, Ginger Dry

P.B. Khamkar & Sons
107, Aharv, 3rd Floor
4th Road Hindu Colony, Dadar
Mumbai - 400014 (M.S)
Curry Powder Chilli Powder
Turmeric Powder Coriander Powder

Panchsheel Trading Co.
G-28, APMC Market -I
Phase-II Vashi, Mumbai - 400705
Ph. 7653353, 7666501
Black Pepper, Safron, Cumin White
Fennel Seed, Ginger Dry

Pravin Chandra Jetha Lal & Company
506 Raigor Chamber Masjid Bandra
Mumbai - 400009 (M.S)
Ph. 3762801

R.C. Shah & Co.
D-1APMC Market - I
Kirana Market Phase- II, Turbe
Mumbai - 400705 (M.S)
Ph. 7662134 , 7666501
Coriander Seed, Fennel Seed

Ramachandra B. Prabhu
2 Datta Niwas, Aarey Road
Goregaon (E)
Mumbai - 400063 (M.S)
Ph. 8747144
Tamarind, Kokam

Ridhi Sidhi Export Corporation
2nd Floor, 12/13
35, Nithaldas Road
Mumbai - 400002 (M.S)
Ph. 20086270

Royal Masala & Exporters Pvt. Ltd.
D-60 APMC Market Vashi
Mumbai - 4000705 (M.S)
Ph. 7665062 , 7662091
Chilli Powder Turmeric Powder
Coriander Powder Curry Powder

S.D. Bakhal & Company
201 Sharda Chambers
15, New Marine Line
Mumbai - 400020 (M.S)
Ph. 2004625 , 2007306

S.V.A. India Ltd.
162-C Mittal Tower, Nariman Point
Mumbai - 400021 (M.S)
Ph. 2830444, 2830455

Sahjanand Enterprises Pvt. Ltd.
142, Panjrapole Road
Mumbai - 400004 (M.S)
Ph. 8552916, 8557262

Samrat Presentations
132/4 Kambeker Street
Mumbai - 400003 (M.S)
Ph. 3741165, 3741166

Sanjiv Kumar Dhanji
3, Chinch Bunder
Mumbai - 400009 (M.S)
Ph. 8727944, 324167

Sat Kamal Exports
98, Kazi Sayad Street
P.B.No. 3431
Mumbai - 400005 (M.S)
Ph. 349098, 324167

Schokhi Industrial Pvt. Ltd.
21, West View 1st Pasta Lene
Colaba, Mumbai - 400005
Ph. 386150, 3868255

Seascope Exports
158/33, Laxmi Industrial Estate
New Link Road Andheri West
Mumbai - 400053 (M.S)
Ph. 6338484 , 6338485

Seeba Exporters
12/47, Yash Want Nagar
Gore Gaon West
Mumbai - 400062 (M.S)
Ph. 6722880 , 6727890

Shashikant & Co.
APMC Market,Shop No.- D-60
Sector -19, Vashi
Mumbai (M.S)
Ph. 7665062
Chilli Dry

Shashvat Gum Industries
155, Jain Society Man Galam
3rd Floor Sion West
Mumbai - 400022 (M.S)
Ph. 4071343,3437777

Sonen Impex
2- Pestom Sarag
Opp-Konica Studio Pllokhande Marg
Mumbai - 400089 (M.S)
Ph. 5561525
Food Processed

Sopariwal Exports
Nirmal P.O.B.No. 9992
21st Floor Nariman Point
Mumbai - 400021 (M.S)
Ph. 2852324
Spices Oil Seed

Spice Exopo House
213, Andamji Building
2nd Floor 413 Narshi Natha
St. Katha Bazar
Mumbai - 400069 (M.S)
Ph. 3422388
Spice

Sidop & Company
5 Lajya Estate Mogra
Road Andheri (East)
Mumbai - 400069 (M.S)
Ph. 8390684, 8390686
Spices

Surendary & Company
18.20 Kazi Sayed Street
Mumbai - 400009 (M.S)
Ph. 8551644 , 8551509

Tech. Know Consultants
B/138 Ghatkoper
Industrial Estate Off. LBS Marg
Ghatkopar, Mumbai - 400086
Ph. 5171842, 5170632
Rosemary Thyme Orengano
Tarragon

The Great Eastern Shipping Co. Ltd.
Hongkong Bank Building
60, M.G. Road
Mumbai - 400001 (M.S)
Ph. 2674869
Spices

Tpi India Ltd.
102, Atlanta Loth Floor
Nariman Point, Mumbai - 400021
Ph. 2873087, 2873088
Spices

Trade Wings International
85/91 Mota Mandir Lane
3rd Bhalwada, Bhuleshwar
Mumbai - 400009 (M.S)
Ph. 3740732, 3740733
Chilli Powder Coriander Powder
Turmeric Powder Cumin Powder
Curry Powder

Trishul Exports
2c, Thakkar Indl. Estate
3rd Floor N.M. Joshi Marg
Lower Parel (E)
Mumbai - 400011 (M.S)
Ph. 3098458,3078178
Spices

Uniexim Ltd.
218, Karsannatha Building
320 Samuel Street

Mumbai - 400003 (M.S)
Ph. 3400270 , 3449281
Spices Pluses

Urmila & Sushma Associates
105, Veena Beena
Opp. Bandra Rly. Station
Mumbai - 400050 (M.S)
Ph. 6260281
Curry Masala

V. N. Thakkar Hingwala & Sons
71, Yusuf Meharalli Road
Majid Bunder
Mumbai - 400003 (M.S)
Ph. 3445110 , 3449930
Asafoodila

Vidi Exports Pvt. Ltd.
20-A Vatsa House Janmabhoomi
Marg Fort, Mumbai - 400001
Ph. 2872173, 2018611

Akshay Exports
7th Floor Tapasya
42, Shivaji Nagar
Nagpur - 440010 (M.S)
Ph. 533523, 523352
Coriander Seed, Chilli Dry
Turmeric Dry, Fenugreck Seed,
Fennel Seed

Arun Madhusudan Bhope
Bhope s House
Near Shriram Mandir
Mangalwari Petty
Nagpur - 441203 (M.S)
Ph. 42548
Chilli Dry

Integrated Markoter & Associate
11, Snehnagar, Wardha Road
Nagpur - 15 (M.S)
Ph. 220095, 720670
Chilli Dry Coriander Seed
Fenugreek Seed , Mustard Seed

Shree Ganesh Food Products
55, Chikhali Industrial Area
Kalamana, Nagpur - 440008 (M.S)
Ph. 781661, 780728
Chilli Powder Turmeric Powder
Coriander Powder Curry Powdor

Jain Industries
Market Yard, Dt-Dhulia
Nandurbar - 425412 (M.S)

Mahender Kumar Bhurabhai & Co.
P.B.No. 35, Market Yard
Nandurbar - 425412 (M.S)

Grapon Foods Pvt. Ltd
Savitri, M.G.Road, Malegaon
Nasik - 423202 (M.S)
Ph. 431240
Dehy. Green Chilli Ginger Dry
Dehy. Garlic Flakes, Cinnamon

Padam Chettri
C/o. Nehru Momorial Sec. School
Umsning, Dt-Ri-Bhoi
Nayabangalow - 793105 (M.S)
Ginger Fresh

A-1 Food Products
10 MIT Corner, Koregaon Park
Pune - 411001 (M.S)
Ph. 6306992, 638203
Herbal

Deelip Godes
Sector-21, Scheme- 9
19/11 Yamunanagar
Nigdi Pradhikaran, Pune - 44 (M.S)
Ph. 772290
Garlic

Nav Maharashtra hakan Oil Mills
Nav Maharashtra House
P.O.Box. No. 571
43, Shaniwar Peth
Pune - 411030 (M.S)
Ph. 212 454450, 454451
Processed Pulses,

Parsi Food Products
Khorshed Lodge, Block No. 2
2414, Fast Street
Pune - 411001 (M.S)
Ph. 648570
Curry PowderMasala, Chilli Powder
Turmeric Powder, Coriander
Powder, Cumin Powder

Fondu Agro
Pawas, Ratnagiri - 412612 (M.S)
Ph. 37263
Kokam Tamarind

Gomati Mills
J-3 MIDC Kupwad Black
Sangli - 412612 (M.S)
Ph. 73870, 76523
Turmeric Dry, Turmeric Powder

Nemani Trading Corporation
Room No-19, Haldi Bhawan
Vakhar Bhag, Sangli - 416416 (M.S)
Ph. 73870, 3400586
Turmeric Dry, Turmeric Powder

Patel Brothers
P.B.No. 178, Mahavir Nagar
Sangli - 416416 (M.S)
Ph. 351162, 77008
Turmeric Dry, Turmeric Powder

Patel Manor Bhai Joitaram
P.B.No - 11.T, Vakhar Bhag
Sangli - 416416 (M.S)
Ph. 77008, 351162
Turmeric Dry

Purushottam Sadanand Dalvi
Arawali, Vengurla
Sindhudurg - 416t518 (M.S)
Ph. 67278

Kokam

Amin Enterprises
102, Modikhana
Shop. No. 2 Meera Apartment
Solapur - 430001 (M.S)
Chilli Dry, Ginger Fresh
Garlic Tamarind, Coriander Seed

Hingmire Trading Company
Market Yard, Dt-Sangli
Tasgaon - 416312 (M.S)
Ph. 40110, 40105
Kismish, Haldi Mirch

Dhana Lakshmi Traders
Sector- 9/C-53/003, Shanti Nagar
Mira Road E, Thane - 401107 (M.S)
Ph. 8115750
Coriander Seed

Ulhas Trade Centre
406, Radha Place, OT Section
Ulhasnagar - 421003 (M.S)
Ph. 556248
Chillli Dry, Ginger Dry, Mustard
Seed, Garlic, Tamarind

Indian Forest Food Industries
Khatri Mansion, Inside Fort
Vidisha - 464001
Ph. 30714
Tamarind Paste

Farm & Forest Pdt. (Surguja)
Ramanuj Ganj Road
Ambikapur - 497001 (M.P)
Ph. 21322, 20666
Ginger Dry, Turmeric Dry, Garlic,
Mustard Seed, Ani Seed

Vinay Tayalji
Sadar Road,Nr. Jayastham Chowk
Dt- Sargooja
Ambikapur - 497001 (M.P)
Ph. 22279
Garlic, Tamarind, Ginger Fresh,
Mustard Seed

Badri Prased Rekhraj
Near Sati Mandir
Dt-Bhatapara (Ralpur)
Bhatapara - 493118 (M.P)
Ph. 21382
Ani Seed

K.K. Masala Prod. Gram Udyog
C/o. Shri Chandra Bhushan
Mishra Jabra Bhushan
Mishra Jabara Road
Street No.3, Bilaspur-490001 (M.P)
Curry Masala, Turmeric Powder,
Dehy. Garlic Powder, Coriander
Powder

Khatri Masala Products
8, 1/A, Industrial Estate
Sirgitti, Bilaspur - 495001 (M.P)
Ph. 23936

Turmeric Powder Chilli Powder
Coriander Powder Curry Powder

Re Acto India
Azad Nagar, Sarjoo Bagicha
Bilaspur - 495001 (M.P)
Ph. 22972, 22198
Tamarind, Rosemary, Thyme
Oregano, Tarragon

Prem Ayurvedic Pharmacy
Tamrahi Mohalla, Chatarpur (M.P)
Coriender Seed, Chilli Dry Ginger

N.S. Sikarwar
60, Sawarkar Marg, Dhar - 454001
Ph. 32566
Chilli Dry, Tamarind

Chetna Masala Udyog
Dt-Raigad, Gadumariya - 496004
Ginger Fresh

Agrawal & Co.
6 Piyu Complex, Laxmi Ganj
Guna - 473001 (M.P)
Ph. 55446,54846
Coriender Powder Curry Powder
Cumin White Fenugreck Seed,
Coriander Seed

Manish & Company
Laxmi Ganj, Guna - 473001 (M.P)
Ph. 56232, 54061
Coriander Seed

Pradeep & Co.
Laxmi Ganj, Guna (M.P)
Ph. 52513, 54513
Coriander Seed

Himalayan Export Mkt. Allied Service
Lohia Bazar, Gwalior - 474001 (M.P)
Ph. 321320
Tamarind, Ginger Fresh,
Asafoetida, Mint, Coriander Seed

Jethalal Nem Chand & Sons
77m, Ushaganj Main, Road Chhawni
Indore - 452031 (M.P)
Ph. 463267, 466536
Chilli Dry, Turmeric Powder,
Dehy. Garlic Powder, Coriander
Seed, Chilli Powder

Mohan Lal Mishri Lal & Sons
8/2 Murai Mohalla,Post Box No. 169
Sanyogita Ganj, Indore - 452001
Ph. 464083, 462408
Chilli Dry

Reliance Corporation
20/8, Yeshwant Niwas Road
Indore - 452003 (M.P)
Ph. 430599, 432864
Chilli Dry, Coriander Seed Frugreck
Seed, dill Seed Cumin White

Prasanth Kumar Rajput
266/1 Near Nagar Nigam
Karyashala, Jabalpur - 482001
Ph. 324673
Ginger Fresh Gralic, Coriander
Seed

Samir Kumar Pal
C/o. Anand Bhandar
Nagar Negam Chowk
Jabalpur - 482001 (M.P)
Ph. 26613, 25377
Mustard Seed, Coriander Seed

Shyam Kumar Shrivastva
1925, Defence Colony
South Civil Lines, Jabalpur (M.P)
Ph. 323031
Coriander Seed, Chilli Dry

Valabh Fruit Processing Unit
7, Arihant Kripa
Co-op Bank Colony,Dt- West Nimar
Khargone - 457001 (M.P)
Ph. 20007
Ginger Dry, Chilli Dry

Mangal Brothers
Payga Street, Dt-Guna
Kumbhraj - 473222 (M.P)
Ph. 43340
Coriander Seed

Kumar Brothers
Sadar Bazar, Mandla - 481661 (M.P)
Mustard Seed, Garlic, Tamarind,
Ginger Dry, Ginger Fresh

Garlico
9/1 Industrial Estate
Mandsaur - 458001 (M.P)
Ph. 53129, 52156
Fenugreck Seed, Coriander Seed
Dill Seed, Ajwan Seed

Kamal Kr. Namichand Kothari
Kothari Bhawan, Jewa Ganj
Mandsaur - 458002 (M.P)
Ph. 52934
Poppy Seed, Ajwan Seed
Fenugreck Seed, Coriander Seed

Ravi Traders
Nai Abadi, Mandsaur- 458001 (M.P)
Ph. 45471, 53230
Fenugreck Seed, Coriander Seed

Sardar Harbhajan Singh
Phuwara Chowk
Manendragarh - 497442 (M.P)
Ph. 52383
Tamarind Mustard Seed

R.N.Ganchi
Shreeram Balm
Udeslya Sahkari-Samiti Ltd.
C/o. Ram Cutplece Centece Centre
Sindhi, Dt-Bazar Marwar Junction
Marwar Junction - 306001 (M.P)

Mustard Seed Cumin White
Fenugreck Seed, Ajwan Seed, Chilli

Rathi Oil Ltd.
Industrial Area, A.B.Road
Morena (M.P)
Ph. 37232, 37295
Mustard Seed Curry Powder

Dr. Raj Thakur
Purani Basti, Ward No. 11
Dt-Mandla
Nainpur - 481766 (M.P)
Ph. 40046
Fenugreck Seed, Mustard Seed

Bafna Traders
Mandi Area, Neemuch (M.P)
Ph. 21582

Hajari Lal Radha Krishan & Sons
29, Station Road
Neemuch - 458411 (M.P)
Ph. 21509
Coriander Seed, Ajwan Seed
Fenugreck Seed, Dill Seed, Poppy
Seed (White)

Raj & Company
Dushera Maidan
Neemuch - 458441 (M.P)
Ph. 21600
Coriander Seed Fenugreck Seed
Cumin Fennel Seed Celery Seed

Saraogi Brothers
Jain Colony, Neemuch (M.P)
Ph. 20298
Garlic

Una Impax
Union Orthoprodic
Hospital Complex
Bungalow - No. 49 Kamal Chowk
Neemuch - 458441 (M.P)
Ph. 21672,21671
Cumin White, Mustard Seed
Coriander Seed, Dehy Garlic
Flakes, Dehy. Garlic Powder

Riddhi Cottage Industries
Krishna Bhawan
Pateratole Pendra Road
Dt- Bilaspur
Pendra Road - 495117 (M.P)
Ph. 435152
Garlic Tamarind Chilli Dry, Coriander
Seed, Fenugeck Seed

Dhananjay Foods Pvt. Ltd.
Plot No- 608, Sector No - 3
Pithampur - 454774 (M.P)
Ph. 435152
Garlic Tamarind,Chilli Dry Coriander
Seed, Fenugreck Seed

Unity Agro Farm
Ring Road No. 2, Industrial Area
Raipur - 493221 (M.P)

Turmeric Dry, Ginger Dry
Ginger Fresh Garlic

Naresh Saklocha
Nandi Grih, 7, Gopal Nagar
Sagad Road, Ratlam - 457001(M.P)
Ph. 31448, 31376
Chilli Dry, Ginger Dry, Cumin
White Fenen Seed Coriander Seed

Shakti Enterprises
PWD/LA-58, Labour
Tenament Industrial Estate
Rourkela - 769004 (M.P)
Chilli Dry, Turmeric Dry,
Mustard, Seed Tamarind

Sunil Kumar
12, Ashok Road
Dr. Satna Singh's Compound
Sagar Kanth - 470001 (M.P)
Ph. 23416
Tamarind

Natural Rural Rosource Resinst
Vangaon Har, Orchha
Tikamgarh - 472247 (M.P)
Ginger Dry Ginger Powder

Mizo. Spices Growers & Mkt. Corp. Soc.
CentOrary Building, Dt- Aizawal
Dawrpui - 796001 (MZ)
Ph. 22742
Ginger Fresh & Dry , Chilli Dry
Turmeric Dry

Cooky Feed Products
Badapandusar, Dt-Nayagarh
Badapandusar - 752068 (Orissa)
Curry Powder Chilli Powder
Turmeric Powder

Smt. Kadambini Das
C/o. D.Das
Akhuapada, Badarak (Orissa)
Chilli Dry, Mustard, Seed

Annapurna Cottage Industry
Neeladari Vihar
4th Lane Tulsi Nagar
Behrampur - 760001 (Orissa)
Ph. 200092
Curry Powder

Dilip Kumar Padhy
Nehrunagar - 9
Behrampur (Orissa)
Turmeric Dry

G.P. Patnaik
Plot. No. 605, Road-8, Unit-9
Bhubaneshwar (Orissa)
Ph. 412282
Chilli, Dry Ginger Fresh

Sabyasachi Satpathi
C/o. 237 Bapuji Nagar
Bhubneshwar - 751009 (Orissa)
Ph. 432681

Chilly, Dry Ginger Fresh, Turmeric
Dry, Mustard Seed, Tamarind
Powder

Sararwati Udyog
Plot No. 312/2533
Baramunda, Bhubneshwar (Orissa)
Ginger Fresh Turmeric Dry

Tribal Dev Coop Corpn Of Orissa Ltd.
Bhubneshwar
Bhubneshwar - 751007 (Orissa)
Ph. 402530
Chilly, Dry Ginger Fresh, Turmeric
Dry, Tararind

Mr. Gopinath Panda
Nayak Street, Dt-Rayagada
Bikrampur - 764062 (Orissa)
Ph. 06857
Turmeric, Dry Chilli, Dry Tamarind,
Curry Powder

Santosh Kumar Mohanty
Kalidas Asuraswar
Cuttack - 754209 (Orissa)
Cordamom (L) Black Peper
Asafodita, Dove, Ginger Fresh
Garli

Trimurty Exporting Agency
Akshya Kumar Mishra
Dlv Of Agri Statistics & Economi
Central Rice Research Institut
Cuttack - 753006 (Orissa)
Ph. 21480
Saffron Chilli Dry, Clove

Orissa Agro Exports Ltd.
Muktadupur Sassan
P.O. Box No-12
Dhankanal 759001 (Orissa)
Chilli, Dry Ginger Fresh, Turmeric
Dry, Coriandir Seed, Mustard Seed

Sunil Kumar Pradhan
Siddharth Nagar
Medical Campus Behrampur
Gangam (Orissa)
Turmeric Dry Ginger Fresh
Mustard Seed

Krishna Murty & Co.
Plot No 77 Phase II
New Industrial Estate, Dt-Cuttack
Jagatpur - 754021 (Orissa)
Ph. 682747
Turmeric Powder Chilli Powder
Cumin Powder Coriander Powder
Curry Powder

V. Laxmipathy Sons
Mill Street, Jaypore - 764001 (OR)
Ph. 22264 , 23260
Chilly, Dry Tamarind, Turmeric Dry
Cardomom (S), Black Paper

L.M. Foods Private Ltd.
Kahnupur- Jaipur Road, Dt- Jaipur
Kahnupur - 755019 (Orissa)
Ph. 06726, 20529
Chilli Dry Powder, TurmericPowder,
Curry Powder, Cardamom S & L,
Mustard Seed

Orissa Mushroom Fruits & Veg Pvt. Ltd.
Plot No. 2/A-B Janla Indl. Estate
Dt- Bhubneshwar
Khurda - 752054 (Orissa)
Ph. 450367
Ginger, Flankes & Pow, Turmeric
Dry Powder, Garlie Flakes

S.K. Food Indusries
Kar & SMS Avenue
At H.B. Colony Gurujanga
Khurda - 752055 (Orissa)
Ph. 20852, 20433
Turmeric Powder Chilli Powder
Coriender Powder, Curry Powder
Cumin White Corien

Ramarao Chaudhary
Pottangi, Koraput -764039 (Orissa)
Ph. 0685387
Ginger, Fresh Turmeric, Dry Curry
Powder, Garlic

Narendra Kumar Sahoo
Kosala Bazar, Dt- Angul
Kosala - 759130 (Orissa)
Ph. 80611
Chilli Dry

Samanwita Gramya Unnayan Samiti
Udayanagiri, Kandhamal
Phulbani - 762100 (Orissa)
Turmeric Dry Turmeric Powder

Grihalaxmi Udyog
Cinema Road, Rajrangpur
Dt- Sudargarh
Rajgangpur - 770017 (Orissa)
Ph. 20620
Turmeric Dry Coriander Seed Chilli
Dry Cumin White Black Pepper

Suvarna Industries
Sabulia 761036, Distt. Ganjam
Dt- Ganjam, Sabulia - 761036
Ph. 87312
Curry Powder, Masal, Turmeric
Powder, Chilly Dry

Mahamaya Training Foundation
Tagore Bhawan, Tulsipur
Dt-Cuttack, Tulsipur - 753008
Ph. 600041 , 602058
Chilli Dry, Turmeric Dry, Cumin
White, Curry Masala

Kamboj Sales Corporation
Krishan Nagar, Taran Taran Road
Amritsar (Punjab)

Ph. 282212 282665
Turmeric, Red Chilli, Curry Masala

Dalchand Mittal & Bros
15-16 Indl. Area, Ferozpura City
Ferozpura -152002 (Punjab)
Ph. 20051, 46247
Curry Powder, Chilly Powder, Turmeric Powder

Bombay Metal Works Pvt. Ltd.
703 Industrial Area -A
Ludhiana - 141003 (Punjab)
Spices

Mahajan Enterprises
145 - I Sarabhai Nagar
Ludhiana - 141001 (Punjab)
Ph. 459459, 451234
Asafoetida, Chilly Dry, Ginger Dry, Cumin, White Funnel Seed

The Mumbai Metal Works P. Ltd.
703 , Industrial Area A
Ludhiana - 141008 (Punjab)
Ph. 61702 , 61705

Ganesh Productions
D-53 Focal Point, Moga - 142001
Ph. 28813 , 28690
Garam Masala, Chana Masala, Chat Masala, Mirch Powder, Dhania Powder

Dipika Masala Udyog
Aaspur Post, Dt-Dungarpur
Aaspur (Rajasthan)

Agro Food Packs
Gali Batesi Wali, Kedar Ganj
Alwar- 301001 (Rajasthan)
Turmeric Powder, Coriander Powder Chilli Powder, Curry Powder, Curry Masala

Arvind Kumar Sekhawath
Thakur Muni Singh Sekhawat
Hajipur, Dt-Alwar, Bansoor - 301402
Chilli Dry, Coriender Seed, Cumin Fenugreek Seed, Mustard Seed

Narayan Lal Ram Goyal
Harnawda Shahji, Baran(Rajasthan)
Ph. 3027, 3027
Coriender Seed, Fenugreek Seed, Mustard Seed, Garlic

Shri Ram Oil & Flour Mill
Chhabra Gujar, Baran - 325220 (RJ)
Ph. 22114, 22031
Coriander Seed, Garlic

Natural Home Products
Somani Sadan, Pratap Talkies Road
Bhilwara - 311001 (Rajasthan)
Ph. 20109
Chilli Powder, Turmeric Powder, Coriender Powder, Curry Masala

P.K. Jain
15/15, Bhupal Ganj
Bhilwara - 311001 (Rajasthan)
Ph. 22929
Coriender Seed, Cumin White Fenugreek Seed, Mustard Seed

Esson Food Spices
Soor Sagar Bikaner - 334001 (RJ)
Ph. 527390
Chilly Dry & Powder Ginger, Dry Turmeric, Dry Powder, Coriender Seed, Pow Cumin White

Rajasthan Masala Trading Co.
Bada Bazar, Bikaner (Rajasthan)
Chilly Dry, Fresh P. Coriender Seed Coriender powder

Kamal and Company
K-10 Kumbha Nagar
Housing Board, Chittorgarh (RJ)
Ph. 40138
Garlic

Ramesh Chander Sharma
C/o. Shree Jagdish Chnader
Sharma Tailmagra, Dt-Rajasmand
Gilond Post - 313207 (Rajasthan)
Chilly Dry Cumini White Fenugrock Seed, Mustard Seed Garlie

Tula Ram Yadava
Via. Palsan, Udalpura
Dt- Sikar, Govind Pura-332402
Chilli Dry Cumini White Fenugreek Seed, Mustard Seed, Garlic

Narayan Lal Ram Gopal
Harnawada Shahji, Dt-Baran
Harnawda Shahji (Rajasthan)
Ph. 3027, 3037
Coriender Seed Fonugrock Seed Mustard Seed Garlie

Satya Narayan Marketing Co.
Station Road New Mandi
Hindaun City (Rajasthan)
Ph. 30447, 31134
Chilly Dry

B & B Exports
Bhandari Chambers, M.I.Road
Jaipur - 302001 (Rajasthan)
Ph. 361150
Turmeric Dry Coriander Seed Cumini White Finnel Seed, Fenugreek Seed

Balaji Sales Corp-Ltd.
43, Santosh Nagar
Ajmer Road, Jaipur-302001 (RJ)
Ph. 368118
Cardamom S&L, Coriander Seed Cumin White Black Papper Chilli Dry Ginger

Chhitramal Bhuramal Jain
B-30 Suraj Pole Mandi
Jaipur - 302006 (Rajasthan)
Ph. 602681, 608184
Cumini White Fennel Seed Coriander Seed Fenugrock Seed Ajwan Seed

G.L.G. Agriculture Pruducts
A/557,Govind Marg, Malviya Nagar
Jaipur - 302003 (Rajasthan)
Ph. 523186, 513757
Chilli Dry Coriander Seed Mustard Seed

Gopi Chand Sardar Mal & Sons
Special D-4 New Grain Mandi
Chandpole Bazar
Jaipur - 302003 (Rajasthan)
Ph. 378534, 361276
Coriander Seed Cumin White Fonugreek Seed, Ajwan Seed, Tamarinal Ginger

Heera Marala Udyog
1707, Near Gopi Nathji Temple
Purani Basti, Jaipur (Rajasthan)
Ph. 320152
Chilli Dry, Coriander Seed Turmeric dry

Krishi Vyawastha
366, Johari Bazar, Jaipur -302003
Ph. 560937, 563814
Coriander Seed Ferugrock Seed Mustard Seed

Madan Lal Malpani & Co.
Dinanath Street, Chandpole Bazar
Jaipur (Rajasthan)
Ph. 310197 , 310637
Turmeric Dry Powder Chilli Dry Powder, Coriander Seed

Rajasthan Fruits Proc. Ltd.
161, Vidyut Nagar B, Ajmer Road
Jaipur - 302019 (Rajasthan)
Ph. 303952, 352881
Coriender Seed, Cumini Seed Fenugrock Seed, Fennel Seed

Sand Gold India
G-20 City Centre, S.C.Road
Jaipur - 302001 (Rajasthan)
Ph. 85248
Chilli Dry Coriander Seed Cumin White Fennel Seed Fenugreek Seed

Shri Manglam Enterprises
B-24 Grain Mandi , Chandpole Bazar
Jaipur (Rajasthan)
Ph. 374485 , 367797
Cumin White Ajwan Seed Fenugreck Seed, Mustard Seed Fennel Seed

The Right Connection
National Industrial Building

Dhamani Street, Choura Rasta
Jaipur -302003 (Rajasthan)
Ph. 311033
Chilli Dry Ginger Dry Garlie Colony Seed Mustard Seed

Anupam Krishi
S-1 Subzi Mandi, Paota Chouraya
Jodhpur - 342006 (Rajasthan)
Ph. 45360, 45209
Chilly Dry Cumin White Garlie

Chaganlal Bhootada
Shamshar Kishorilal
Mani Bazar Mandore Road
Jodhpur - 342007 (Rajasthan)
Ph. 46330
Cumini White

Hi Choice Exports
H-43 Shastri Nagar, Jodhpur
Jodhpur 342003 (Rajasthan)
Ph. 33933
Chilli Powder

Jangid & Company
37, Subhash Nagar
Jodhpur -342008 (Rajasthan)
Ph. 41021, 42039
Chilly Dry Ginger Fresh Turmeric Dry Coriander Seed Cumin White

Jassaram
Bidg No. 273(A)
(Near Chaupasani School)
Hospital Road. Modi Nagar
Jodhpur (Rajasthan)
Ph. 39628
Cumin White Chilly Dry, Fennel Seed, Garlic

Keshri Impex
53, Nehru Park
Jodhpur - 342003 (Rajasthan)
Ph. 32738
Cumin White Fenugrock seed Coriander Seed Chilli Dry

Marwar Spices & Industries
G-35 Rlico Industrial Area
Marwar Mathania
Jodhpur (Rajasthan)
Ph. 383443, 621942,
Cumin Seed Fonnel Seed Dill Seed Coriander Sed Rad Chilli

Namdev & Co.
Bageria, Via Gopalgarh
Jodhpur- 342603 (Rajasthan)
Ph.86817
Cumini White Chilli Dry Coriander Seed Fonugrock Seed Garlie

Sincere Industries
Section Of Plot No. 36
New Power House Road
Jodhpur - 342003 (Rajasthan)
Ph. 26541
Chilli Dry Coriender Seed

Cumini White Fenugrock Seed Garlie

Sudhan Fashions
18/825 Nandawan, Chopasani Rd.
Jodhpur - 342008 (Rajasthan)
Ph. 36461, 540134
Ginger Dry & Fresh Turmeric Dry Coriander Seed Cumini White, Fenugrock Seed

Kedar Lal & Sons
Sadar Bazar, Dt-Ajmer
Kekkari - 305404 (Rajasthan)
Coriander Seed, Cumini White Garlic, Fungreek Seed

Ranjay Khandelwal
Shree Mahalakshmi Kirana Bhand
Sadar Bazar Kekkari, Dt- Ajmer
Kekkari (Rajasthan)
Ph. 20465, 20411
Chilly Dry, Ginger Fresh Coriender Seed Cumin Whito Mustard Seed

Aggarwal Brothers
Kherli, Dt-Alwer
Kherli - 321606 (Rajasthan)
Ph. 20046,20446

Rakesh Vijay & Sons
Chhipabaroad Post, Dt-Baran
Khhipapard Post - 325221
Ph. 4414
Garlie, Coriender Seed

Shree Ganesh Trading Co.
Madan Ganj, Kishan Garh
Dt-Ajmer
Kishan Garh - 305801 (Rajasthan)
Ph. 2245, 2273
Cumin White

Agro Forestry Divistion
Umesh Sadan Jhalawar Road
Kota (Rajasthan)
Mustard Powder, Corrender Seed

Gorwal Enterprises
F-9, H.W.P.Colony, Rawat Bhata
Kota - 323305 (Rajasthan)
Ph. 33092
Garlic,Coriender Seed

National Products
G -11, Opp. Multimetal Indl. Area
Kota - 324003
Ph. 436556
Chilli Powder Turmeric, Powder Coriender Powder Curry Powder Garlie Powder

Orient Spices India
Sivaji Market, Purani Dhanwandi
Kota - 324006
Ph. 23668
Coriender Seed, Turmeric Seed Chilli Dry Ajwan Seed Aniseed

Shree Ganesh Udyog
G-18A, Industrial Area
Kota (Rajasthan)
Turmeric Powder Chilli Powder Coriender Powder

Vyapar Doot
39 New Grain Mandi
Kota - 324007
Ph. 450212
Coriender Seed Coriender Powder

Raj Luxmi Spices (India)
H-1/23 To 26, Industrial Area
Mathania -342305 (Rajasthan)
Ph. 22062
Turmeric Powder Dr Chilli Powder Coriender Powder Cumin Powder White Fennel Seed Powder

Balkishan Bhauja
Pipli Gali, P.B.No . 21
Nagour - 341001 (Rajasthan)
Ph. 43343
Cumin white

Madhuvan Spices Growers & Suppliers
Krishna Kunj Lal Bhag
Dt-Nathdwara (Rajasamandi)
Nathdwara (Rajasthan)
Ph.30003
Chilly Dry Garlie Fonugrock Seed Mustard Seed Ajwan Seed

Shri Krishna Spices Suppliers
1st Floor Krishna Krishna Kunj
Lal Bagh, Dt- Raja Aaman
Nathdwara (Rajasthan)
Ph. 30003
Garlie Turmeric Dry Chilli Dry Ajwan Seed Mustard Seed

D.S. Enterprises
Tongya Bhawan, Bada Bazar
Dt-Tonk, Newai - 304021
Ph. 31012 , 31298
Chilli Powder Coriander Powder Turmeric Powder Cumin Powder Curry Masala

Gandhi Spices (India)
R-400, Mandia Road
Pali Marwar - 306401 (Rajasthan)
Ph. 31012, 31298
Chilli Powder Coriander Powder Turmeric Powder Cumin Powder Curry Masala

Baheti Brothers
High School Road, Pratapgarh
Ph. 22052
Fenugrock Powder Cumin Powder Curry Masala

N.L. Garjar (Engineers)
Krishna Kunj, Lal Bagh
Dt- Nathdwara, Raja Aaman
Ph. 86817

Cumini White Coriender Seed
Chilly Dry Coriander Seed
Fonugreek Seed

Sudhir & Co. Gandhi Spices (P) Ltd.
Para Bazar, Golpith
Rajkot - 360001 (Rajasthan)
Ph. 223945, 232473
Haldi Mrichi, Jeera Masalas

Kirti Trading Company
Ramganj Mandi (Rajasthan)
Ph. 20017, 20228
Coriander Seed

Desort India Spices Growers & Supplie
C/o. Prakesh Telecom Aircuit
House Road, Dt-Jodhpur
Ratnade (Rajasthan)
Ph. 530107
Cumin White Muatard Seed
Chilly Dry Coriander Seed Garlic
Fonugreek

Satyanarayan & Brothers
F-64, Industrial Area
Sajat - 306104 (Rajasthan)
Ph. 22001 22601
Ajwan Seed Curry Powder

Panpaluja Enterprises
Karsi Mandi Shanti Nagar
Dt-Jalore, Sanchora - 343041
Ph. 22268
Cumin White

Ganga Bishan Periwal & Sons
160, New Mandi Yard
Shri Ganganagar-335001
Ph. 21293, 22168
Mustard Seed

Mahaluxmi Oil & Masala Product
G-13, Jalamata Industrial Area
Dt-Pali, Sumerpur - 306902
Ph. 44103
Chilly Dry Coriender Sead
Turmeric Dry Cumini White
Forungreek Seed

Kumbha Exclusives
23, Karjali Cardones, Sardarpura
Udaipur - 313001 (Rajasthan)
Ph. 539986
Poppy Seed

Rajasthan Agriculture Depot
27-28, Karjali Gardones
Sardarpura, Udaipur - 313001
Ph. 411185, 561822
Chilli Dry Ginger Dry/Fresh
Turmeric Dry Cornator Seed,
Cumin Ferungreek

Sahu Masala Udyog
10, Cement Road Kali Bawadi
Near Arban Bank
Udaipur - 313001 (Rajasthan)
Ph. 421523
Mirchi Powder, Black Salt, Long-Kali, Haldi

Deep Chand Joshi
North Sikkim, Sikkim
Ph. 34249
Cardamom (Large)

Cordamom Products P. Ltd.
2/174 Subbiah Nadi
Industrial Complex, Pudupatti
Dt-Madurai
Arumbamur - 625107 (T.N)
Ph. 822731, 822823
Cordamom Oil

Chakra Traders
95-B, Kamarajanar Road
Dt-Salom, Attar- 636102 (T.N)
Ph. 41338, 40168
Turmeric Dry Chilly Dry

Ambikai Traders
22/4, P.H.Road, Gandhi Nagar
Bodinayakkanur - 626513 (T.N)
Ph. 20880
Cardamom (S)

K.Ulagunathan
8/10 Subbaraj Nagar
Bodinayakkanur- 626513 (T.N)
Cardamom

Kerala Cardimom Prod & Mktg Soc. Co. Ltd.
118, Subbaraj Nagar
Bodinayakkanur - 626513 (T.N)
Ph. 20763, 20765
Cardamom (S) Black Papper

N.Marutha Muthu
Naga Illam, Melachokanathapuram
Bodinayakkanur - 626513 (T.N)
Ph. 20997
Cardamom L&S Black Paper
Ginger Fresh

Pareek Sones
Post Box No- 01, Dt-Madurai
Bodinayakkanur - 626513 (T.N)
Ph. 21387 , 20078
Cardamom (S)

R. Suresh
Gurukkalaiah Street
Bodinayakkanur - 626513 (T.N)
Cardamom (S)

Spices Trading Co. Ltd.
North Raja Street
(National Building)
Bodinayakkanur - 626513 (T.N)
Ph. 20571
Cardamom (S)

Sri Luxmi Traders
No-3 Valayat Karalna
Bodinayakkanur - 626513 (T.N)
Ph. 20545 , 20779
Cardmom (S)

Shri Raja Traders
1012, Church Road
Bodinayakkanur (T.N)
Ph. 20849, 20779
Cardmom (S)

V.Nirmala Agency
10, Kaspa Maniqm House
South Raja Street, P.B.No. 25
Bodinayakkanur- 626513 (T.N)
Ph. 20303
Cardamom (S)

V.S. Radhakrishanan
12/10 Nadar Street
Thinumalapuram
Bodinayakkanur - 626513 (T.N)
Ph. 20738
Cordamom (S)

A.M. Ahemed & Co.
103, Linghi Chetty Street
P.B.No. 1792
Chennai - 600001 (T.N)
Ph. 5230066, 5230803

Aitha Ramanatham Chetty & Co.
26, Chinnathamtri, Mudali Street
Chennai - 600079 (T.N)
Ph. 5228261
Coriender Seed

Bajaj & Co.
3, Chinna Thumbi, Mundu Street
Chennai - 600079 (T.N)
Ph. 522436
Spices, Chilli Dry

Beauty Exports Indian Pvt. Ltd.
168/2, Poona Make High
Road Kilopauk, Chennai - 600010
Ph. 8522134, 8522175
Spices

Channa Leathers
9/AF Veerasomy
Pillai Street Periamet
Chennai - 600003 (T.N)
Ph. 582263
Turmeric Powder Cardamom (S)
Black Paper

Deekay Exports
135, Kholan Street, A.T.Nagar
Chennai - 600087 (T.N)
Ph. 40541, 21605
Chilli Dry Ginger Dry
Turmeric, Dry Coriender Seed,
Fenugreek Seed

Ganesh Rajah Organisations Pvt. Ltd.
558, Anna-Salai, Teynampet
Chennai - 600018 (T.N)
Spices

M.S. Vijjai Kumar & Co.
No-94, Saran Walls Street
Chennai - 600001 (T.N)
Ph. 534010
Garlie Turmeric Dry
Cumin White Tamarind Fonugreek Seed

Miki Moto Exports Pvt. Ltd
12, Lakshminarsibaham Street
T.Nagar, Chennai - 600017
Ph. 8281212, 8284242
Black Paper Chilli Dry
Cumin White Coriender Seed
Turmeric Dry

S. Abdul Saleem
P.B.No. 3484, Chennai-600040
Ph. 62122[illegible]

Sam Enterises Pvt. Ltd
133, Linghi Chettyst
Chennai - 600001 (T.N)
Ph. 5224918

Suresh N. Suresh Exports.
7 Damodaron Street, Chetpet
Chennai (T.N)
Chilli Dry (Gunfur & Sannam)

Tiruvidum Eovuitable Exim Pvt. Ltd.
4/238 D Anna Salai, Palavakkam
Chennai - 600041 (T.N)
Spices

Spider Chemicals
131, Iyah Mudali Street, Dt- Madras
Chintadripet - 600002 (T.N)
Ph. 835720
Dill Seed, Ajwan Seed, Herbal Spices

C.P. Paulsons & Company
Gali 1780, Fire Station Road
Pudamodi, Coimbatore - 641004
Ph. 530957
Black Paper Ginger Dry Chilli Powder Coriander Powder
Turmeric Powder

Mathur Murugam Mills Ltd.
No-46 B, Dr. Raja Naidu Road
Coimbatore (T.N)
Ph. 235247, 430650
Turmeric Dry Tamarind Chilly Dry

S. Venkateshwaran
5/28 Ramchettiar Street
Dellachi, Dt-Anaimalai
Coimbatore - 642104 (T.N)
Turmeric Dry Chilly Dry

Vinayak Imex Agencies
22, Arunachalam Street
K.K.Pudur, Coimbatore - 641038
Ph. 443607, 22136
Chilli Dry Tarmaric Asafoetida

Modern Farms
180 Ramalayam, Tankasi Taluk
Courtallom - 627802 (T.N)
Ph. 24975
Chilly Dry Garlie
Tamrind Clove

S. Rajamani
Pallaniappa Ghee Store
21 Vadur Street
Devakotta - 630302 (T.N)
Ph. 72810
Corinder Powder Chilli Powder

Vijyalakshmi Conidiments
6 Therason Lane
Dindigul - 624001 (T.N)
Ph. 21396
Curry Powder, Curry Masala

Aditya Trading Company
6, Therason Lane
Dindigul - 624001 (T.N)
Ph. 21396
Curry Powder Curry Powdor

Lancho Packers
9 Qttukari Chinnaiya Street
Post Box No. 549, Erode - 638003
Ph. 214851, 214611
Chilli Dry Chilli Powder
Turmeric Dry Turmeric Powder

Reshmi Food Products
44, Thanga Perumal Street
Dt-Eroda Periyar
Erode - 638007 (T.N)
Ph. 219310
Chilly Dry Turmeric Dry Curry Powder

Shri Jagdamba Traders
900, Park Road, Erode - 638003
Ph. 212228, 213273
Haldi Powder

Sai International
No. 20, V.O. Street, Desurpattai
Gingee - 604202 (T.N)
Ph. 22259, 36567
Chilli Dry, Turmeric Dry, Garlic

G. Thirumonirajan
Vargunaramapuram, Rajapalayam
Dt- Komarojar
Gopalapuram - 626136 (T.N)
Spices, Chilli Dry Coriender Seed

Thirumalai Trading Co.
93, Palayako Hai Road
Dt- Periyar
Kangayam - 638701 (T.N)
Ph. 20233, 20663
Turmeric Dry, Tamarinol

Cozy Agro Expo.
36/2, Kamoraja Puram West
Karur- 639002 (T.N)
Ph. 40541, 21605
Black Paper, Cardamom S&L
Chilli Dry & Fresh Ginger Dry

R.P.Selva Kumar & Co.
140, Dhanuskodia Puram Street
V.O. Chidambarnar
Kavilpathi - 628501 (T.N)
Ph. 20081, 22930
Chilly Dry Coriander Seed
Cordamom (S)

Rajarathinam
7, Appark Nadar Lane, Dt- Madurai
Kooraithurai - 625001 (T.N)
Ph. 34127, 36737
Asafoetida

Littlo Flower Cottage
Kootangal Viali, Fathima Nagar
Dt-K.K.
Kollemcode - 629160 (T.N)
Ph. 68090
Paprika Tamarind

Kanya Kumari Market Commitee
Dt-Kanya Kumari, Nagarcoli (T.N)
Tamarind

Priyha Raja & Co.
No.55 Chetty Street, Vadasory
Nagarcoil - 629001 (T.N)
Turmeric Powder Chilli Powder
Coriender Powder Cumin Powder
Fenneal Powder

Rajaganapathy
Kottar, Nagarcoil - 629002 (T.N)
Ph. 31112, 3295
Chilli Dry

Vijay Enterprises
52, Court Road, Nagercoil - 629001
Ph. 23785, 23885
Clove, Black Pepper

Eno Exports
65,B Sankari Road, Dt-Eroda
Pallilallayam - 638006 (T.N)
Ph. 42079
ChilliDry&Powder, Turmeric Dry & Powder Tamarind Curry Powder
Ginger Dry & Powder

Ambu Agencies
5754/3 Santhanapuram
3rd Street
Pudukkottal - 622001 (T.N)
Ph. 20469, 23229
Curry Powder Cury Masala

Nandini S. Agro Foods
153, Rice Mill Road
Rajapdayam - 626117 (T.N)
Ph. 20469, 23229
Curry Powder Cury Masala

Hira Lal & Company
392/2 Suranjanglam, Main Road
Salem - 636009 (T.N)
Cassia Curry Leaf Basil, Thyme,

Dill Seed Nutmeg

Suman Traders
16,A Dolvanayagam
Street Shevepet
Salom (T.N)
Ph. 210921, 53696
Turmeric Dry Turmeric Powder

A. Gurusamy Chattlar
36, Aruman Sannaty Street
Sankarankovil - 627756 (T.N)
Ph. 22565 , 22412
Chilly Dry Coriander Seed

Max Exports
4/57, Sasee Nagar, Dt-Sivakashi
Siturajapuram - 626123 (T.N)
Ph. 20124
Ginger Dry & Powder, Chilly Dry
Turmeric Dry Chilli Powder

Sidhna Agencies
187 A/5 P.K.N. Road
Sivakasi - 626189 (T.N)
Ph. 23071
Chilly Dry Ginger Dry Turmeric Dry
Mustard Seed Garlic Powder

P. Ramamoorthy
Johnson Complex, Dt-Kamjakumar
Thadikkaramkonam (T.N)
Clove

K. Haldoral
Thambatty, P.O. Numthala
The Nilgiris - 643003 (T.N)
Rosemary Thyme
Sage Basil Marjoram

S. Noorunisha
No.555 Part-1, TNHDB
Dt-N.Arcot Ambedkar
Thiruppatur - 635601 (T.N)
Tamerind, Turmeric Dry

Lakshmi Exporters
5-A Erattai Pillaiyar, Kovil Street
Tiruvannamali - 606601 (T.N)
Ph. 22961

Peevee Enterprises
162/7 Big Bazar, Trichy - 620008
Ph. 22961 (T.N)
Curry Masala

AKhilesh Exports Pvt. Ltd.
315, South Cotton Road
Tuti Corin - 628001 (T.N)
Ph. 23496, 24105
Chilli Dry Red Turmeric Finger
Pepper Black Grount Nut Kernel

A. Mangalraj
No. 114 South Raja ST
Tuticorin - 628001 (T.N)
Ph. 21758, 22988

S.V.S. Natarajam & Son
71/1 Tovipuram Main Road
Dt-Toti Corin
Tuticorin - 628003 (T.N)
Ph. 21598, 22398
Turmeric Powder Chilli Powder
Coriander Poder, Curry Powder
Curry Masala

Turicorin Marine Products
7, Manal Street
Tuticorin - 628001 (T.N)
Ph. 20615, 25616
Spices Pulses

Saravana Traders
11, Telungar Street
Tuticorin - 628001 (T.N)
Garlic

Vignesh International
285/P. Main Road, Dt-Tirunelveli
Vallioor- 627117 (T.N)
Ph. 20614, 202168
Turmeric Dty Tamerinal
Black Papper Ginger Dry Fresh
Coriander Seed

V.P.S.A. Paramasiva Nadar & Co.
35-M.C. Chidambaram Nadar
Street, Virudhu Nagar - 626001
Ph. 43714
Oil Seed

A.P.A. Sivamourya Nadar & Co.
14. Malal Kavil Street
Virudhunagar (T.N)
Ph. 43442
Cardomom (S)

U. Karunakaran
15, T.C. Godown Street
Virudhunagar - 626001 (T.N)
Ph. 44240
Black Pepper Cardamom (S)
Chilly Dry Gringer Dry Turmeric
Dry Tamar

Devi Industries
2/176, Subbiah Naidu
Industrial complex
Papupati Arumbanur Post
Dt-Madural
Y. Papupati - 762507 (T.N)
Ph. 822731, 822823
Cardomom Oil

Nitap Chandra Saha
Kamarukupar, AA Road
PO Agartala College
Agartala - 799004 (T.N)
Ph. 0381-228343

Ranjit Ranjan Paul
S.P. Mukherjee Road
Dharamanagar Bazar
Dharama Nagar - 799250 (TR)
Ph. 22568
Chilli Dry, Gringar Fresh
Tamerind

Biswajit Aditya
C/o. Rohini Kumar Aditya
Dt-Tripura West, Khowal -799201
Ph. 22568
Chilli Dry Ginger Dry

Kamal Chemical Works
1/32, Taksal Gali
Johri Bazar, Agra - 282001 (UP)
Harar

Raj Kumar C/o. Ram Singh
Sikkri Gowda, Aligarh - 202923
Maee, Turmaric Dry Chilli DDry
Coriander Seeds, Curry
Massala

Vimal Kumar Jindal
Madhur Steels, Opp. Gandhi Park
Azad Road
Aligarh - 202001 (U.P)
Black Paper Cordamom (S.L)
Chilli Dry Ginger Dry & Fresh
Turmeric Dry

Pankaj Srivastava
Opp. District Hospital
Harra Ki Chungi
Asamgarh - 276001 (U.P)
Ph. 201000, 200639
Chilli Dry Ginger Dry Fresh
Turmeric Dry Coruiander Seed,
Fenugreek Seed

Durga Trading Co.
130/8 Adarsh Mandi Sathai
Bareilly (U.P)
Ph. 456431, 472898
Fennal Seed Chilli Dry

Parvati Overseas
437, Shivaji Marg, Alam Giri Ganj
Bareilly- 243005 (U.P)
Ph. 475568 , 472069
Curry Powder Pepper Powder
Chilli Powder Turmeric Powder
Coriander Powder

Shri Hari Baba Gramodhyog Sansthan
Raja Ki Sivapuri
Bareilly - 243303 (U.P)
Coriander Seed, Fennel Seed
Chilli Dry Fenugrock Seed

Jagdish Sahai Kamal Kishore Kanigo
New Subzi Mandi Barusagar
Dt-Jhansi, Barusagar - 284201
Ph. 835353, 835345
Ginger Fresh

Brah Saini
Aryanagar, Massepur Morridder
Road, Bhandawali
Bijnaur (U.P)
Chilli Powder Turmeric Powder

Relaxo Herbs
Opp. Anup Shahar Bus Stand
Bulandshahar - 203001 (U.P)
Ph. 6274
Black Paper Cordimom (S)
Chilli Dry Turmeric Dry Coriander Seed

Rakesh Chemicals
Kayastan Street
Chandausi - 202412 (U.P)
Ph. 50008, 51098
Chilly Dry Coriender Seed
Fennel Seed Mustard Seed

Tirupati Overseas
3/17 Mazid Street
Farrukhabad -209625 (U.P)
Ph. 25489
Garlic

Zian Brothers
Mohalla Jatwara, Karim Ganj
Farrukhabad- 207502 (UP)
Ph. 2088
Garlic

V.N. Enterprises
30 2nd Floor, Palika Bazar
G.T.Road, Ghaziabad -201001
Ph. 726772
Black Papper Chilli Dry
Coriender Seed Cumin White,
Aniseed Mustard

N.A.Jain & Co.
Ghirror, Dt- Manipuri
Ghirror- 205121 (U.P)
Ph. 84450 , 84490
Garlic

Natural Health Care Foundation
Aonla Nagar Gonday
Dt-Partap garh
Gonday - 230143 (U.P)
Curry Powder Chilli Powder
Turmeric Powder Ginger Powder

Vinod Ideal Products
C/o. House Of Ankur Masala
Near Sanskrit Pathshala
Turkmanpur, Gorakhpur (U.P)
Curry Masala

M.B. Group
A-25. Industrial Estate
Hathras -204101 (U.P)
Ph. 20145, PP. 20390
Asafoetida

Siddiqui Agro Farm
Moh. Azad Chowk
Islam Nagar - 202523 (U.P)
Ph. 5412051
Chilli Dry Coriender Seed
Ginger Dry & Fresh Fennel Seed
Turmeric Dry

Khajuraho Distillors Pvt .Ltd
39/1 Pasrot, Jhansi - 284002 (U.P)
Ph. 443806
Ginger Powder, Ginger Oil
Ginger Oleoresin

Sujat Kumar Jain
1054, Station Road Babeena
Jhansi - 284401
Ph. 846682
Ginger Fresh Mustard Seed

Yuva Adikta Sangarsh Samiti
Dariapur Bikkoo
Kakar Ghata (Shahabad)
Dt- Hardol, Kakarghata (U.P)
Ginger Fresh Garlic, Coriander
Seed Turmeric Dry Fennel Seed

Anand Enterprises
54/27, Nayaganj, Kanpur
Kanpur (U.P)
Ph. 364669
Turmeric Powder Chilli Powder
Curry Powder Coruiander Powder

Anuradha Masala Udyog P. Ltd.
59/132 A L-2-4, Akash Deep Bldg.,
Purani Dal Mandi, Naya Ganj
Kanpur - 208001 (U.P)
Ph. 363106, 318377

Anuradha Traders
54/27, Nayaganj Kanpur
Kanpur (U.P)
Turmeric Powder Chilli Powder
Curry Powder Coriander Powder

Family Food Products
53/30, Naya Ganj, Dt-Kanpur
Kanpur (U.P)
Ph. 319187
Gaham Masala, Subji Masala,
Meat Masala, Kitchen King, Chhole
& Chat Masala

Hiltex Exports
26/50, Birhana Road
Kanpur - 208001 (U.P)
Ph. 368167
Spices

Manni Lal Suraj Prasad Company
54/27 Naya Gani
Kanpur- 208001 (UP)
Ph. 318249
Jari Booti Katha

Narmada Sales
128/D/123, Kidwai Nagar
Kanpur - 208011 (U.P)
Ph. 20118
Curry Powder, Chilli Powder,
Turmeric Powder, Ginger Powder

Neha Exports
111/106, Ashok Nagar
Kanpur - 208012 (U.P)
Ph. 294411
Spice

Purnima Sewa Ashram
70/34, Shutarkhana
Kanpur (U.P)
Ph. 354648 PP
Black Pepper

Shee Neeraj Enterprises
51/7, Ram Ganj
Kanpur -208022 (U.P)
Ph. 361117

Vikas Grah Udyog Pvt. Ltd
4, N Block Kidwai Nagar
Kanpur - 208011 (U.P)
Ph. 272397
Turmeric Dry Chilli Dry
Curry Masala Papper Powder

Suneet Dutt Giri
D-1137, Indira Nagar
Lacknow (U.P)
Ph. 382388
Ginger Fresh Mustard Seed
Dehy Garlic Powder

Industrial Acid Chemicals Ltd.
17, Gokala Vihar Marg
Lakhnow - 226001 (U.P)
Ph. 272845
Spice

Gihar Spices Suppliers
C/o. G.D. Gihar
D-1139, Indira Nagar
Lucknow - 226016 (U.P)
Ph. 388309
Garlic, Dehy Garlic Powder

Lucknow Kiran Company
88, Subhash Marg
Lucknow - 226003 (U.P)
Ph. 2665216, 265219
Parsely Cinnamon
Saffrom, Pepper Long Ginger Dry

Rahul & Brothers
289/10, Moti Nagar
Lucknow - 226004 (U.P)
Ph. 265870, 219538

Reliable Spices Supplier
Reliable Paint Industry
A-66 Govt Industrial Estate
Lucknow (U.P)
Ph. 259764
Chilli Dry Ginger Dry & Fresh
Turmeric Dry Coriender Seed
Mustard Fresh Garlic

Season Specialist India
L-11, F 382, Aashiyana
Lukhnow - 226005 (U.P)
Ph. 250414
Turmeric Powder Chilli Powder
Coriander Powder

Sree Annapurni Intustries
61, Ram Bhawan Purana Kila
Lukhnow (U.P)

Ph. 389201
Coriander Seed Cumin White
Ani Seed, Curry Masala

Tirupati Traders & Distibuters
C-257 Nirala Nagar
Lukhnow (U.P)
Ph. 389201
Black Paper Ginger Dry
Coriander Seed Chilli Dry Turmeric Dry

Best Cold Storage & Vegetable Dehydrates
Lalpur Sirsaganj Road
Post Box No. 001
Mainpuri -205001 (U.P)
Ph. 34138, 34139
Dehy. Gaglic Flakes, Chilli Dry, Dehy. Green Chilli, Tamarind

M.S. Mani
C/o. Ratna Singh
PAC Vijaypur, Ram Bagh
Mainpuri -231303 (U.P)
Parsaley Ginger Fresh
Black Pepper Nutmeg

R.P. Dwivedi
Moh. Khera, Karhal
Mainpuri - 205264 (U.P)
Ph. 315741
Chilli Dry Turmeric Dry
Mustard Seed Garlic Herbal Spices

Saroj Industries
Anugrah Bhawan, Bartan Bazar
Mooradabad - 244001 (U.P)
Ph. 315741
Chilli Dry Turmeric Dry. Mustard Seed Garlic Herbal Spices

Rajneesh Kumar Jain
Jain Niketan, 232 Krishana puri
Muzaffar Nagar -251002 (U.P)
Ph. 25327, 409827
Black Pepper Cardamom (L)
Chilly Dry Ginger Dry & Fresh
Turmeric Dry Powder

Singhal Food Products
155/1 Almaspur Chowk
Kukra Road
Muzaffarnagar - 251001 (U.P)

Swastik Products
6th Km. Saharanpur Road, Rampur
Muzaffarnagar (U.P)
Black Paper Carda Chilli Dry
Coriander Cumin White Fennel Seed Fenugrock Seed

Chandra Kottra Industries Pvt. Ltd.
Wotwali Road, Nazibabad - 246763
Ph. 20200, 20111

Hitech Food
B-19 Sector-3, Noida -201301 (U.P)
Ph. 521624

Tera Taste Foods Ltd.
F-2 Sector - 6, Noida -201301 (U.P)
Ph. 521729

T.R. Grinders
Bhawani Ganj
Dt- Ram Nagar (Naintal)
Ram Nagar - 244715 (U.P)
Ph. 35518
Cumin White Mustard Seed
Fenugreek Seed Fenugreek Seed Anu Seed Fennel Seed

Indus Hortics
Jail Road, Rampur (U.P)
Ph. 25367
Chilly Dry Coriander Seed
Turmeric Powder Fenengreek Powder Tamarind

Rajendra Kumar Harsi Kumar
Miston Gnaj
Rampur - 244901 (U.P)
Ph. 26951, 23722
Chilli Dry Coriander Seeds
Turmeric Dry

Bhagwati Trading Co.
Himmat Nagar
Saharanpur - 247001 (U.P)
Ph. 722210
Chilli Powder Turmeric Powder
Coriander Powder

Avedesh Kumar Misra
Alha Ganj, Shahjahanpur
Shahjanpur (U.P)
Parsely Coriander Seed
Ani Seed

Sharda Brothers
Tanakpur, Dt-Nainital
Tanakpur - 262309 (U.P)
Ph. 59022, 59295
Tejpat, Curry Leaf

Dhanvantari Sara Sansthan
Murtaja Nagar Unnar
32, Sekhwade
Unnar - 209801 (U.P)
Ph. 820591, 820498
Coriander Seed, Chilli Dry
Fenugreek Seed, Ginger Fresh
Turmeric Dry

Rajeev Mohan
K-67/113, Easwar Ganji
Varanasi - 221001 (U.P)
Chilli Dry

Heeramoti Spices Pvt. Ltd.
1054, Industrial Area Phase-II
Chandigarh (UT)
Ph. 6540012, 654013

Special Spices Industries
243 , Industrial Area
Phase-I, Chandigarh - 160002 (UT)
Ph. 0712-655194, 650820

Candid Services
57, Girish Mukharjee Road
Dt-Kolkatta
Bhawanlpur - 700025 (W.B)
Ph. 4654
Chilli Dry

Sarda Kanta Roy
C/o. Deshurathi Choudhary
Ravindra Pallij
Birbhum (W.B)
Chilli Dry Turmeric Dry
Ginger Dry Ginger Fresh

Agro Tropicana
25, Hindustan Road
Kolkatta - 700029 (W.B)
Ph. 4641166
Rosemary Thujme
Oraegane, Tarragon, Besil

Apurva Export Pvt. Ltd
7, Munshi Prem Chand Sarani
Hastings, Kolkatta - 700022 (W.B)
Ph. 220016, 220018
Spices

Behari Lal Hamraj
176, Jamuna Lal Bajaj Street
Kolkatta - 700007 (W.B)
Herbal Spices

D.G. Sales & Marketing
2/21, Jogendra Basak Road
Kolkatta - 700036 (W.B)
Ph. 5572528
Chilli Dry Ginger Dry & Fresh
Turmeric Dry Coriander Seed,
Cumin White

Dehshree Export & Holding Pvt. Ltd.
75-C, Park Street 7th Floor,
Kolkatta - 700016 (W.B)
Ph. 292086, 293762,

Eastern Udyog
B-14/19, Rabindra Pally
Jijangra Post, Bagulali
Kolkatta - 700059 (W.B)
Ph. 3828
Ginger, Fresh Garlic, Cumin White
Coriander Seed ,Turmeric Dry

Indian Products Ltd
Jay Complex, 3rd Floor
46, B.B. Gauguly Street
Kolkatta-700012 (W.B)
Ph. 274775

J.K. Traders
61, Kali Krishna, Tagore Street
Kolkatta - 700007 (W.B)
Ph. 2390582, 332552
Jeera

Jai Mica Supply Company Pvt. Ltd.

62, Beutick Street
Kolkatta - 700069 (W.B)
Ph. 277295

K.K. Gupta & Co.
21/3A, Gariehat Road
Kolkatta - 700019 (W.B)
Ph. 4408349
Cardomom(L) Ginger Fresh
Ginger Dry, Tamarind, Garlic

Kanchan Traders
20, Kumar Tully Steet
Kolkatta - 700005 (W.B)
Ph. 5517020, 5513046
Onion Fresh,GarlicTamarind Ginger

Kejri Wal Chemical & Pappers Ltd.
6, Lyons Range, 5th Floor
Kolkatta - 700001 (W.B)
Ph. 2205590 , 2200102
Chilli Dry Turmeric Dry Kekam ,
Rosemary Thyme Oregano

Krishna Traders
20-Hara Chandra Mullick Street
Sova Bazar, Kolkatta - 700005
Ph. 544288, 543793

Ma Saradamayee Spice Mills
P-42 Raipur, Kolkatta - 700084
Ph. 725072
Turmeric Powder, Chilli Powder
Cumin Powder Coriander Powder
Pepper Powder

Madhu Jayanti International Ltd.
Jay Complex, 3rd Floor
46, B.B.Ganguly Street
Kolkatta - 700012 (W.B)
Ph. 270021, 2256534
Spics

Mines Agencies
71, Ganesh Chandra Avenue
Kolkatta - 700013 (W.B)
Ph. 272261, 261178
Seeds Soyabean

N.R. Exports
P-299, Parnasree, Pally Behala
Kolkatta - 700060 (W.B)
Black Papper Cardamom (S&L)
Mustard Seed Clove Chilli Dry

New Punjab Traders (India) Pvt. Ltd.
26/1, Strand Road
1st Floor P.B.No. 2593
Kolkatta - 700001 (W.B)
Ph. 2203892,2214594
Black Paper Cardamom (S&L)
Ginger Dry& Fresh, Mustard Seed,
Chilli Dry

Omega Traders (India)
16 A, Synagogue Street
Kolkatta - 700001 (W.B)
Ph. 2422858, 2434820
Cardamom(L), Ginger Fresh
Ginger Dry, Tarragon

Oriental Products
55B. Peary Mohan Roy Road
Kolkatta - 700027 (W.B)
Ph. 4797385
Curry Powder Turmeric Powder
Chilli Powder Coriander Powder
Cumin Powder

Shaw Wallace & Company Ltd.
1, Bankshall Street
Kolkatta - 700001 (W.B)
Ph. 285601, 289151

Sona Enterprises
167/4, Lolin Sarani
2nd Floor, Room No. 25
Kolkatta - 700072 (W.B)
Ph. 271671
Chilli, Dry Ginger Fresh,
Mustard Seed, Garlic, Herbal
Spices

Snurise Spices Limited
46, Pathuriya Ghat Street
Kolkatta - 700006 (W.B)
Ph. 2393163, 239487

Tata Iron & Steel Co. Ltd.
Engg. Exports Dept. Tata Centre
7 Floor 43, Chowringhee Road
Kolkatta - 700071 (W.B)
Ph. 2049131, 2043453

Tirupati Niryat Pvt. Ltd.
21 A Shakespeare, 2nd Floor
Kolkatta - 700017 (W.B)
Ph. 404735,404882

Vijay International Traders
5/3C/3, Uma Kant Senlane
Kolkatta - 700017 (W.B)
Ph. 5568560
Turmeric Dry

Mohammed Samad Tejmall
Ratanpur Station Rod
Dt-Dhulian (Murshidabad)
Dhulia - 742202 (W.B)
Turmeric Dry

Gulab Chand Tejmall
130, Hillcart Road
Ghoom, Darjeeling, Dt Darjeeling
Ghoom - 734102 (W.B)
Ph. 2042,3220
Cardomom(L), Ginger Dry
Ginger Fresh

Prosan Choudhary
Kotwani, Malda - 732144 (W.B)
Ph. 2578
Turmeric Dry, Turmeric Powder
Ginger Fresh

Satya Ranjan Das
Baikunthapur
P.S. Contal, Midnapore
Midnapore (W.B)
Chilly Dry, Tamarind

Bivas Kumar Saha
Karimpur, Lakhmipura
Nadia (W.B)
Ph. 55128
Turmeric Dry, Coriander Seed
Cumin White

Tapan Kumar Haldar
Betal Bazar, Betal
Nadia - 741163 (W.B)
Cumin White, Mustard Seed
Garlic

Deep Enterprises
Supreme Furniture & Timber Mart
Dhowmatha Bazar
Halishar Station Road
Dt-24, Parganas (North)
Naganagar - 743136 (W.B)
Ginger Dry & Fresh Chilli Dry
Garlic Mustard Seed

Sadhu Enterprises
Narayanpur, Dt-Birbhum
Narayanpur - 731239 (W.B)
Chilli Dry Ginger Dry & Fresh
Turmeric Dry, Coriander Powder,
Papper Powder

North East Martketing Bureau
S.Road, Raiganj
Raiganj - 744134 (W.B)
Ph. 52042
Chilly Dry Turmeric Dry
Ginger Dry, Coriander Seed,
Mustard Seed

Bikash Roy
102, Aghor Sarani, Barandra Para
Raipur (Sonarpur)
Dt-Parganas (South)
Raipur - 743358 (W.B)
Chilli Dry Mustard Seed

Deokinandan Amit Kumar
Gaushala Complex
Bardwan Road, Jalpaimore
Siliguri - 734405 (W.B)
Ph. 432824, 27828
Spices

Nem Chend Jain & Sons
Naya Bazar, Siliguri - 734105 (W.B)
Ph. 433090 , 25299
Cardamom (L)

Punam Chand Jain
Naya Bazar, Siliguri - 734405 (W.B)
Ph. 436640, 436641
Cordamom (L)

Shanti Enterprises
S.F.Road, Siliguri - 734405 (W.B)
Ph. 431330
Cardamom (L)

47

SPICES BOARD

The following addresses will help the entrepreneurs/ industrialists to avail more relevent informations related with spices/masala.

Spices Board
Sugandha Bhavan
Kochi N. H. Byepass Road
Palarivattam Post,
Post Box No. 2277
Kochi - 682025
Ph:. 484-333610 (6 Lines)
Fax : 484-331429/4429

Spices Board
Pancholi Hospital Building
2nd Floor,
90 Feet Road
Ghatkopar East,
Mumbai - 400 077
Ph:. 22-5153771
Fax : 22-5143673

Spices Board
No.1, 95A,
Park Street
2nd Floor,
Kolkatta - 700 017
Ph:. 33-280430
Fax: 33-2479736

Spices Board
13, 1st Floor,
2nd Street East
Abhirampuram,
Mylapore
Chennai - 600 004
Tele Fax : 044-4991448

Spices Board
A-428, Defence Colony
New Delhi - 110 024
Ph:. 011-4623597, 4611510
Fax : 011-4621359

48

SPICE RESEARCH CENTRES IN INDIA

	Name of the Centre/ University	Agro-Climatic Zone	Spice Crops
1.	**Pampadumpara** Cardamom Research Station	West Coast	Cardamom
2.	**Mudigere Reg. Res.** Statics (UAES-13)	West Coast	Cardamom
3.	**Yercaud** Horticultural Research Station (TNAU)	East Coast Plains & Hill Region	Cardamom Tree Spices
4.	**Panniyur** Pepper Research Station (KAU)	West Coast Plains & Ghats Region	Black Pepper
5.	**Sirst** Regional Agricultural Research Station (UAS)	West Coast Plains & Ghats Region	Black Pepper
6.	**Chiniapahi** Regional Agricultural Research Station (APAU)	Southern Plateau & Hill Region Clay Loam	Black Pepper
7.	**Solan** Dept. of Vegetable Crops (Dr. YSPUHF)	Western Himalayan Region	Ginger & Turmeric
8.	**Pottangi** High Altitude Research Station (OUAT)	Eastern Plateau & Hills Region	Ginger Turmeric

9. **Jobner** SKN College of Agriculture (RAJAU)	Western Dry Region	Cumin Coriander Fennel Fenugreek
10. **Jagudan** Spices Research Station (GAU)	Gujarat Plains & Hills Region	Cumin Coriander Fennel Fenugreek
11. **Coimbantore** Horticultural College (TNAU)	East Coast Plains & Hills Region	Coriander Fenugreek
12. **Guntur** Regional Agricultural Research Station (APAU)	East Coast Plains & Hill Region	Coriander Fenugreek
13. **Jagtial** Regional Agricultural Research Station (APAU)	Southern Plateau & hills Region	Turmeric
14. **Gangtok** ICAR RC for NEh Region	Eastern Himalayan Region	Large Cardamom
15. **Hissar** CCS Haryana Agricultural University (CCSHAU)	Trans Gangetic Plains Region	Coriander Cumin Fennel Fenugreek
16. **Dholi** Tirhul College of Agriculture (RAU)	Middle Gangetic Pains Region	Turmeric Coriander Fenugreek
17. **Dapoli** (KKV)	Western Plateau & Hills Region	Black pepper Clove, Nutmeg & cinnamon
18. **Raipur** Indira Gandhi Krishi Vishwa Vidyalaya	Central Plateau & Hills Region	Ginger Turmeric Coriander & Fenugreek
19. **Faisabad** (NDUAT)	Upper Gangetic Plains Region	Fennel & Fenugreek
20. **Nadia** (BCKVV)	Lower Gangetic Plains Region	Black pepper Ginger Turmeric & Cinnamon

EIRI PROCESS TECHNOLOGY BOOKS

CHEMICAL/ DYES/ PETROCHEMICALS/ LUBRICANT/ ELECTROPLATING

01 Small Medium & Large Chemical Industries
02 Industrial Chemicals Technology Hand Book
03 Modern Technology of Organic & Inorganic Chemicals
04 Hand Book of Electroplating Anodizing & Surface Finishing Technology
05 Hand Book of Agro Chemical Industries (Insecticides & Pesticides)
06 Technology of Synthetic Dyes, Pigments Intermediates
07 Petrochemicals, Lubricants, Greases & Petroleum Refining
08 Hand Book of Lubricants, Greases & Petrochemicals Technology

GUMS, ADHESIVES AND SEALANTS

01 Technology Of Gums, Adhesives & Sealants With Formulations
02 Hand Book Of Adhesives With Their Formulaes
03 Adhesives Technology & Formulations Hand Book (Hand Book of Adhesives)
04 Technology of Glue and Adhesives with Adhesives Bonding and Formulations

SMALL SCALE INDUSTRIES/ STATIONERY/PAPER/ INKS/ CANDLES & EXPORT BUSINESS

01 Start Your Own Export Business (How To Export)
02 Start Your Own Small Business And Industry
03 Candle Making Processes & Formulations Hand Book
04 Stationery, Paper Converting & Packaging Industries
05 Modern Inks Formulations & Manufacturing Industries
06 Profitable Businesses To Start For Entrepreneurs
07 Modern Small & Cottage Scale Industries
08 Profitable Small Cottage Tiny & Home Industries

BIO FUEL & BIOPROCESSING

01 Technology Of Bio-Fules (Ethanol & Biodiesel)
02 Modern Technology Of Bioprocessing

PRINTING, SCREEN PRINTING & PACKAGING

01 Hand Book of Printing Processes Technologies & Industries
02 Hand Book Of Printing Technology (Offset, Screen, Flexo, Gravure, Inkjet & Digital)
03 Hand Book Of Offset Printing Technology
04 Screen Printing With Processes & Tech.
05 Hand Book Of Prepress
06 Hand Book Of Packaging Technology
07 Modern Packaging Technology for Processed Food, Bakery, Snack Foods, Spices and Allied Food Products
08 Hand Book Of Food Packaging Technology
09 Modern Technology of Printing Inks

PAINT, VARNISH, SOLVENTS, COATING & LACQUERS, POWDER COATING

01 Paint Pigment Varnish & Lacquer Manufacturing
02 Paint Varnish Solvents & Coating Technology

EIRI PROCESS TECHNOLOGY BOOKS

03 Paint, Pigment, Solvent, Coating Emulsion, Paint Additives & Formulations
04 Technology Of Coating, Resins, Pigments & Inks Industries
05 Manufacturing Technology & Formulations Hand Book On Thinners, Putty, Wall & Industrial Finishes And Synthetic Resins
06 Technology of Synthetic Resins and Emulsion Polymers
07 Technology of Paints and Coatings with Formulations
08 Powder Coating Technology Hand Book

PLASTIC/POLYMER PROCESS, COMPOUNDING, INJECTION MOULDING, ROTATIONAL MOULDING, PLASTIC FILM, FIBRE GLASS, PLASTIC WASTE RECYCLING, MOULDS, PET & RESINS INDUSTRIES

01 Moulds Design & Processing Hand Book
02 Hand Book Of Plastic Materials & Processing Technology
03 Injection Moulding Of Plastics
04 Plastic Processing and Packaging Industries
05 Plastic Waste Recycling Technology
06 Technology Of Plastic Films
07 Rotational Moulding Technology Hand Book
08 Plastic Compounding, Master Batches, Pet & Other Plastics
09 Synthetic Resins Technology With Formulations
10 Technology Of PVC Compounding And Its Applications
11 Hand Book of Polymer And Plastic Technology
12 Hand Book of Fibre Glass Moulding
13 Technology of Reinforced Plastics
14 Plastic Additives Technology Hand Book
15 Technology of Pet Bottles, Preform and Pet Recycling
16 Modern Technology of Extrusion & Extruded Products
17 Technology of Synthetic Resins & Emulsion Polymers
18 Technology of Plastic Additives with Processes and Packaging
19 Technology of Disposable Medical Products

BAKERY, CONFECTIONERY & BREAKFAST, PASTA & CEREALS

01 Hand Book Of Bakery Industries
02 Hand Book Of Confectionery With Formulations
03 Breakfast, Dietary Food, Pasta & Cereal Products Technology
04 Hand Book Of Modern Bakery Products
05 Modern Bakery Technology & Fermented Cereal Products With Formulae
06 Technology of Confectionery, Chocolates, Toffee, Candy, Chewing & Bubble Gums, Lollipop and Jelly Products with Formulations

AGRO CULTIVATION, ANIMAL FARMING, AGRO PLANTATION & AGRO CHEMICAL/ PESTICIDES/ FLORICULTURE & BEE KEEPING

01 Poultry Farming & Feed Formulations
02 Hand Book of Pig Farming
03 Agro Based Hand Book of Plantation, Cultivation & Farming
04 Agro Based Plantation Cultivation & Farming
05 Agro Chemical Industries (Insecticide & Pesticides)
06 Modern Bee Keeping & Honey Processing

EIRI PROCESS TECHNOLOGY BOOKS

07 Technology Of Modern Rice Milling And Basmati Rice
08 Hand Book Of Goat Farming
09 Floriculture Hand Book (Flowers Growing Technology)
10 Aloe Vera Cultivation, Processings, Formulations And Manufacturing Technology
11 Poultry Farming, Hatchery and Broiler Production

DAIRY FARM, MILK PROCESSING AND ICE CREAM

01 Hand Book of Dairy Formulations, Processes & Milk Processing Industries
02 Milk Processing And Dairy Products Industries
03 Hand Book Of Dairy Farming to Produce Milk with Packaging
04 Hand Book Of Ice Cream Technology And Formulae
05 Hand Book Of Milk Processing Dairy Products And Packaging Technology
06 Dairy Farming for Milk Production Technology
07 Commercial Dairy Farming with Project Profiles

HERBS & MEDICINAL CULTIVATION

01 Herbs, Medicinal & Aromatic Plants Cultivation
02 Aushidhi And Sungndhit Paudho Ka Vaysayik (Hindi)
03 Hand Book Of Aromatic & Medicinal Plants And Biodiesel (Jatropha)
04 Hand Book Of Medicinal & Aromatic Plants (Cultivation, Utilisation & Extraction Processed)

FOOD & AGRO PROCESSING, PRESERVATION, SNACK FOOD, DEHYDRATION, FRUIT BEVERAGE, POTATO, MAIZE, MEAT PROCESS

01 Fruits & Vegetables Processing Hand Book
02 Fruit Beverage & Processing With Mango
03 Food Processing & Agro Based Industries
04 Manufacturing Technology of Snacks Food, Namkeen, Pappad & Potato Products
05 Preservation & Canning Of Fruits and Vegetables
06 Hand Book of Food Dehydration & Drying
07 Meat Processing & Meat Products Hand Book
08 Technology of Food Preservation & Processing
09 Hand Book of Food Packaging Technology
10 Agro Based & Processed Food Products
11 Potato & Potato Processing Technology
12 Technology of Maize & Allied Com. Products
13 Technology of Food Processing Industries
14 Technology of Sweets (Mithai) with Formulae
15 Modern Technology of Frozen Food Products
16 Technology of Water and Packaged Drinking water
17 Complete Hand Book on Frozen Food Processing and Freeze Drying Technology
18 Technology of Sweets (Mithai), Namkeen and Snacks food with Formulae
19 Complete Book on Banana Cultivation, Dehydration, Ripening, Processing, Products and Packaging Technology

EIRI PROCESS TECHNOLOGY BOOKS

20 Technology of Chicken Meat and Poultry Products
21 Agro Food Processing and Packaging Technology
22 Modern Technology of Tomato Processing and Dehydration (Ketchup, Juice, Paste, Puree, Soup and Drying)
23 Modern Technology of Agro Processing and Food Packaging Products with Project Profiles
24 Start Your Own Coffee and Coffee Processing

SOAPS & DETERGENTS

01 Household Soap. Toilet Soap & Other Soap
02 Profitable Small Scale Manufacture Of Soaps & Detergents
03 Synthetic Detergents With Formulations
04 Modern Technology of Acid Slurry, Surfactants, Soap and Detergents with Formulae

ORGANIC FARMING AND FOOD

01 Hand Book Of Organic Farming And Organic Foods With Vermi-Composting And Neem Products

FISH FARMING & FISHERY PRODUCTS

01 Hand Book Of Fish Farming And Fishery Products

COSMETIC (SYNTHETIC & HERBAL)

01 Cosmetics Processes & Formulations
02 Herbal Cosmetics & Beauty Products With Formulations
03 Profitable Small Scale Manufacture Of Cosmetics (Synthetic & Herbal)
04 Hand Book Of Synthetic & Herbal Cosmetics (How to Make Beauty Products)
05 Technology Of Herbal Cosmetics & Toiletries Products With Formulae

OIL AND FATS

01 Hand Book of Oils, Fats And Derivatives With Refining & Packaging Technology
02 Technology of Oilseeds Processing, Oils & Fats and Refining

ESSENTIAL OILS & AROMATIC

01 Essential Oils Manufacturing & Aromatic Plants
02 Modern Technology Of Essential Oils
03 Technology Of Perfumes, Flavours & Essential Oils
04 Essential Oils Processes & Formulations

PERFUMES AND FLAVOURS

01 Hand Book Of Flavours & Food Colourants Technology
02 Hand Book Of Perfumes & Flavours
03 Hand Book of Perfumes With Formulations
04 Technology Of Perfumes, Flavours & Essential Oils
05 Hand Book Of Flavours Technology

BUILDING MATERIALS & CHEMICALS

01 Technology Of Building Materials & Chemicals With Processes